T0245625

"The kind of book that robs you of your peace. It unpacks—tale after heart-breaking tale—how 'court guilt' can blow the doors off judicial safeguards and overwhelm innocence with ease. Long before your jaws rehinge, the truth hits: guilt often comes down to gamesmanship, we live a hairsbreadth from the unthinkable, you might go to prison even if you haven't done a thing."

CATHERINE PUGH, Attorney, formerly with the Department of Justice Civil Rights Division, Special Litigation Section

You Might Go to Prison, Even Though You're Innocent

Justin Brooks

UNIVERSITY OF CALIFORNIA PRESS

University of California Press
Oakland, California

© 2023 by Justin Brooks

Cataloging-in-Publication Data is on file at the Library of Congress.

ISBN 978-0-520-38683-9 (cloth : alk. paper)
ISBN 978-0-520-38684-6 (ebook)

32 31 30 29 28 27 26 25 24 23
10 9 8 7 6 5 4 3 2

For Heidi, of course. The love of my life. The person who picks me up and keeps me going in this work and this world.

Contents

Foreword

I first met Justin Brooks in 1998 at an extraordinary event in Chicago. It was a gathering of lawyers, academics, and innocent people from across the United States who had been exonerated after being sentenced to death. It was heartbreaking and inspiring to see each one of them take the stage knowing they came close to being executed. At the time Justin was working to free an innocent woman from death row in Chicago. I'm sure the event gave him hope that freedom was possible, even against all odds.

The next year, in 1999, Justin cofounded the California Innocence Project. He joined a small group of us who started projects around the country. We were mostly criminal defense attorneys and law professors, and our projects were attached to clinical programs at law schools. We worked together and shared resources. Our group soon became known as the Innocence Network.

For the better part of the next two decades, I served on the board of the Innocence Network with Justin as we watched our small group of lawyers doing innocence work grow into an international movement. More than sixty projects emerged in the United States, while projects began in Europe, Asia, the South Pacific, and Africa. Justin led not only the efforts in California, but he also initiated and coordinated the efforts of twenty-five innocence organizations in Latin America.

You Might Go to Prison, Even Though You're Innocent is the culmination of everything Justin has learned doing innocence work and a powerful indictment of our criminal legal system. Justin skillfully weaves together his personal experiences representing innocent people with research and cases from around the world, leaving no doubt that no one is safe from being wrongfully convicted.

Barry Scheck
Cofounder
The Innocence Project

Introduction

In May of 1872, William Marion and his friend John Cameron traveled to Kansas from Nebraska with plans to work on the railroad for four or five weeks. Several days later, Marion returned to Nebraska alone but with Cameron's horses and harnesses. Marion claimed he'd purchased them from Cameron.[1]

A decomposed body found in the desert with a bullet in the skull that could have come from Marion's gun led to murder charges. He was convicted, sentenced to death, and executed by hanging. Four years after the execution, Cameron reappeared alive and well. He told authorities he sold his horses and harnesses to Marion and fled to Mexico to avoid a shotgun wedding. One hundred years later, the Governor of Nebraska pardoned Marion.[2]

Wrongful convictions are nothing new. And yet, when I began my criminal defense career thirty-two years ago, I often had conversations with people who were deeply cynical about the idea that innocent people are convicted in our criminal legal system.

In the 1990s, DNA technology changed the discussion. People began to be released from prison based on definitive scientific proof of innocence—nearly as definitive as John Cameron showing up alive after William Marion's execution.

Since the 1990s, thousands of innocent people have been freed from prison.[3] And yet, those freed people, those exonerees, are simply the tip of the iceberg. They are the lucky ones.

It's hard to tell someone who is innocent and has spent years in prison they are lucky, but they are. They are lucky the evidence from their trial wasn't thrown in the trash. They are lucky they didn't get killed in prison. They are lucky they found a competent lawyer to listen to their pleas of innocence. They are lucky the lawyer spent time and resources on their case. They are lucky their case was assigned to a judge who would grant a hearing. And ultimately, they are lucky they were able to jump over the many barriers in our legal system to gain their freedom. The unlucky ones, regardless of innocence, die in prison.

Despite the thousands of documented cases of innocence, there's still a cynicism surrounding the notion that innocent people are wrongfully convicted. Although the claim that innocent people *never* go to prison has softened, many still believe such instances are exceedingly rare or it only happens to people "who must have done something wrong." This dismissive attitude results in the conclusion that "it happens to some people, but it won't happen to me."

That's the reason I wrote this book. The criminal legal system is imperfect. No matter what country, state, city, or town you live in, you can be wrongfully convicted. This imperfect system acts on your behalf. It protects your family, your home, and your life. This imperfect system also can take away everything you have ever loved and cared for.

I'm confident once you read the stories of injustice that fill this book, you will see the possibility that you or a loved one could be the victim of a wrongful conviction. Each chapter will take you through causes of wrongful convictions that are typically beyond the control of those who suffer the fate of landing in prison as an innocent person. Maybe it's getting the wrong lawyer, living in a neighborhood that is over- or under-policed, finding a dead body, or a host of failings by government entities and pseudosciences. Even though the statistical chances of this happening to you change based on factors such as race, gender, age, socioeconomic standing, education, and who you associate with, anyone, including you, can be wrongfully convicted.

I personally litigated many of the cases discussed in this book, but all the successes I've had over the past two decades were the result of teamwork by the lawyers, law students, volunteers, and administrative staff of the California Innocence Project (CIP), an organization I'm honored to direct.

When I cofounded CIP in 1999, I was a thirty-four-year-old lawyer with aggressively thick brown hair and an attitude to match. Both have softened over the years. My hair has greyed, and I've learned more persuasive and less in-your-face approaches to freeing innocent people from prison. My cofounder, Jan Stiglitz, was a perfect partner. His hair had already greyed, and his relentless reasonableness rubbed off on me. At the law school, Jan was Professor Kingsfield from the movie *Paper Chase*. He was well known for making students cry in his Civil Procedure class, but he had a huge heart which was always on display when he was around his wife and two daughters. When I pitched him the idea of CIP, he immediately said he wanted in. After years as an appellate lawyer, he'd only been able to reduce outrageous prison sentences. He wanted to free innocent people.

Kim Hernandez was the third member of our team. We hired her as a part-time administrative assistant, but she soon became so much more. She was a mother of five who had no experience in criminal law, but a lot of experience in business and organizing children. Those skills came in handy as we created an organization with the capacity to screen, investigate, and litigate innocence claims based on the thousands of letters we received while also training and managing a group of inexperienced law students.

After we raised some money from grants and the generosity of guitarist Joe Walsh and the rock band The Eagles, we added two lawyers to the staff. I convinced Jeff Chinn, my best friend from law school, to leave his cushy job in career services at American University in Washington, DC, and join us. He was, and is, incredibly patient. If he could sit at a desk and listen to music while he dug through the piles of innocence claims we received, he was happy.

The second lawyer we hired was Alex Simpson. Alex distinguished himself as the best of our first clinical students, and he is one of the smartest, funniest, most sarcastic people I've ever met. Alex shared an office with our first investigator, Craig Woolard. Craig had been a law student but realized his skills, interest, and personality were much more suited to tracking down witnesses, stakeouts, and finding the truth on the streets. Jan, Kim, Jeff, Craig, and a few other great lawyers and staff we've had over the years have moved on to other work, but they've all been part of the story of CIP and our successes. Alex and I are the two who have remained.

I'm proud of all the work done by the students, lawyers, and administrative staff who have made CIP part of their education and career over the past two decades. I'm particularly proud of the work of our current team of outstanding lawyers who have been with the project for many years. They comprise the greatest group of advocates and friends I could hope for. Alex Simpson, Alissa Bjerkhoel, Raquel Cohen, Mike Semanchik, and Audrey McGinn are people I'd trust with my life, something our clients do every day.

As I've said, every success we've had in our office has been a team effort involving many people and, if I fail to mention all their names in conjunction with a particular case I'm discussing in this book, let it be known that we all work on every case (see fig. 1).

Beyond the exonerations we've obtained, I'm also proud of the policy changes we've been a part of. Jasmin Harris, a former pancake restaurant owner/manager for many years, came into our office after the breakfast rush was over. She volunteered all day reviewing cases and helping out any way she could. She spent so many unpaid hours at CIP and did such great work; I was thrilled when we were able to hire her to lead both our policy efforts and our development team. As a result, CIP has been part of changing criminal legal policy in California, including laws related to new evidence standards to reopen old cases, preservation of evidence after trial, post-conviction DNA testing, police identification procedures, and compensation for innocent people who have lost years of their lives in prison.

Although this book is dedicated to the causes and devastating effects of wrongful convictions, I don't want to leave you with the impression that wrongful convictions are the only problem with the criminal legal system. There's a great deal wrong with our system beyond convicting the innocent. Our unending devotion to antiquated notions of punishment in the hands of bureaucratic government agencies, combined with overwhelming political influences, has left us with a system that is often both impractical and cruel. In the United States, decades of tough-on-crime policies

Figure 1. The California Innocence Project Team. Top row from left: Alex Simpson, Mike Semanchik, Audrey McGinn, Jasmin Harris, Jolena Pamilar, Raquel Cohen, Sydnie Mitchell. Bottom row from left: Alejandro Romero, Claudia Salinas, Justin Brooks, Alissa Bjerkhoel, Ruby Anaya. Photo credit: Heidi Brooks.

have created the largest prison system in the world, disproportionally filled with people of color, that incarcerates a higher percentage of our population than any other country.

We must not only address the issues in this book that lead innocent people to prison, but also holistically examine the criminal legal system and ask hard questions. What behaviors should be criminalized to truly serve society? What processes and resources are needed to serve justice? What sentences and remedies are reasonable responses to criminal behavior? What type of correctional system will return a person back to society who is less likely to commit more crimes? It is only by answering these questions that we can create a system that is just.

1 You Hired the Wrong Lawyer
(Pleas with No Bargain)

MARILYN MULERO

In 1994, I was a twenty-nine-year-old law professor living in East Lansing, Michigan, when I read about a young Puerto Rican woman named Marilyn Mulero awaiting execution in Chicago. The article said she was *sentenced to death on a plea bargain.* You read that right: a bargain. For death.

I thought that couldn't be accurate. The media often gets legal proceedings wrong. Why would anyone give up the right to trial and appeals and plead to the death penalty? If she'd gone to trial, even if she was guilty, she might have won, or she might have received a lesser sentence. And, even if she lost, she'd have the right to appeal, and she'd be alive during the many years her case slowly worked its way through the appellate system, again with the chance of success.

By pleading guilty, she'd given up all these rights and opportunities with nothing in return. There was no "bargain" in the plea bargain. It simply guaranteed a quick death sentence.

I did some research and found out the article was, in fact, accurate. I needed to know how this young woman, who was twenty-one years old at the time of her arrest, ended up on death row without a trial in the United States of America. I didn't want to know. I needed to know.

I read about Marilyn's case just a year and a half after I'd moved from Washington, DC, to suburban Michigan. In DC, I worked as a court-appointed criminal defense lawyer and ran a prison education program in DC's notoriously violent Lorton Prison. On a daily basis, I moved between the prison, the courts, and crime scenes in what was then known as the "Murder Capital of the World." I was tempted away from my life in DC, immersed in the criminal legal system, by the prospect of a beautiful Victorian house in Michigan that cost only $89,000, a public school a safe walk away where our children could get a decent education, and a cushy job teaching law.

Yet, eighteen months into my new life, I was sucked back into my old life by Marilyn's story. I don't exactly know why. Maybe I felt a kinship with her because she was from Puerto Rico, my island home throughout high school. Maybe I was already bored of suburban living and needed some action. I still don't know exactly why I took on her case, but it changed the entire direction of my life.

I first met Marilyn in the Dwight Correctional Facility, one hundred miles outside of Chicago. Dwight was a women's prison in the middle of endless farmland that was shut down in 2013 for budget reasons. It was a typical place for a prison in the United States, far from the city where most of the residents came from, built with no concern for poor families without decent cars, or money for gas, to make the long journey to visit their loved ones.

As I approached the prison, the guard towers rose above the cornfields like silos. I pulled into the visitor parking lot, where a group of incarcerated women in white jumpsuits raked the gravel lot.

"Can I help you?" asked the serious-but-bored-looking officer at the front gate. His expression was exactly what you would expect from someone who stared at grey walls all day.

"I'm here to see Marilyn Mulero." I showed him my state bar license, driver's license, and a memo from their legal department confirming my visit.

He glanced at the documents for a moment. "You're going to meet her in the cafeteria."

The cafeteria? That seemed very odd. If she was a man, our meeting would have been through the bars of a cell or in a highly secure attorney room in a specific unit built for death row. But there was no specific unit for women on death row. There were too few of them.

I was escorted to the cafeteria and waited for Marilyn on an uncomfortable metal folding chair. I looked around at bright artwork and motivational posters on the walls, including the classic cat hanging from a wire with bold orange letters declaring *Hang in There!* There were sad looking pieces of streamers stuck to tape on the walls from some past holiday celebration.

I could smell some nondescript food being cooked nearby and heard some distant shouting, a constant sound in correctional facilities. I was thinking about what to say to Marilyn and whether I was making a terrible mistake getting involved in her case when I saw her for the first time. Two guards led her into the cafeteria, one on each side. She was half the size of the guards, and yet her wrists and ankles were shackled, causing her to shuffle across the polished linoleum floor.

Marilyn wore layers of clothes under her drab, oversized, blue prison jumpsuit. Her freckled face made her look even younger than she was. Her dark hair was neatly braided, and she wore thick eyeliner. I could tell she'd spent some time on her hair and makeup for the visit. That always saddens me. Everyone's life should involve better things to get made up for than a prison visit with a lawyer.

"Hello, Mr. Brooks." She nervously smiled, trying to shake my hand while one of the guards handcuffed her to the table.

"How are you, Marilyn?" A seemingly absurd question for someone in her situation, but even in prison there are good days and bad days. "How are you being treated?"

She shrugged her shoulders. "I'm getting by."

We talked for half an hour before I started to ask about her case. I always begin my client visits by talking about their lives, classes they are taking, work they are doing, and prison visits they've had with family and friends. I talk to them about anything but their case for as long as I can. I care about them as human beings, and it allows me to try and develop a bit of trust before they have to open up about the worst experience of their life, and often, the worst choices they've ever made.

Marilyn indulged me and told me about the certificates she'd earned taking correspondence courses from a junior college. She was upbeat, and it felt like she was excited to be talking to someone from the outside world. We talked about Puerto Rico and places we both knew from my time going to high school there and her time bouncing back and forth between Chicago and a Caribbean mountain village. She talked about her time in prison and the other women who were housed with her—the fights, the relationships, the general drama. We talked about everything except why she was facing execution until the conversation ran out of steam.

"What can you tell me about your case?" I asked, shifting gears.

"I'm innocent." She nervously laughed and stared directly into my eyes.

I was deeply cynical about this statement. It made no sense to me that an innocent person would plead guilty with no better sentence than death on the table.

"Then why did you plead guilty?" I asked.

She started to look angry. "My lawyer told me it was the best way to go. He said no matter what I did, I was leaving prison in a body bag. If I plead guilty, I had a chance of living out my life in prison. If I fought the case, I was going to be executed."

"Yet, you pleaded guilty and got the death penalty."

"Yep." She lowered her head and started tearing up. She wiped her eyes with a tissue and, with each stroke, her efforts at applying makeup for our visit disappeared.

"How did you get this lawyer?"

She looked back up at me with smeared eyeliner and watery eyes. "I had a public defender, but my friends told me I needed a real lawyer, so I fired her and got a private lawyer."

This was a tragic statement I'd heard too many times. There are three types of lawyers who work in the criminal legal system. Private lawyers hired by people charged with crimes, private lawyers appointed and paid for by the court, and public defenders. Unfortunately, Marilyn, like many people, held the mistaken belief that public defenders are not "real lawyers," and she'd be better off with private representation. She'd fired her public defender, who I later learned was one of the best in Chicago, and her friends found a lawyer with an office in their neighborhood. They paid him a $10,000 retainer and, for that, Marilyn got a plea and the death penalty. She had, in fact, hired the wrong lawyer.

THE RIGHT TO COUNSEL

The right to a criminal defense lawyer in the United States has a sketchy history. In the 1930s, in the case of *Powell v. Alabama,* three Black men were sentenced to death for allegedly raping two White women.[1] Their trials began and ended with death sentences in a single day with practically no assistance from lawyers. For the first time, the US Supreme Court said that states had to provide some form of legal services in their criminal courts to defendants in similar situations. However, it wasn't until the 1960s, in the case of *Gideon v. Wainwright,* that the Court specifically ruled that states had to provide lawyers for any cases that resulted in any prison time.[2] This is why you don't get a lawyer for traffic court, but you do get a lawyer if you are charged with a serious crime.

When the US Supreme Court ruled that states had to start providing lawyers for criminal defendants, public defender offices and court-appointed lawyer programs cropped up all over the country. Public defenders were nothing new; more enlightened jurisdictions had been providing their services for decades.

It's true that most public defenders are overworked and underpaid. Many have horrendous caseloads that make it very difficult to give their full attention to all their cases. Some are exhausted and on the edge of burnout after years of working too hard for too little. And, yes, a few are incompetent, but at no greater level than you find incompetence in all professions.

The overwhelming majority of public defenders get into the work because they want to help people. They are typically well-credentialed, committed, and smart. Getting a job as a public defender is more difficult than most people think. Public defender offices receive many more applications from lawyers looking for work than they can hire, so they can be selective. Public defender offices do lots of training, the lawyers have a great deal of experience, and the junior lawyers are supervised by senior lawyers.

Private lawyers are often excellent, but they also often lack the experience and training of public defenders and operate without supervision. In some systems, court appointed lawyers are paid by the hour, whether the case settles quickly or goes to trial. In other systems, there is a flat fee per case, which encourages lawyers to settle quickly and move on to the next case.

I am certain Marilyn's case would have had a better outcome had she not fired her public defender and hired a private criminal defense attorney. And, I say that having practiced as a private criminal defense attorney.

AN INAUSPICIOUS BEGINNING

In the early 1990s, I was on the list of private criminal defense attorneys in DC who got paid by the city to take on court-appointed cases. We were a motley crew. Some in our group were highly competent lawyers who loved the independence of running a law practice with no boss. Others appeared unemployable and were on the list because they had no other choice. Today, in most jurisdictions it's much more difficult to get on court-appointed lists, and it requires years of experience. When I got out of law school, all you needed was a bar card and a couple of days of training.

There was an older female attorney whom I'll never forget. When her cases were called, she never responded to the judges because she never knew her clients' names. The clerk would have to tell the judge the client was one of hers, and the judge would shout her name out, often disturbing her from near slumber. Her bumbling and confused representation of clients seemed sort of comical at the time. It's not so funny after decades of witnessing the devastation that results from bad lawyering.

I wasn't much better than some of the unemployables in my early days in court. As soon as I'd passed the bar, I'd taken the two-day course required to be on the list. The training was conducted by an eccentric Mexican American lawyer who went over basic court procedure and demonstrated some dramatic lawyering. He had perfect, unaccented English, but he talked about how sometimes he used a strong Mexican accent to appear folksy and relatable to jurors. To illustrate this point, he proceeded to give a sample closing argument, using a heavy accent, for a case where he wanted the jury to understand why an innocent person might run:

> When I was a young boy living in Mexico, I was a good boy, but Pablo was a very bad boy. One day Pablo threw a rock at a truck. The driver slammed on his brakes and jumped out. He was huge! The biggest man I'd ever seen! He was running toward us! Pablo ran as fast as he could in the opposite direction, but I froze. I thought to myself, "Why should I run? I've done nothing wrong. Pablo threw the rock. I'll just explain that it wasn't me." But, as the huge man got closer and closer, I got more and more frightened. And, when he was ten feet away, I turned and ran. Not because I was guilty, but because I was afraid.

He then continued, easing off on the accent,

> Ladies and gentlemen of the jury, my client didn't run because he was guilty. My client ran because he was afraid. He was frightened about what the police might do if they caught him, just like I was frightened of that giant man the day Pablo threw that rock.

He was a good teacher. I loved the class. But two days of training wasn't enough.

On my first day in court, I thought I was ready. I'd purchased the two-volume, purple manual that all the DC defense lawyers used. It allegedly contained all the secrets I needed to be a great lawyer. I'd read the chapters covering arraignments and was good to go. Or so I thought.

In reality, I knew next to nothing about arraignments. I only knew there were two purposes for them that I'd jotted down in my training notes:

1. To decide if the arresting officer had probable cause; and
2. To decide whether the person should be held in jail until trial, released on bail, or released on their own recognizance with no bail.

When I showed up in court that morning, I saw my name next to three cases on the assignment list. I was excited to get going as I headed to the lockup to interview my new clients and prepare them for arraignment.

From my two-day training and my purple books, I learned that I needed to get as much information from my clients about their family, work, school, and ties to the community so that, at arraignment, I could argue for their release pending trial.

Any plan I had went out of the window when I met with my first client, Mrs. Johnson. She was an elderly woman arrested for screaming drunkenly at a neighbor and throwing garbage on her neighbor's front yard.

"Hi, my name is Justin Brooks. I've been assigned to represent you," I said cheerfully through the jail bars.

"Assigned, what does that mean?" she growled. "You don't want to represent me!"

"No, of course I do," I sputtered. "I just mean the court has appointed me."

"Has appointed you what?"

"To represent you. They've appointed me to represent you."

"Represent me in what?"

"In court. You are going to court today."

"Where?"

"Court."

Forty-five minutes later, I had still learned nothing about her, and she was equally uninformed about me and why I was bothering her. With fifteen minutes to go until I had to be in court, I ran to the men's side of the jail and used the little time I had left to get basic and inadequate information from my other two clients. One had been charged with car theft. The other faced a drug charge.

I rushed to the courtroom. Mrs. Johnson was the first case called. She was brought into the center of the courtroom, and then the judge ordered her released before I could even say a word. I failed to learn what the letters "NP" meant, which were clearly written next to her name on the arraignment list. She'd been "No Papered," which meant a prosecutor had reviewed the police report and decided not to charge her, even though she'd been arrested. I wasted most of my morning talking to a client I didn't need to talk to and would never see again instead of talking to my clients who I needed to represent. I was lamenting my misstep and reading quickly through the police reports of my other assigned cases when one of them was called.

"Mark Taylor!" the bailiff yelled.

Mr. Taylor was led into the courtroom as his newly minted twenty-five-year-old lawyer approached counsel table.

"Your honor, I'd like to waive further reading of the complaint, enter a plea of not guilty, and request a speedy trial," I said, parroting my training manual.

The judge looked up from his paperwork and stared down his nose at me through his wire-rimmed glasses. He was straight out of central casting: old, White, and grumpy. He turned to his bailiff and said sarcastically, "Have we started reading the complaint?"

"No, Judge," the bailiff answered, shaking his head, and laughing.

"Mr. Brooks," the judge continued, "how can we 'waive further reading of the complaint' if we haven't started reading the complaint?"

"I'm sorry, Judge," I said quietly, determined to soldier on. It was the first, but certainly not the last time I apologized to a judge.

The point is, I don't believe a public defender would have made my rookie mistakes. They go through much more extensive training and shadowing before they fly solo in court. Then, they have supervisors who monitor them and give them continuous training. I think I eventually became a good lawyer, as I believe most lawyers do. But, left to their own devices, with no supervision and little training, lawyers get sloppy, cut corners, or simply don't know any better. I didn't know the failings of Marilyn's lawyer when I first met with her, but the more she talked, the more I became convinced something had gone desperately wrong.

And that was before I went to the crime scene.

A TWENTY-FIVE-YEAR ODYSSEY

The day after meeting with Marilyn, I told my first-year criminal law students her story.

"There's a woman on death row in Illinois who is scheduled to be executed, and she says she's innocent. Who wants to help me represent her?" I announced to my class.

Four brave souls raised their hands. That night, we met at my house, where we sat around my kitchen table, hatching an investigation and litigation strategy.

I knew reversing a death penalty case would take a herculean effort. In death cases, there were supposed to be so many safeguards built into the system that no innocent person could possibly be sentenced to death.

In 1972, the United States Supreme Court suspended the death penalty in the case *Furman v. Georgia* due to concerns about how it was being administered. The Court found that the sentence of death was being given in an arbitrary and capricious manner, and thus the punishment was violative of the Eighth Amendment's ban on cruel and unusual punishment.[3]

In 1976, however, the Court brought the punishment back based on Georgia's new death penalty procedure in the case of *Gregg v. Georgia*.[4] Under the new procedure, death cases had two phases. First, there is a guilt/innocence phase, like a regular trial. Second, there is a separate sentencing phase that is much more involved than a traditional sentencing. During the sentencing phase, prosecutors could introduce aggravating factors to justify a death sentence. The defense could argue mitigating factors to justify a lesser sentence. The law also required automatic review of all death cases by the state supreme court.[5]

We now know that the promise of *Gregg v. Georgia* didn't become a reality as 4 percent of the people sentenced to death in the United States were later proven innocent and released.[6] And, when I worked in Chicago, more people were found innocent and released from death row than were executed. At that time, a lawyer could turn to their client after they received a death sentence and say, "The good news is that it's 50/50 as to whether you will be executed or go home."[7]

In Marilyn's case, she benefitted from none of these procedures. Her case involved a plea bargain, a short sentencing hearing, and she was sent to death row.

The weekend after the students volunteered to work on the case, I piled the four of them in my Jeep Cherokee and drove to Humboldt Park in Chicago, the scene of the crime that landed Marilyn on death row. For years, the park had been a battleground between two Puerto Rican street gangs (Maniac Latin Disciples and Latin Kings) who both claimed the territory.

Marilyn and her friends associated with the Maniac Latin Disciples. They weren't members of the gang. There were no female members, but they dated members of the Disciples, and the Disciples controlled their neighborhood.

Marilyn's case began when she was driving in the Humboldt Park area with fifteen-year-old Jackie Montanez and another teenage girl. At a stoplight, they started talking to two male Latin King members, rivals of the Disciples, and the group decided to go hang out at the park together. Jackie went into the men's bathroom with one of the men and shot him in the back of the head while he was urinating.

There are two conflicting stories as to what happened next:

The first story, which Marilyn confessed to after many hours of interrogation, was that Jackie walked out of the bathroom, handed her the gun, and Marilyn shot the second man.

"That's not what happened," Marilyn told me the first day I met her in the cafeteria. "Jackie killed the guy in the bathroom and then walked out and shot the second guy. I freaked out and ran."

There was one eyewitness who claimed to see the second shooting. She told the police she looked out of her apartment window after midnight and saw Jackie (whom she described as the tall girl) walk out of the bathroom and hand a gun to Marilyn (whom she described as the short girl), who then shot the second man.

It's true Marilyn is significantly shorter than Jackie, but there was a small problem with the witness statement. When my students and I stood in front of her apartment building on a sunny day, you could barely see the bathroom where the shooting occurred. When we measured the distance between the apartment building and the bathroom, it was more than 400 feet.

The witness's statement claiming she saw the passing of the gun at night, 400 feet away, was the equivalent of sitting behind one end zone in an unlit football stadium at night and seeing someone pass a hot dog behind the opposite end zone. It was impossible.

Later in the investigation, we learned this eyewitness, the only person in the entire city of Chicago who claimed to see the shooting, also happened to be the girlfriend of one of the victims. This fact was conveniently left out of the police reports.

Marilyn ended up on death row because there was no investigation into her case. Her lawyer later admitted that he didn't investigate the crime scene, even though his office was nearby. If Marilyn had kept her public defender as her attorney, an investigation would have occurred by a trained investigator, another resource that public defenders have that private attorneys often don't.

It took a few months to track down Marilyn's lawyer. He'd ended his legal career when Marilyn was sentenced to death and began studying to be a priest. Probably a job where he could do less damage. Perhaps an opportunity for penitence. Who knows?

Fortunately, due to mistakes made by the prosecutor at Marilyn's sentencing hearing, the Illinois Supreme Court reversed and remanded her case for a new sentencing proceeding, but they refused to allow her to withdraw the plea. I worked with my law students and Chicago public defenders on the resentencing. We presented her case to a new jury, but since the plea "bargain" was still in effect, under Illinois law, they only had the choice of life or death. We anxiously awaited their decision.

Even though it was more than two decades ago, I vividly remember the moment in 1998 when the jury returned to the courtroom with Marilyn's sentencing decision. It was one of those intense moments when you can hear your pulse in your ear, the world freezes, and you are hyper-aware of everything around you. Marilyn was shaking. I felt the vibration of her leg knocking against the counsel table where we sat. I put my hand on hers to attempt to give her some comfort that I knew was unattainable in that moment.

"Have you reached your decision?" the judge asked the jury foreman.

"Yes, your honor," answered the electrician turned decider of life and death decisions.

"And what is it?" the judge asked.

"We have decided the defendant should be sentenced to life in prison."

Never, before that case, could I have imagined a sentence of life would be great news. Life meant life and not death. Life meant Marilyn would live, and there would be an opportunity to keep fighting. It was the best choice they could make. I hugged Marilyn and promised to keep fighting for her freedom.

It was a bitter cold Chicago winter day as I left the courthouse. It was just past 4:30 in the afternoon, but it was already dark. As I stumbled toward my car, trying not to slip on the icy sidewalk, I made a life-changing decision. I wanted to spend the rest of my life working on cases like Marilyn's. I wanted to free innocent people from the nightmare of wrongful incarceration.

I also decided I wanted to do the work with students. In a classroom, I couldn't teach them the skills they needed. I learned how to be a lawyer in the real world of crime scenes, jailhouse interviews, and the courtroom, and that was where they would learn as well.

The following year, in 1999, I cofounded the California Innocence Project. California was the belly of the beast. In the country with the largest prison population in the world, California incarcerated more people than any other state. California had it all—the death penalty, three-strikes laws, and mandatory minimums. It was the perfect place to look for innocent people among the nearly two hundred thousand who were residents of the California prisons at that time. Since then, our office has freed dozens of innocent people. But I never abandoned Marilyn. Reversal of the death sentence was not enough. I needed her to be free, and I would not stop fighting until she was.

Marilyn sat in prison waiting while I continued to litigate her case. I failed in state court repeatedly, but I was hopeful when I got to argue the case in federal court. I was confident federal judges would see how the representation she received fell below what is required by the Sixth Amendment.

To get a criminal case reversed based on a lawyer's incompetence, the following must be proven:

1. A lawyer's handling of a case was below an objective standard of reasonableness; and
2. There is a reasonable probability that if the lawyer had performed adequately the result would have been different.[8]

This is a technical way of saying your lawyer did a bad job and, if they hadn't, you wouldn't have been convicted. In general, I disagree with this standard because, while it appears to be an objective standard, it still comes down to what the judge thinks is *reasonable* work by the lawyer, and it's difficult to prove that a jury would have done something different based on a different presentation of evidence.

I hoped the judges would agree with me that Marilyn's trial lawyer's work did not resemble the word "reasonable." He did no investigation. How could that be reasonable? That hope began to fall apart when the first judge asked a question.

"Counsel, wasn't it your client's choice to plead guilty?"

"Your honor," I answered, "that's like being taken to a hospital and a doctor mistakenly telling you immediate emergency heart surgery is necessary, or you will die. Should you or your doctor be held responsible for your choice based on the misdiagnosis? Is that truly a choice?"

The judge seemed unimpressed with my answer. That was confirmed when the ruling once again was a loss. The conviction remained intact.

I still believe that no competent lawyer would ever allow a client to plead guilty in a death case with no guarantee of a lesser sentence. And, a reasonable lawyer would have at least obtained a better deal, if not an acquittal.

For twenty-five years, I lost that argument in Marilyn's case in every court I argued it. I lost all her appeals, clemency petitions, and my petition for review by the United States Supreme Court. I even filed a petition with the United Nations, asking for a finding that the Illinois criminal legal system operated in violation of principles of international human rights law. Within its system, a young, innocent woman was sentenced to death without any investigation into her case. To this day, that petition hasn't been ruled on.

Of course, it wasn't just the defense attorney in Marilyn's case that caused her to get a death sentence. Blame can also be allocated to the lawyers on the other side of the courtroom. The prosecution did little to determine the truth. Once they were presented with a case where they got an easy plea of guilty, and thus no need to prepare for a trial, they focused their attention on making sure Marilyn got the maximum sentence. The possibility that she was innocent wouldn't have even been considered. In the psychological warfare waged in our criminal legal system, there is little room for prosecutors to consider whether a person who confesses to a crime and pleads guilty may, in fact, be innocent.

Mark Godsey, a former federal prosecutor who founded and now directs the Ohio Innocence Project at the University of Cincinnati Law

School, describes this psychology in his book *Blind Injustice*. Professor Godsey, using his own experience as a prosecutor, discusses in detail how confirmation bias, cognitive dissonance, administrative evil, bureaucratic denial, and dehumanization, among other factors, combine to cause prosecutors to not see and/or not act on indicators that a person they are prosecuting might be innocent. He also describes the competitive atmosphere of a prosecutor's office and the drive to win:

> Simply put, there is great atmospheric pressure to win cases and appear tough and aggressive. Everyone in my office was ambitious and competitive. Everyone wanted to look good. Everyone cared about his or her reputation. Everyone wanted to advance. If you loafed around and were not aggressive with your cases, you would not gain a reputation for being a strong "prosecutor's prosecutor." If you lost a case, people would talk. If you lost more than a case or two in a short time period, people would start to question your competence or dedication. So we all did our best to make sure that didn't happen.[9]

Without competent counsel and up against aggressive prosecutors looking to get a death verdict, Marilyn had little chance of avoiding a death sentence. With the luck of the draw, she also drew a tough-on-crime judge who was a former police officer. He allowed the death sentencing procedure to go forward, knowing the prosecution and defense hadn't even spoken about the option of pleading and obtaining a lesser sentence. And the detective who investigated her case was later revealed as one of the most corrupt officers in Chicago history. More on him later.

Finally, in 2020, at the height of the COVID-19 crisis, I got the call I dreamed about during the twenty-five years I worked on Marilyn's case. I had filed yet another clemency petition with the help of two amazing sister organizations—the Illinois Innocence Project and the Exoneration Project. We argued that the detective in Marilyn's case had been linked to dozens of wrongful convictions similar to Marilyn's. There was a clear pattern of police misconduct that undermined confidence in the conviction.

Lauren Myerscough-Mueller was one of the lawyers I worked with. "Marilyn's going home!" she screamed into the phone.

"What?" I could hardly speak. I felt my eyes well up with tears.

"The governor is granting our petition, and she's going home!"

It's impossible to describe the feeling I had as I heard this news. Shock, joy, elation, relief—none of these words do justice. I had worked on the case for twenty-five years. I talked about it to anyone who would listen. It was part of me. I could barely remember a time when I wasn't fighting to free her.

Sadly, due to COVID, I couldn't walk her out of prison. But she called me as soon as she was home and safe with her family. We talked for the first time outside prison walls and without our conversation being recorded by the Illinois Department of Corrections.

I often tell students if they want to have a calm, even-keeled life, a life where you go to work and your days are predictable, don't become an innocence lawyer. My life is filled with incredible highs. The days I get to walk innocent people out of prison and bring them home to their families after many years of incarceration are some of the best days of my life. I also have incredible lows. Those are the days when we lose cases I know we should win, and an innocent person continues to waste away in prison.

Traditional criminal defense is hard, but when you know your client is guilty, and they go to prison, if you've done your best, you can live with that. But when you know your client is innocent and they are still in prison, it's much more difficult. And it's tough not to blame your own inability to make things right.

There is no way of overstating the importance of having a competent lawyer to represent you if you are charged with a crime, whether you are innocent or guilty. Our criminal legal system is complex, biased, overloaded, and geared toward pushing you into a plea bargain. Without a competent lawyer, it will run over you without tapping the brakes, and you may find yourself wrongfully convicted.

I finally got to see Marilyn outside of prison on August 7, 2021. I flew to Chicago with my son Zach who was born the year before I took on the case, but by then was a third-year law student. Instead of meeting in a prison cafeteria surrounded by guards, we planned to meet at a restaurant surrounded by family and friends.

I saw her through the restaurant window and ran out to greet her. As she walked toward me, I flashed back to a quarter of a century earlier when she was walking toward me in the prison cafeteria. Instead of a

Figure 2. August 7, 2021. Meeting Marilyn outside prison for the first time. Photo credit: Justin Brooks.

prison jumpsuit, she was wearing a bright tee-shirt with the words "She is fearless" emblazoned across the front (see fig. 2).

She was older, we both were, but I could see the weight of her long incarceration lifted off her. She was excited and energetic, smiling and laughing. We hugged for a long time. Again, I was at a loss for words.

2 You Live in the Country or the City

Angel Reséndiz

"I beat that girl in the head with a brick until I saw her brains, and she survived. That's a beautiful thing."

I nodded my head, wondering how long I'd have to listen to this man talk about killing people until I got the information I needed. He kept diverting away from the case I wanted to talk about to tell me about other killings he'd committed. And he told his stories with no bravado and no shame. He was just matter of fact about it, like he was telling me stories about countries he'd visited on vacation or foods he liked to eat.

It didn't help that it was incredibly hot—Texas hot—and I was sweating through my suit. I imagined for a moment how great it would be to be with my wife and kids enjoying a day on the beach in San Diego instead of sitting on death row in Texas interviewing a sociopath.

"Sure," I answered. "But what can you tell me about these crime scene photos?"

I lay the pictures of Pamela Richards's dead, half-naked body on the table. "Do you remember doing this?"

He put on his glasses and studied the photos, intently trying to cut through the hazy memories of so many dead bodies.

"She does look familiar. I can't remember if I killed her. I used to do a lot of drugs."

"Okay, but she looks familiar?"

"Yes. I might have killed her." He kept studying the photo.

"Is there a reason you think you might have killed her?"

"I don't know. But look at this shirt she's wearing. It says, *'Shady Lady.'* That's disrespectful."

I stared at him, words failing me. I wanted to run out of that prison as fast as I could.

Angel Reséndiz, better known as the "Railroad Killer," was executed by the state of Texas not long after this meeting. His appellate attorney had allowed me to meet with him, reasoning that implicating Reséndiz in a murder investigation in California could delay his execution.

Reséndiz was a prolific serial killer. He traveled around the country on freight trains and killed women who lived near the tracks. He would knock on doors and ask for work doing odd jobs. At just over five feet tall, he was unthreatening and had a big smile. Women who were home alone would let him in their houses.

It's unknown how many women Reséndiz killed, but at least fifteen of them were beaten to death with rocks and blunt objects. A signature of his killings was overkill, where victims were often beaten after they were already dead.

When I read about his modus operandi, it caught my attention. The California Innocence Project was representing a client, Bill Richards, who was convicted for a murder committed in just the same manner in a rural area with train tracks nearby. The fact that the crime was committed in a rural area was a significant link to Reséndiz, but it was also significant in that the low quality of the police and prosecution work reflected what I've often seen in rural areas.

Bill Richards

August 10, 1993, started as a typical day for Bill and Pamela Richards. Neighbors reported that the couple were holding hands and walking around the property where they were building a new home in Summit Valley, a remote and sparsely populated California desert community in San Bernardino County. Construction had begun, so they were living in a motor home on the property.

Pamela worked as a waitress at an Olive Garden fifty miles away, and Bill worked as an engineer at a power plant forty-five miles away. Pamela didn't work that day. She planned on doing some errands, including going to the laundromat. Bill worked the late afternoon and evening shift at the plant.

Bill's shift was ordinary. Coworkers later reported that he didn't seem agitated or act in any way but his usual self. He clocked out at around the normal time (11:03 p.m.), and before he went home, he filled his cooler from an ice machine at work because there was no refrigeration in the motor home.[1]

Bill got home just before midnight and found his property, including the motor home, in complete darkness. He thought that was odd because Pamela was supposed to be home. He went to the shed where they kept their generator and restarted it. Then, he walked in the darkness toward the motor home and tripped over Pamela's body.

Panicked, Bill rolled his motionless wife over, placed his hands on her head to see if she was still alive, and cradled her body in hopes she would wake up. Large portions of her skull were missing, her ear looked like it was torn off, and her eye was hanging out of her skull.

Bill ran to the motor home and called 911 at 11:58 p.m.

"Ah Christ, I don't know what to do," he told the dispatcher. "I just came home. My wife is dead. She fell off the step. She's got a hole in her head."

The dispatcher said they were sending the police immediately, but more than half an hour passed, and no one had arrived. Bill hit redial.

"This is Bill Richards calling again. Is somebody coming? Things don't look right here at all, I thought she slipped and fell, but there's things moved."

The dispatcher warned Bill not to touch anything and reassured him that help was on the way.

Several minutes passed with no signs of emergency service lights. Bill called again.

Finally, at 12:36 a.m., San Bernardino County Sheriff's Deputy Mark Nourse arrived. In his opinion, Pamela's body wasn't cold to the touch, but it also wasn't warm. To Nourse, that meant she died recently. No official time of death analysis was ever conducted. In fact, Deputy Nourse skipped several steps that would happen in a normal investigation. No formal measurements of any type were taken. He failed to take the liver temperature or the core temperature of the body. He failed to assess rigor mortis. And, although Pamela's car door was open, he didn't even check to see if the engine was still warm.

Around 1:00 a.m., a homicide detective was called to assist in processing the scene, but the detective got lost searching for the property. He didn't arrive until almost 3:15 a.m. and didn't begin processing the scene until 6:00 a.m.

Investigative mistakes piled up throughout the early morning as more officers arrived at the crime scene. No fingerprinting was done. The officers walked all over the scene, possibly destroying footprint evidence. Perhaps most egregious, Pamela's body was left uncovered and not protected. Neighborhood dogs began to bury her head in the dirt.

Over the next few days, detectives focused their investigation on Bill and repeatedly interrogated him. Ultimately, they built a case against him based on his presence at the scene, allegations of problems in the marriage, a thread wedged under Pamela's fingernail that matched the color of Bill's shirt, and Pamela's blood on Bill's shirt. The prosecution also presented a recorded statement that Bill gave noting the lack of emotion in his voice after discovering his wife's dead body. When I listened to the statement it simply sounded like a man suffering from shock while dealing with an unimaginable situation. People often assume that the only normal reaction to losing a loved one to a homicide is sobbing and tears, but shock and shutting down emotionally is how your brain can protect you from facing the reality of a tragedy.

The District Attorney brought the case to trial. It ended in a hung jury.

The District Attorney brought the case to trial a second time. It ended in a hung jury.

The District Attorney brought the case to trial a third time. The judge recused himself during jury selection, ending the trial.

The District Attorney brought the case to trial a fourth time with evidence that hadn't been heard before. Dr. Norman "Skip" Sperber, a forensic odontologist (bite mark expert) who testified in both Jeffrey

Dahmer's and Ted Bundy's murder trials, testified that a mark on Pamela's hand was a human bite mark from the bottom dentition of a set of teeth. He made this conclusion by merely eyeballing a photo of the injury. He further testified that the bite mark was consistent with Bill's dentition because the mark revealed an unerupted canine tooth similar to Bill's. Dr. Sperber opined that this variant would only be found in 1–2 percent of the population.

"So, if it was a hundred people that we took in here," he testified, "I doubt that we would see in a hundred people one tooth lower, submerged like this. It might be one or two or less. That's kind of a unique feature."

At the end of the trial, the jury was deadlocked. The trial judge sent them back to deliberate further, and they found Bill guilty. Bill was sentenced to twenty-five-years-to-life in prison.

In 2001, Bill reached out to the California Innocence Project. I vividly remember reading his letter and going through the case file for the first time. The crime scene photos were some of the worst I'd ever seen. Absolutely gruesome. I remember thinking, why would a guy who has no history of violence do this to his wife? And if he did, why would he call the police? Why wouldn't he drive her body into the desert, dig a deep hole, and leave her there?

"We never thought Bill was guilty," Pamela's sister told me over the phone not long after we took on the case. "The District Attorney didn't care what the family had to say."

When we started to investigate, the District Attorney's Office was similarly not interested in our opinions. After taking four trials to get a conviction, they had no interest in revisiting the case.

"I'm happy to cooperate," the Deputy District Attorney assigned to deal with habeas petitions to reopen old cases told my law partner, Jan Stiglitz, and me on the phone.

"Great, will you agree to do DNA testing on the evidence from the crime scene?" I asked.

"No."

"Will you agree to give us access to the evidence that was collected from the crime scene?" I asked.

"No."

"How exactly do you define cooperation?" Jan asked.

"I will do what the judge orders me to do."

I was pretty new to California at the time of this conversation. I hadn't yet truly understood that there were two Californias. The further you got from the ocean, and the deeper you ventured into the California desert, the weirder it got. The desert jurisdictions are far more conservative, and the voters expect their elected prosecutors to be tough-on-crime. This is common throughout the United States, where rural areas tend to be more conservative.[2]

San Bernardino is no exception.

We had to litigate to get access to the evidence.

We had to litigate to get DNA testing.

Even worse, we had to litigate as to whether DNA was a valid science. Walking into that hearing, I remember asking the Deputy District Attorney whether he had thought about the implications if he won.

"What do you mean?" he asked.

"Well, if you win, we'll be sending the ruling to every criminal defense attorney in the country. A lot more people have gone to prison based on DNA than have been freed."

We won that hearing, and the judge ordered testing of the paving stone the police had concluded was used in the murder, as well as a human hair found underneath one of Pamela's nails. Often, a victim will have hair and skin from their attacker under their nails from their attempts to defend themselves. The judge ordered that the testing be done by the California Department of Justice (CDOJ), and we naively thought that was a good idea.

CDOJ delayed the testing over and over again. We filed multiple motions asking the court to demand they complete the testing. We asked for sanctions. Nothing happened.

This was the early 2000s when DNA testing was still a novelty. Today, we would just have the testing done by a private lab and get the results within weeks, possibly even days.

It took four years to get the results. Four years Bill sat in prison. Male DNA was found on the stone, but it wasn't Bill's. The hair found under Pamela's nails was neither his nor Pamela's.

While we were waiting for the test results, we continued to pursue other aspects of the case. We looked closely at the photos of Pamela's fingernails and the blue thread that allegedly matched Bill's shirt. We found photos where the finger was no longer attached to her hand (from the autopsy), and the blue thread clearly appeared, but we also found a photo with the finger still attached—so obviously taken first—and no thread seemed to be in the nail. We blew the photo up, and we still couldn't see it. Then, we had an expert analyze the photo, and he reported that the color of the thread didn't appear in the photo.

Based on these results, we concluded that the thread had been planted. We didn't know exactly by whom, but we knew there had been allegations of fabricating evidence in another case against the criminalist who processed the thread evidence.

Next, we looked at the bite mark evidence. Some of the most notorious wrongful convictions in the United States involved bite mark testimony. I often say that many of the forensic odontologists who testify in these cases are bored dentists with too much time on their hands, who love the TV show *CSI*.

We had an expert look at the bite mark photos. He told us the photos were taken at an angle that distorted the bite mark, but he could correct it using Photoshop software. When he did, he concluded that the dentition didn't match Bill Richards at all. In fact, it excluded him.

Skip Sperber, the forensic odontologist who testified for the prosecution in Bill's case, was thought by many to be the best forensic dentist in the world. He'd been a practicing dentist in San Diego since he left the Navy in 1956, where he served as a dental officer. He was the Chief Forensic Dentist at the California Department of Justice, where he developed a Dental Identification System. He testified as an expert in more than two hundred trials and was on the scene at Ground Zero after the attacks on 9/11, where he helped identify fifteen hundred victims.

My friend Mario Conte handled a case where Skip testified. Mario was the director of the Federal Defenders of San Diego office for many years. His organizational skills, preparation, and attention to detail made him a great trial lawyer. He approached each trial like a prizefighter preparing for a fight. With his grey hair slicked back, always impeccably dressed, he would even click his neck like a fighter as he began his cross examinations. He said, "Skip is a great guy. Let's have lunch with him and talk about the case."

And so, we did. And over lunch, I showed Skip the evidence we'd developed, including the adjusted photo of the bite mark. Skip agreed to study everything, read the trial transcript, and then meet with us again.

At that next meeting, Skip agreed the bite mark wasn't a match, and he should never have testified in support of Bill's conviction.

The combination of the DNA results from the murder weapon, the hair from under Pam's fingernails, the exclusion of Bill from the bite mark, and evidence the blue fiber was planted was certainly enough to prove Bill's innocence. The blood on Bill's shirt was also easily explainable based on him cradling her body. But, to leave no question, we wanted to find the actual killer.

Angel Reséndiz looked good for the crime in so many ways. He'd been in the area and knew it well. The train tracks curved behind the Richardses' property, and neighbors said sometimes people jumped off the train there. Angel gave us blood and saliva samples, but we couldn't match them to the murder weapon or hair. In fact, he kept sending multiple samples to our office to the shock of the students opening letters. We had to put a sign up in the mailroom: DO NOT OPEN MAIL FROM ANGEL RESÉNDIZ!

We hired a dentist in Texas to go to death row and get a sample of Reséndiz's bite mark before he was executed. At first, the dentist was enthusiastic at the prospect of meeting the famous killer until he got to the prison parking lot, and it became real.

"Is he a biter?" he asked me over the phone.

"Well, he killed at least a dozen women with his bare hands, but I'm not sure," I answered.

The bite mark was inconclusive.

In 2007, with the DNA, bite mark, and thread evidence, we were ready to present our case for innocence in court. After an extensive hearing, a judge reversed the conviction, partly on the basis that Skip had provided false testimony. It was finally over . . . or so we thought.

Michael Ramos, the San Bernardino District Attorney at the time who later falsely bragged on his office's website that they had never convicted an innocent person, couldn't let the ruling stand. So, he appealed and challenged whether an expert's prior testimony could be considered false evidence. With bail set at $1,000,000, Bill waited in jail while the appeal played out.

It would be six years, ten months, and eleven days from the time Bill Richards's conviction was reversed until the day he was freed. And, for most of that time, he was housed in a county jail where he couldn't take classes, work, or have contact visits, and where he had to constantly deal with new cellmates who were often drug-addicted and violent.

We lost our initial appeal, with the state appellate court concluding that recanted expert testimony could not be deemed "false" under California law. After all, an expert's opinion was just that—an opinion. It wasn't "evidence" that could be either true or false. The appellate court seemed concerned about a flood of cases being reopened when new experts testified that other experts at trial had testified falsely. But that was not our case. We didn't have a new expert testifying that another expert at trial testified falsely. We had the prosecution's own trial expert saying he testified falsely. It was a very rare situation.

The argument also didn't hold up when it was compared to other types of false evidence. For example, an eyewitness could come into court and say, "That identification I made ten years ago, that was wrong," and that could be considered false evidence, but an expert recant could not.

Jan Stiglitz argued all the appeals in the case. We were confident the California Supreme Court would see it our way.

They didn't. The court ruled against us 4–3. The dissent agreed with us and concluded that the majority of the court was making an untenable distinction between the testimony of "lay witnesses" and "expert witnesses."

In the spirit of never giving up, we decided we were going to change the law, and in 2015, we went to the California state legislature and got the "Bill Richards Law" passed. The dissenting opinion in the Richards case became the backbone of the law which now specifically states that expert trial testimony can later be deemed false evidence if it is recanted and shown to be false.

We went back to the California Supreme Court arguing the application of this new law to Bill's case and won in a unanimous decision. Bill was freed, but the San Bernardino District Attorney's Office threatened to put him on trial again. The case was finally dismissed after we filed a vindictive prosecution motion.

Since his release, Bill has been doing his best to make up for the decades he lost in prison. He's been riding his motorcycle around California and traveling around the world. Nothing will bring back the time or bring back his wife. That devastation can clearly be seen on his face every time I see him.

The fifteen-year battle to free Bill was an example of how difficult it is to win the reversal of cases in rural California. The district attorney fought us at every stage, from access to the evidence through all the appeal processes. But, perhaps more importantly, Bill's case illustrates how easy it is to be wrongfully convicted in rural areas where the police do not have as much training, expertise, or experience in processing violent crime scenes and thus make more mistakes.

Had Bill's case been investigated in a large city, it is much more likely there would have been a quicker response and better trained and more experienced officers who knew how to process a murder scene.

Botched criminal investigations by the police are a common problem in rural areas. John Grisham explored this theme in his true-crime book *An Innocent Man,* which takes place in the rural town of Ada, Oklahoma, with a population of roughly sixteen thousand.[3] Ronald Williamson, once a prospect of the New York Yankees before a career-ending shoulder injury, and his drinking buddy Dennis Fritz, became suspects based on police officers' perceptions that they were the local alcoholics and troublemakers. Those perceptions led the police down a path filled with flimsy evidence that confirmed their biases and ultimately led to the wrongful conviction of both men. Fritz and Williamson spent eleven years in prison before they were exonerated by DNA evidence. Williamson, at one point, had come within five days of being executed.[4]

Rural populations, and their corresponding tax revenues, have continued to decrease over recent decades, contributing to the lack of resources for rural policing.[5] The Bureau of Justice Statistics estimates that expenditures for police officer training, salaries, and other expenses in rural areas are half the expenditure per officer in urban areas. The amount spent per resident on policing is also significantly lower. Police departments serving populations under twenty-five hundred residents spend $95 per resident per year on policing, while urban areas with populations greater than one hundred thousand spend $144 per resident.[6]

Rural police officers also have less education than urban police officers. While 36 percent of urban police officers in the United States have a bachelor's degree, only 12 percent of rural officers have graduated from a four-year university.[7] Rural police officers also have less technical training and less access to high-tech police investigation tools.[8]

Rural communities have fewer crimes than urban areas, and it has been suggested that one of the reasons for this is due to the interpersonal bonds in a small town.[9] These same bonds that help reduce crime, however, can also result in the sheriff creating a suspect list from the town roster of perceived suspicious characters. "Round up the usual suspects," the line from the classic film *Casablanca,* can be the response in small towns where the police know the community well and have established biases.

Another example is the "West Memphis Three" case, a tragic story that was the subject of three documentaries. When young boys were found bound, naked, and murdered in West Memphis, a town with a population of roughly twenty-eight thousand, police interviewed Damien Echols simply because they believed him to be a troubled teen. Echols, and his friends Jason Baldwin and Jessie Misskelley, were seen as outliers in the community with their dark clothes and fondness for heavy metal music. This was somehow twisted into a theory that the three of them committed the murders as part of a satanic ritual.

All three were convicted. Echols was sentenced to death, and Baldwin and Misskelley were sentenced to life in prison. It would be eighteen years until they were released after DNA testing excluded them from the crime scene.[10]

Similarly, when a sixty-five-year-old woman was found brutally raped and murdered in her apartment in Beatrice, Nebraska, a town with a population of roughly twelve thousand the sheriff pursued six mostly poor, troubled people. The "Beatrice Six" would spend a combined total of seventy-seven years in prison before being exonerated by DNA evidence.[11]

While there is not enough research to assert that wrongful convictions happen at a higher rate in rural communities due to these biases, you certainly don't have to look very hard to find them.[12] And, there is no doubt that in cases like that of Bill Richards, the lack of training, experience, and resources to handle homicide cases in small communities can lead to wrongful convictions.

YOU LIVE IN THE CITY

George Johnson

Unfortunately, living in an urban area to avoid the types of wrongful convictions that occur in rural areas can bring on entirely new challenges. Whereas rural areas may suffer from inadequate investigative ability and are less friendly to reviewing old cases, urban areas have their own problems.

My first innocent client wasn't facing the death penalty. His name was George Johnson, and he was facing prison for possession of crack cocaine. It was 1990, and he was one of the thousands of criminal defendants who overwhelmed the police, the courts, and the prisons in Washington, DC, as the "War on Drugs" began to rage. It was the year after President George H. W. Bush went on national television with a bag of crack cocaine seized from a dealer in Lafayette Square Park across from the White House.

"This is the first time since taking the oath of office that I felt an issue was so important, so threatening, that it warranted talking directly with you, the American people," the president declared.

He pulled out the bag of crack cocaine.

"It's as innocent-looking as candy. But it's turning our cities into battle zones."[13]

Just as in all battle zones, there are innocent victims. George Johnson was one of them. He was approaching seventy years old when he decided to move to a small apartment after living in the same house in Washington, DC, for most of his life. A good friend offered to lend him a truck to make the move, and George was walking over to the friend's house to pick it up when suddenly police cars came out of every direction. An officer with a bullhorn screamed for everyone to get on the ground. George was frightened and complied. Soon, he was in handcuffs, along with several young, Black teenagers.

At the police station, George was booked in with the rest of the group for drug dealing. Several of the teenagers had crack cocaine in their possession, and there was a large quantity found in an abandoned house nearby, where they were allegedly keeping the drugs and then bringing it to purchasers who drove up in front of the house.

When I practiced in DC, these types of mass arrests were common in heavily policed inner-city neighborhoods. The goal was to round up as many defendants as possible, and this tactic didn't even require probable cause to initiate. In fact, the more aggressively the police approached a scene, the better, because it would often cause suspects to run, throw evidence on the ground, or do something else that could be deemed as incriminating.

The US Supreme Court endorsed this approach to law enforcement in the case of *California v. Hodari D.* in 1991.[14] The Court held that if an officer attempts to arrest someone and they flee, then there isn't an arrest—there is an *attempted* arrest. Thus, probable cause isn't required.

In other words, if the police try to pull your car over for no reason at all, and you instead keep driving and speed away, they can now legally stop you for speeding. It isn't relevant that they initially had no valid reason to stop you. And, if they have no reason for raiding your neighborhood with bullhorns, guns, and squad cars, but you later give them a reason to arrest you by running and throwing evidence, then their initial lack of probable cause is irrelevant.

Another interesting tool in the "War on Drugs" is the concept of constructive possession, where you can be charged with possessing drugs that are "not on your person." These laws are used around the country to address the strategy of drug dealers not carrying drugs on them, or just carrying a small amount for a single sale and then running back and forth to a location where the drugs are kept. Constructive possession is fine in theory, but also subject to mistakes because people can be charged with possession for drugs they aren't carrying and don't even know about.

Thus, living in neighborhoods where drugs are being sold can subject innocent people like George to be swept up in mass arrests, and constructive possession laws can lead them to be convicted for possession of drugs they know nothing about.

Fortunately for George, he didn't look like the rest of the teenagers. He had a grey afro and deep lines on his face reflecting a tough life. I convinced the prosecutor to dismiss the case. I explained that George lived in DC his entire life without even getting a traffic ticket. I also had credible witnesses who would testify George had never been involved with drugs and that George was in the neighborhood to pick up the truck.

My defense wouldn't have worked if George had any priors, a weak story for being in the neighborhood, or if he was similar in age to the teenagers. Perhaps one of the teenagers was also just walking through the neighborhood when the bust occurred. If so, it would be tough to prove innocence.

There is a common complaint of inner-city residents in the United States that their neighborhoods are often under-policed and over-policed. Under-policing leads to hours of waiting for police responses to calls, unsolved crimes, and residents feeling unsafe in their neighborhoods. Over-policing leads to mistakes, fear of the police, wrongful convictions, and sometimes even death.[15]

There is no more notorious example of this than the murder of George Floyd (discussed further in chapter 10) by Minneapolis police officer Derek Chauvin. After a convenience store employee claimed Floyd had purchased cigarettes with a counterfeit twenty-dollar bill, Floyd was arrested. Chauvin then pinned Floyd to the ground, pressed his knee against Floyd's neck for more than eight minutes, and killed Floyd while multiple officers stood around watching.[16] Chauvin was convicted of second-degree murder and sentenced to more than fifteen years in prison based on video footage of the incident, but far too many of these incidents are undocumented.[17]

A 2014 US Department of Justice investigation of the Newark, NJ, Police Department concluded there was a "pattern or practice of constitutional violations in the NPD's stop and arrest practices, its response to individuals' exercise of their rights under the First Amendment, the Department's use of force, and theft by officers."[18] The report also found "deficiencies in the NPD's systems that are designed to prevent and detect misconduct, including its systems for reviewing force and investigating complaints regarding officer conduct."[19]

A national study of deaths that occurred during police interactions in the United States revealed that 90 percent of the fatalities occurred in urban areas.[20] This study could be dismissed as being based simply on the fact that more violent crimes occur in inner cities, however, the lack of familiarity and relationships urban police officers have with people in the community can also lead to more violent interactions. Increasing familiarity with community residents is one of the principles of the community policing movement, which focuses on improving policing by decreasing violent interactions between the police and the public.[21]

There are positive signs there is a trend toward less violent interactions between the police and citizens in inner cities. This has been attributed to improved training since the George Floyd murder. Sadly, at the same time, killings by police in suburban and rural areas have increased.[22]

Although there are problems that are unique to urban versus rural criminal legal systems, wrongful convictions regularly occur in both environments. The bottom line is that wrongful convictions happen everywhere.

3 You Are in a Relationship and Live with Someone Who Is Murdered

Bill Richards isn't the only person to come home, find a dead spouse, and ultimately be wrongfully convicted of murder. More than half of all female homicide victims are killed by their partners.[1] As a result, the police are always focused on the partners, particularly when they claim to have found the dead body, and thus can be put at the crime scene.

Like Bill Richards, Kim Long was convicted of killing her boyfriend Ozzy after she came home and found his dead body. Kim's conviction was largely based on the fact that she had an argument with Ozzy earlier in the day. Like Bill's case, there was sloppy police work and questionable time of death analysis.

Our advocacy in Bill's and Kim's cases went beyond the courts. We took both cases to the governor's office and sought clemency. Clemency gives power to every governor in the United States to free innocent people from prison in the state systems and the president of the United States to do the same in the federal system. It is the fail-safe power that can be used to remedy wrongful convictions.

The power to grant clemency and give pardons comes from British law, where the kings and queens, through the ages, have always had the power to free anyone they choose from prison. In Britain, it's known as the "Royal Prerogative." We brought that power from Britain to the colonies and enshrined it in our federal and state constitutions. Every US President always has his list on the last day in office, where typically well-connected people are cleared of federal charges. Every Thanksgiving, it's traditionally used to save the life of one lucky turkey. Governors have the same power over people locked up in state prisons.

A MARCH FOR INNOCENCE

Knowing how difficult and political the process of getting clemencies and pardons is, as well as the number of petitions filed in the state with the largest prison population, and my lack of connections to the governor, I decided I needed to perform a grand gesture to get the governor's attention.

It came to me one night—I'd walk the petitions of Bill Richards, Kim Long, and ten other innocent clients from our office in San Diego to the governor's office in Sacramento (more than five hundred miles away). I'd speak about the wrongful conviction of our clients at high schools, colleges, and anywhere I could get a crowd. I'd make as much noise as I could, with the media reporting on why this crazy law professor was walking across the state. The message would be simple and clear. If anyone should receive clemencies and pardons, shouldn't it be those who have strong claims of factual innocence and not those who have strong political ties to power?

I told my staff about the idea, half hoping they'd talk me out of it. Instead, they were all interested in participating in what came to be known as the "Innocence March." Alissa Bjerkhoel and Mike Semanchik walked the entire way with me.

The march ended up being far more than 500 miles once we figured out the only route where we could avoid dying of heatstroke in the desert was 712 miles long. On April 27, 2013, we started walking from San Diego straight up the California coast. Families of our clients joined us, as did all the clients we'd freed over the years.

Alissa and Mike were the two perfect companions for this adventure. Alissa is a five feet ten, tough and strong woman of Norwegian descent. She loves karaoke and can often be found playing the trumpet at Norwegian festivals. She is perhaps the most detail-oriented and organized person I've ever met. Her office is always immaculate, and she has literally no email in her inbox at the end of each workday. Alissa grew up in Truckee, California, a mountain town where the pioneers known as the *Donner Party* became trapped in snow in 1846 and turned to cannibalism.

Mike is from Pittsburgh. He's an All-American former Eagle Scout. Mike's ability to manage budgets and grants led to his promotion to managing attorney in our office. He is likely the only managing attorney in the United States who wears flip-flops to work every day. For 712 miles, we debated daily the distinction between orange and banana peels thrown on the side of the road and whether one was litter and the other was not.

The three of us were equally determined to walk every step of the journey. When we were told there was a tunnel along the Central Coast that we couldn't walk through, and we needed to get in a car to get through it, we decided to spend an extra day hiking over a mountain range to get around having to drive. We learned later that we'd received bad information, and there was a footpath next to the road going through the tunnel.

The first couple of hundred miles were tough as we trudged through San Diego County, then Orange County, then Los Angeles County, and continued up the coast. Eventually, we fell into a rhythm with the road. We talked and laughed and reflected on our work and the reason we were pushing our bodies to the limits. It felt invigorating to do something physical to help free our clients as opposed to sitting in our offices writing petitions the courts often ignored.

We met amazing and generous people along the way. People gave us food and let us use the bathrooms in their homes when they learned what we were doing. In Los Angeles, we had a massive press conference at the Santa Monica pier where radio, TV, and newspaper media showed up.

Fifty-five days after we began, we entered Sacramento with more than one hundred people walking behind us in support of our clients who had become known as the "California 12" (see fig. 3). I felt like Forrest Gump as I led the group to the capitol building. Due to all the media coverage of the march, we were able to get a meeting with Governor Jerry Brown's staff to hand deliver the clemency petitions. We were also given the opportunity to put on a presentation about the cases.

For each of the twelve clients, we explained in detail the facts supporting their innocence to the governor's team. They nodded their heads, asked questions, and then told us they would consider the petitions and follow up with questions. We flew home, excited that our mission was completed, and it appeared to be effective.

And then, radio silence. We heard nothing from the governor's office for weeks, and no response to multiple calls and emails. Finally, I learned that most of the team we had presented the cases to had been moved to positions outside the clemency process. Governor Brown eventually only granted one of our clemency petitions, reducing the sentence of Quintin Morris and making him eligible for release.

Quintin is one of the many victims of misidentification, a topic I go into in depth in the chapter "You (Kind of) Look Like Other People in the World." Quintin was identified in a highly suggestive identification procedure after he was detained by the police in connection with a shooting, even though neither he, nor the car he was in, matched the witnesses' descriptions. After he was convicted by a jury, the trial judge—a former police officer who worked in the area where the crime occurred— expressed "grave concerns about the sufficiency of the evidence." And, even after the real shooter was discovered and confessed, Quinton sat in prison while appeals were litigated. He was finally released on January 10, 2019, after serving twenty-seven years in prison for a crime he did not commit.

Governor Brown's successor, Gavin Newsom, was much more generous with clemencies. With the help of people like Jason Flom, a tremendously successful record company executive who hosts a podcast called *Wrongful Convictions with Jason Flom*, we obtained clemency for four of the "California 12," while at the same time we freed six others through litigation. Like Bill Richards, Kim Long was an innocent client we freed through litigation.

Figure 3. Marching to Free the California 12. From left: Dani Dauntless, Katherine Bonaguidi, Dana Garber, Justin Brooks. Photo credit: Heidi Brooks.

KIM LONG

Kim grew up in a hardworking middle-class family in the desert town of Corona in Riverside County California. She was an adventurous and vivacious child, with loving parents. Kim loved desert living, particularly riding motorcycles down dusty two-lane roads. She also loved helping people, which led to a career as a nurse.

Kim and her boyfriend Ozzy were childhood friends. As they grew older, they dated on and off, but eventually found long-term relationships with other partners.

In 2002, Ozzy and his girlfriend ended their ten-year relationship. Around that same time, Kim and her husband divorced, and Ozzy and Kim found their way back to each other.

In April of 2003, Ozzy and Kim moved in together. This upset Ozzy's former girlfriend. At one point, Ozzy's ex took a black marker and wrote "asshole" and "deadbeat" on Ozzy's white truck in permanent marker and stuck super glue in the door key locks. She left messages on the couple's home phone threatening to kill them.

Kim and Ozzy changed their phone number multiple times and reported this behavior to the police, which infuriated Ozzy's ex-girlfriend even more. She wrote a long, profane, threatening letter to Kim, claiming that she was still having sex with Ozzy, and signed the letter with, "Bitch. Truly yours." Kim and Ozzy filed for a restraining order against her.

Nine days later, Kim and Ozzy joined a group of friends for some day-drinking and barhopping. The day started at a bar called Chuck Wagon around 10:00 a.m. and continued to three other bars throughout the evening. At the final bar, Kim was slurring her words and visibly drunk.

Between 10:00 p.m. and 11:00 p.m., the group decided to get on their motorcycles and leave, but Kim refused to ride home with Ozzy because she thought he was too drunk. The couple got into an argument, and Kim ended up taking a ride from a friend named Jeff. Back at her house, she had another argument with Ozzy, and then Jeff took her to his house.

Around 2:00 a.m., Jeff dropped Kim off at her house, where she found Ozzy slouched down on the couch. She thought he was asleep, but when she checked on him, she saw a large blood stain on the arm of the couch and blood coming from his ear. Ozzy was dead.

Kim called 911.

The police officers and first responders found her in a hysterical state. They noticed she smelled of alcohol, but they didn't see any blood on her or note any injuries.

When paramedics arrived on the scene, they noticed Ozzy had a penetrating injury to the back-right side of his head, he was abnormally pale, and cold to the touch. Based on the lack of blood flow from the wound, and the spots of coagulated blood, the paramedics determined Ozzy had not died recently. Later, an autopsy revealed that he died from blunt force trauma. The criminalist believed he was struck at least three times with an object like a bat, large stick, brick, or golf club. It could have been up to eight times.

The house was covered in blood. There was 360-degree blood spatter on every wall of the living room, as well as on the curtains, the coffee table, and the television. While neither Kim nor Ozzy smoked, there was a Turkish Gold cigarette butt in the incense tray on the coffee table. Additionally, there were several items missing, including a change bowl that was kept in the kitchen, the center console of a stereo, and a shotgun that was usually stored in Kim's closet.

The police didn't find any sign of forced entry. They didn't find any weapons in the house, garage, or surrounding neighborhood. The criminalist didn't recover any usable fingerprints from the crime scene, and didn't notice any footprints around the house. No blood was found on Kim's clothing, hats, shoes, or motorcycle helmet.

Detectives took Kim into the station for questioning. In between tears, she explained the long day and night of drinking, and the argument with Ozzy. As the questioning started to focus on her actions that night, she consistently maintained that she didn't kill Ozzy, and she suggested the police look for Ozzy's ex-girlfriend.

The police brought in Ozzy's ex-girlfriend, and she gave the questionable alibi that on the night of the murder, she was at a hotel with a man she was dating. When police followed up on the alibi, the hotel manager didn't remember them coming in that day, and there were no records indicating a room was rented by Ozzy's ex-girlfriend, or her date, on that night.

Regardless of the motivation of the ex-girlfriend and her weak alibi, the police focused their attention on Kim. The police believed Kim had a motive due to the argument, and she could be put on the scene of the crime. Kim's alibi was also challenged when Jeff claimed he dropped Kim off at the house around 1:30 a.m., which contradicted Kim's account that it was around 2:00 a.m., just minutes before she called 911. Police investigators believed this thirty-minute gap was enough time for Kim to murder Ozzy and get rid of the evidence.

Kim was charged and tried for murder. After several days of deliberations by the jury, they couldn't reach a unanimous decision. Nine jurors
were adamant Kim hadn't killed Ozzy, while three believed she was guilty.

Kim was put on trial a second time. The prosecution's case was based
on Jeff's time line, giving Kim the opportunity to kill Ozzy, but the defense
wasn't given an opportunity to challenge that time line because Jeff had
died in a motorcycle accident before the trial began.

The jury came back with a guilty verdict. Kim's trial counsel filed a
motion for a new trial, based on the grounds that the verdict wasn't supported by the evidence. The statements from the two alternate jurors were
introduced. Both had contacted Kim's attorney and stated they would
have acquitted her. Unfortunately, the trial judge denied her motion for a
new trial, even while saying on the record, "To make a perfectly clear
record in this matter, if this was a court trial, if the court would have heard
the evidence in this case, I would have found the defendant not guilty. I
would have found that the evidence was insufficient to prove beyond a
reasonable doubt."

When we took on Kim's case, we found two independent time-of-death
experts who supported Kim's account of events. Both experts reviewed
Kim's file and concluded Ozzy was dead long before Kim could have
arrived home. They both determined Ozzy died at least an hour before the
1:30 a.m. time line the prosecution presented. This new time of death
bolstered Kim's alibi, which was already supported by her passing polygraph tests.

In the habeas corpus hearing, we argued that, with the 360-degree
blood spatter on the crime scene, there was no way Kim did the killing
because she would have had blood on her. The prosecution argued that
Kim must have changed her clothes before the police arrived, but witnesses had described Kim as wearing a unique T-shirt and jacket earlier in
the day, and it was the same outfit she was wearing when the police photographed her that night.

We presented this evidence in front of the original trial judge, and
he reversed her conviction based on the legal theory that Kim's lawyer
didn't provide effective assistance of counsel under the Sixth Amendment.
There were multiple failures, including the failure to present time of death
experts and the failure to present the evidence that showed Kim didn't

change her clothes that night. Kim was free after more than seven years in prison for a crime she did not commit.

Still not satisfied with the result, the District Attorney's Office appealed the reversal, and the appellate court determined the defense attorney did a good enough job to satisfy the Sixth Amendment. Fortunately, Kim wasn't sent back to prison while we appealed that decision, but she wasn't truly free. She lived every day wondering if that was the day she would lose her freedom.

Kim was finally vindicated when the California Supreme Court, in a unanimous decision, reversed the appellate court decision and the Riverside District Attorney decided not to retry the case. I had the pleasure of calling her and giving her the great news.

"It's over," I said into the phone. "The case is over!"

"What!" she screamed. "Oh my God!"

I then heard a bunch of yelling and commotion. Apparently, she'd run into the street and was shouting with joy. I wish I'd made a video call and recorded it as a pick me up to watch when cases looked like they would never end. Like many of the struggles I've watched our clients deal with, I couldn't imagine how she'd stayed sane through all the years the case had been hanging over her head.

The parallels between Kim Long's and Bill Richards's cases are crystal clear. They both went to prison based on the false belief they killed their partners. They were both convicted based upon evidence of problems in their relationships. Both cases had time-line issues, making it highly improbable they had the opportunity to commit the killings. Both cases involved interpretations of physical evidence made to fit with the prosecution's theories. And most significant, is the fact that the physical evidence in both cases just put them at the scene. It didn't confirm they committed the murders.

In Bill's case, there was a specific time he clocked out of work, leaving a very limited window between that time and the time he called 911. In that small time frame, he would have needed to drive home, brutally murder his wife, and tear her clothes off. Presumably, there would also have been time for whatever altercation led to the murder.

Once Bill was the suspect being pursued, the police and prosecution looked to match the physical evidence with their narrative. For example, although Pamela's blood on Bill's shirt was easily explained as resulting from him cradling her head after he tripped over her body in the yard, the allegation was that the blood came from the murder. The prosecution actually created a papier mâché doll, filled it with ink, and dropped a brick on it to show that the blood on Bill's shirt could also have been from him beating Pamela to death. That inanely unscientific experiment was presented to the jury.

The police and prosecution built their narrative from the only evidence they had: Bill was at the crime scene (his home), and there were problems in the relationship.

Kim's case was the same story. She was on the scene. They had a flimsy motive. That was enough for a conviction.

The fact that the crime scenes in both cases were the homes of both the victims and the people convicted of their murders is sobering. It's easy to see how anyone in a cohabitating relationship could find themselves in the nightmare that Bill and Kim suffered: coming home to find your partner murdered, being convicted of their murder, and going to prison for a crime you didn't commit.

Another commonality in these cases, and in every case where a loved one is the victim of a violent crime, is the difficulty of participating in your own defense when you are deeply traumatized. Both Bill and Kim lost loved ones in brutal ways. It's hard to imagine that their abilities to combat the state of California were not impaired when the full force of the government came down on them.

It's easy to dismiss these cases as being extraordinary, but they are far too common. Bear in mind, in writing this book, I didn't go out and look for cases where partners were wrongfully convicted after finding their dead loved one. Both these cases are from my office—one of more than sixty innocence organizations in the United States. There are many more of these cases among the thousands of documented cases of wrongful conviction.

You will also learn in chapter 10 that poor people and people of color have a much higher rate of wrongful conviction, yet both Bill and Kim are middle-class White people. Kim was a nurse and Bill was an engineer. Anyone can be wrongfully convicted.

4 You (Kind of) Look like Other People in the World

On the morning of November 24, 2004, sixteen-year-old Natalie[1] was enjoying her Thanksgiving break in Lemon Grove, California, a small city in San Diego County. She decided to walk to her friend's house, about a mile away, to help with some painting. It was a bright and sunny day, so she grabbed her CD Walkman and began walking.

On her way, a light-colored truck with a camper stopped three feet in front of her. The man driving the truck stared at her, but when she realized she didn't recognize him, she quickly walked around the truck. At the next intersection, she noticed the man had circled around and was again staring at her. She started to feel concerned, but she continued walking and listening to music. She walked under an overpass and was walking up a hill when she was grabbed from behind and felt a stubbly beard rubbing on the left side of her face. The attacker started to grope her and told her not to scream. He started pulling off her clothing while she fought back. She hit him in the face with her CD player and was able to break away from him.

Natalie ran up the hill in the middle of the street wearing only one flip flop. The attacker chased her, caught up, and threw her into the bushes by the side of the road. Natalie felt the stabbing of sticks and rocks as she landed on her back. He tore her clothes and underwear and penetrated her with his fingers while she fought and screamed for help.

"Stop screaming," he ordered. "I will hurt you!"

Natalie saw a car coming up the hill. She kept screaming and fighting and was able to break away again. She ran to the car and started beating on the window screaming, "Please let me in!"

The woman driving the car let her in, locked the doors, and drove away.

When Natalie got home, she immediately called the San Diego County Sheriff's Department. She told the deputies the attacker was in his mid-twenties and described him as a White male, with a medium build, brown hair, and facial hair.

The deputies took Natalie around the neighborhood and pointed out men who fit the description provided, but Natalie couldn't identify any of them. She drew a picture of the attacker, but there was no detail in the drawing beyond a man with a goatee. She also made a drawing of the truck with the camper which was circulated around the community.

URIAH COURTNEY

Several weeks after Natalie was attacked, detectives received information about a possible vehicle matching the description. The owner didn't match Natalie's description of the attacker, but his stepson Uriah Courtney did. A mugshot of Uriah was available because he had a prior drug offense. Deputies placed Uriah in the fourth position of a photo array that was shown to Natalie to identify the attacker (see fig. 4).

The photo array was highly suggestive. There was only one detail in Natalie's drawing: the attacker's facial hair. Uriah was the only man who matched it. One, two, and five had no facial hair. Three only had hair on his chin and six had a space between his mustache and the hair on his chin.

Even though Uriah was the only one who matched Natalie's description, she was still tentative in her identification of him. She said she was, "not sure, but the most similar is number four."

Confidence in the identification grew throughout the trial proceedings, as Natalie identified Uriah at every stage. Uriah presented evidence to

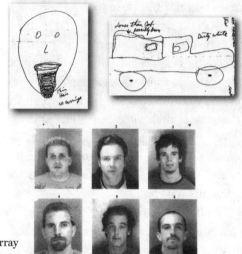

Figure 4. Drawings and photo array
used to identify Uriah Courtney.

prove he was working a construction job, and he went out to lunch with his girlfriend on the day of Natalie's assault. Uriah's stepfather told the jury that while Uriah had driven his truck in the past, Uriah returned the keys months before the day of the assault, and he didn't have access to the truck on that day. Several witnesses testified in support of Uriah, but none could specifically account for his whereabouts at the exact time of Natalie's attack. The jury convicted, and the court sentenced Uriah to life in prison for kidnapping and rape.

In 2010, Uriah reached out to the California Innocence Project. Alissa was assigned the case because she is not only an amazing walker, but she is also the DNA expert in our office. Luckily, the government had not yet destroyed Natalie's clothing from the day of the attack, so there was a possibility of getting DNA from the attacker off her clothes.

Alissa filed a motion for testing that was granted, and the results revealed male DNA that didn't match Uriah. Unfortunately, that result alone was not very compelling. It was great Uriah's DNA didn't show up on the clothing, but an argument could be made that there was no transfer of DNA during the attack, and the biological material on her clothes came from some random male. Everyone has DNA from other people on their clothes from daily activities like riding the subway or sitting on a chair where someone else has left DNA.

Through the miracle of modern technology, however, we were able to find the actual perpetrator of this crime using CODIS, the Combined DNA Index System. CODIS is software that makes it possible to search the National DNA Indexing System, a databank of DNA profiles from incarcerated people, missing persons, and crime scenes throughout the United States. On the day the DNA results from Natalie's clothing were entered into the database, there were more than 10 million profiles in the databank. The DNA profile from the clothing matched the profile of a man who was approximately Uriah's age, lived in the area, matched the general description, and had prior sexual assault charges.

Alissa and I went to see Uriah at Donovan Prison as soon as we got the results. Although I like to visit all our clients, particularly at Christmas time when I spend a couple of weeks driving across the state to see as many as possible, it wasn't typical for me to show up for an impromptu visit.

When Uriah came into the attorney visiting room, he was surprised to see me.

"I have really good news," I told him.

"What is it?" His eyes filled with hope and tears.

Again, there is no way to describe moments like that. Giving hope to the near hopeless is something I'll never tire of.

Nonetheless, when we approached the San Diego County District Attorney's office with this evidence, we received resistance from the deputy district attorney who handled the case at trial.

"My victim made a good identification," she kept insisting when we met.

"She was a scared sixteen-year-old girl," I answered. "And, we have DNA that proves it wasn't Uriah."

Fortunately, we had two allies in the district attorney's office. The first was Brent Neck, a gentle and thoughtful man who defies stereotypes of brash, aggressive prosecutors. Brent was assigned to review potential innocence cases and he'd methodically reviewed all the facts and made sure all the testing of the evidence was completed. He believed in Uriah's innocence, but the deputy district attorney who prosecuted Uriah was adamant that neither she nor the victim had made a mistake. In contrast to Brent, she was hostile, confrontational, irrational, and in denial. Brent brought the case to our second ally, Bonnie Dumanis, the County District Attorney—the one person who had the ultimate say in whether Uriah would go home.

Bonnie had a remarkable story. She started her government career as a typist and rose to the level of district attorney of the fifth largest county in the United States. She was the first openly gay elected district attorney in the country, and the first woman to obtain the position in San Diego. She has a tough, independent spirit that matches the strong Boston accent she hasn't lost after decades on the West Coast. Although she was a deputy district attorney for many years, she came to the top job after sitting as a judge, which gave her a different perspective on cases.

Bonnie overruled the deputy district attorney who handled the case at trial, rejecting the claim that Uriah was guilty, and joined us in a motion to vacate the conviction and dismiss the case. Uriah was freed after serving eight years in prison for a crime he did not commit.

The greatest moment in representing innocent clients is the moment they walk out of the gates of the prison into freedom. The first steps. The first breath of air. The first glances through squinted eyes up at a vast blue sky. The first tears that come streaming down their faces. The realization that it is finally over. Those are the moments we live for. The culmination of a job well done.

Alissa and I missed Uriah's release. We were walking across the state trying to free other clients. Uriah came up and joined us at a rally in Santa Monica. His freedom gave us fuel to keep going. He understood better than we ever could what it meant to be innocent in prison. Even though he'd just been released after eight years of wrongful incarceration, instead of spending time with the friends and family he had so desperately missed, he wanted to be with us helping others to gain the freedom he'd gone so long without.

I learned something valuable in Uriah's case. No matter how strong the exonerating evidence is, it's still difficult for prosecutors who personally handled cases to accept they put an innocent person in prison.

This phenomenon is explained in Mark Godsey's book *Blind Injustice*. He describes the resistance to innocence evidence presented on behalf of his client Clarence Elkins: "The prosecutor did believe what he was saying. He wasn't putting on an act. And he wasn't evil. Because Elkins's innocence conflicted with everything he had internalized for years about the system to which he had dedicated his life, he was in a form of psychological denial that prevented him from evaluating the evidence objectively. He literally could not mentally or emotionally accept the truth."[2]

What made the prosecutor's denial in our case particularly troubling was that, by 2010, when we were arguing about Uriah's innocence, there had been substantial research demonstrating that identification procedures were deeply flawed. In fact, in the first 180 DNA exonerations in the United States, bad identifications were the cause of the wrongful conviction in more than 75 percent of those cases.[3]

Uriah's case had all the earmarks of a bad identification. A frightened young victim, a vague description of the attacker, and a suggestive photo array.

TIM ATKINS

We faced the same resistance in the Tim Atkins case. Tim was a seventeen-year-old Black teenager living in Los Angeles when a Mexican couple were attacked in his neighborhood. The couple were picking up their baby from a babysitter when two Black men snuck up alongside their car. One of the attackers put a gun to the back of the wife's head, while the other man pulled the husband out of the car, shot him in the chest, took his wallet, and threw his body on top of his wife. It was a dark street, and the wife, with a gun to her head, said she looked back and saw her attacker for no more than a few seconds.

After the shooting, Denise Powell, a drug-addicted sex worker, was walking in the same neighborhood. She came across Tim hanging outside his house, and they had a short conversation about the shooting. Denise proceeded to falsely brag to other people that she knew who the shooter was. Someone called the police, and they picked her up. Officers told her they were detaining her until she revealed who the shooter was.

With her addiction calling her back to the streets and remembering the conversation with Tim that night, Denise falsely claimed Tim told her he was the shooter. Tim was then identified by the victim's wife using a six-pack photo array with a photo taken when Tim was fourteen years old.

At trial, the victim's wife couldn't identify Tim. The prosecutor asked for a recess, and when court resumed, she miraculously identified him.

Denise didn't show up for trial, and the judge allowed the prosecutor to read her statement from the preliminary hearing to the jury. Tim was convicted and sentenced to thirty-two-years-to-life in prison.

We were able to free Tim after he'd spent twenty-three of those years behind bars. One of our law students, Wendy Koen, found Denise Powell. We brought her to court, and she confessed to fabricating her statement. We also presented evidence that established it was highly unlikely any identification could have been made after the violent encounter twenty-three years earlier. Tim was seventeen on the day of his arrest. The day he went home, he was forty.

When I told Tim the case was over and he would be released, I could tell he didn't believe me. He just looked at me with a blank expression. After twenty-three years in prison, his entire adult life, it must have been a surreal moment for him. He didn't show any emotion until he had taken a few steps out of the jail. He then fell into the arms of his family, and he broke down among their flood of tears.

Judge Tynan, the judge who heard Tim's original trial, was also the judge who released him. He knew how weak the case was to start with, and with what we'd learned about the problems with identifications in the ensuing decades, coupled with Denise Powell's recantation, he knew Tim was innocent. The Los Angeles District Attorney's Office, however, refused to accept this. Even after the judge reversed Tim's conviction, the assistant district attorney handling the case announced in court that his office still believed Tim was guilty, even though they were not seeking re-prosecution. And for more than a decade, the California Attorney General's Office fought against compensating Tim under a state law mandating compensation for innocent people who are wrongfully convicted.

The fundamental problem with identification evidence is that jurors give it much more weight than it deserves. Even in the face of powerful evidence of innocence, jurors will convict based on even a weak identification.

RAFAEL MADRIGAL

Rafael Madrigal was convicted of a drive-by shooting in East Los Angeles in 2002, even though he was thirty-five miles away from the crime scene working at a factory at the time of the shooting, and there was no physical evidence or motive linking him to the crime.

In our habeas hearing, Rafael's supervisor testified that he was a hands-on manager, he supervised a small staff, and Rafael was most certainly at work at the time of the shooting. The supervisor produced both time cards and production records that specifically documented tasks Rafael completed during the day in question. Most powerfully, the supervisor testified that if Rafael had not been at work at the time of the shooting, the entire production line would have shut down because Rafael was the only employee trained to operate a laminating machine that was part of the production process.

Additionally, there was a codefendant in Rafael's case. In a recorded jailhouse conversation, this codefendant admitted to his girlfriend that he and another gang member committed the shooting, not Rafael. He complained to his girlfriend about Rafael's family and friends asking questions and trying to figure out who actually committed the crime. He worried that their inquiries might lead to additional evidence against him and the actual shooter.

Considering the evidence of innocence and lack of evidence of guilt in Rafael's case, why was he convicted? First, Rafael's trial lawyer did not fully investigate and present the exonerating evidence to the jury. Second, a witness identified Rafael from a photo taken of him when he was a teenager.

Even with strong evidence of innocence, the jury convicted Rafael based on a flimsy identification from an old photo, and the court sentenced him to twenty-five-years-to-life in prison. He was released in 2009 after spending nine years in prison for a crime he did not commit.

GUY MILES

In 1999, a jury convicted Guy Miles of robbing a savings and loan company in Orange County, California. The judge handed down a sentence of seventy-five-years-to-life in prison even though Guy had never even been to Orange County. The facts of the robbery would be comical if they hadn't led to Guy's wrongful incarceration for eighteen years.

Bernard Teamer financed his car through the savings and loan company. When he was making his monthly payments, he noticed that the company had a great deal of cash, so he decided to rob them. The employees knew Bernard, so he recruited two friends to do the robbery while he waited outside and served as the getaway driver.

During the robbery, Bernard became bored or anxious or nervous or something. Instead of waiting for his cohorts to return and flee the scene, he got out of the car, locked it, and went into an auto parts store where he asked about car parts for a very specific car with a very specific problem. He had a 1975 Chevy Caprice Classic with a 454 cubic engine that was backfiring.

While Bernard was talking to an employee of the store, his partners in crime returned to the getaway car only to find it locked and Bernard nowhere to be seen. The employee saw the two men outside trying to get into the car and told Bernard, "I think your friends are looking for you." Bernard ran outside and the three men left in the car. But for Bernard's shopping detour, the three perpetrators would have gotten away with the crime.

Descriptions of Bernard, his car, and his statements to the auto parts store employee quickly led the police to Bernard. For the other two perpetrators, police had nothing but general descriptions—one short and stocky, one tall and thin. The investigating detective created six-pack photo arrays to show the savings and loan employees and the auto parts store employee. However, instead of using photos in the arrays that matched the descriptions given by the employees, he simply used photos of anyone associated with Bernard.

If you lived in Bernard's neighborhood, your photo went into a six-pack. If you were friends with him or friends of his friends, your photo went into a six-pack. Although six-packs are only supposed to contain one suspect, these contained up to four. And what was worse, most of the people in the photo arrays looked nothing like the descriptions given by the employees. In the photo array that included Guy, who lived in Bernard's neighborhood and was loosely associated with him, he was the only one who matched the general description of the short and stocky robber.

Guy was initially identified using this suggestive photo array. At trial, one of the employees looked at him and said, "I'm not certain that that's him," and nine witnesses testified that Guy Miles was in Las Vegas at the time of the robbery. However, the jury still convicted him.

After nine years of investigation, we finally located the two other men who committed the robbery, and they both confessed to the crime. Incidentally, two eyewitnesses had tentatively identified one of the actual robbers before Guy's trial. And, amazingly, both tentatively identified the third robber nearly twenty years after the crime. Nonetheless, we got no cooperation from the Orange County District Attorney's Office in reversing the conviction, nor from the original trial judge who denied our claim in 2011 after presenting our evidence in a habeas hearing.

With her typical tenacious, never-give-up attitude, Alissa immediately appealed the decision. After several more hearings ordered by the appellate court, they reversed Guy's conviction in 2017.

But we still weren't done. Even with all the exonerating evidence, and the reversal of Guy's conviction, the prosecution told us they would re-prosecute Guy in a new trial. This was a despicable move. It was strategic pushback due to the successes of our innocence organization and others like us around the country.

Prosecutors' offices have two options. The first is cooperating with innocence organizations and working together to exonerate innocent people as Bonnie Dumanis had done in San Diego in both the Ken Marsh and Uriah Courtney case. The second is to fight every post-conviction process, and then if they lose, re-prosecute the case.

The Orange County District Attorney's Office figured they had nothing to lose. If they won, he went back to prison. If they lost, he'd be released just like he was going to be if they didn't retry the case.

But, of course, very few cases go to trial. This retrial was no exception. They offered Guy a deal he could not turn down—plead guilty to the robbery, and they would agree to a sentence of time served. If he rejected the offer and was convicted in the new trial, he could spend the rest of his life in prison.

With a new trial pending, the judge set a million-dollar bail. There was no way Guy's family could pay it, so even if we were successful in the retrial, he'd sit in the jail for months awaiting trial. And even though we were confident we had a great case, and he wouldn't be convicted, there is no way to guarantee what a jury might decide.

Alissa and I met with Guy in the county jail while he faced retrial to discuss his options. He sat nervously on a metal chair welded to the

Figure 5. Walking Guy Miles out of prison after eighteen years of wrongful incarceration. Photographed by the California Innocence Project.

ground. His knee was shaking. His hair had greyed from the past two decades he'd spent in prison. He was a grandfather.

"You need to do what's best for you," I told him through the thick glass on the jail phone. "If you decide to take this deal, we'll understand and support you." Alissa nodded her head in agreement, so he knew that, even though she'd fought for his innocence for years, she understood his desire to go home.

"Thanks for saying that," he said with tears welling up in his eyes. "I've been trying to find a way to tell you both that I want to take this deal. I don't want to let you down."

"Of course, you aren't," I said, looking into his eyes. "This isn't about us. It's about you and what's best for you and your family."

Guy took the deal. You can watch a very emotional video of Alissa and me bringing him home to his family on YouTube.[4] He's doing great, but he shouldn't have had to take that deal (fig. 5). He shouldn't have the conviction for armed robbery on his record. The prosecution should have done the right thing and dismissed the case.

CROSS-RACIAL IDENTIFICATIONS

A common element in Tim's, Rafael's, and Guy's cases is that they all involved cross-racial identifications. In my experience, these are the worst type of identifications, and defense lawyers don't do a good enough job educating jurors about the difficulties of identifying someone who is not of your own race.

Discussing race is always challenging, but jurors must understand the difficulty in cross-racial identification doesn't come from being racist; it's simply based on exposure, especially at an early age. Studies have shown that we learn most of what we will learn in life in the first three years.[5] Babies are sponges. At the same time that they are learning how to speak, how to walk, how to use a spoon, and how to identify all the objects that surround them, they are also developing their facial recognition software.[6] If mom is White, dad is White, their siblings are White, and most of the children they are exposed to are White, for the rest of their lives, they will not be able to identify non-White people as accurately as identifying White people. This phenomenon applies to all races.[7]

THE PROBLEMS WITH MEMORIES

Even when the suspect is of the same race as the victim, many factors still lead to misidentification. Memory is not as certain as most people think. Memory is composed of bits of information that we take in through our five senses (sight, sound, touch, smell, and hearing) and store in different parts of our brain.

Smell is the strongest memory source.[8] Smells can link you to the past when you've smelled the exact scent, allowing you to identify it immediately. I often tell students they can use smell to study if they put a strong-smelling marker in front of their nose while a professor explains a complicated concept and then use the same marker on their final exam. The smell will attach to the information and help with recall.

The process of recall is reconstructive. We pull together the bits of information from different parts of our brains and put the memory together. We've all experienced the strain of trying to reconstruct a memory as we think as hard as we can, but the pieces just don't come together. During this process, there are ample opportunities to reconstruct the memory incorrectly, particularly if there are influences on the reconstruction, like a police officer feeding misinformation.

It is even possible to distort our memories without outside influences. For example, if you tell a story repeatedly and change facts, after a while it's difficult to remember the truth.

With children, it's easy to distort their memories (something I will discuss more in chapter 8). For example, if you have a four- or five-year-old who wants to go to Disneyland, you can convince that child with false suggestions that he or she has already gone to Disneyland.

You say, "Remember I bought you that red dress in Disneyland?"

The child will be confused because you did, in fact, buy a red dress, but not at Disneyland. While the child is trying to reconcile the true fact with the false one, hit them with another question.

"Remember, I bought you that Cherry Coke at Disneyland?"

In fact, you bought the Cherry Coke at a movie theater. With a couple more similar combinations of fact and fiction, the child will create a memory of a trip to Disneyland that never happened. On the plus side, it's cheaper than actually going, and there are no lines to stand in.

In scientific terms, there are three stages to memory: encoding, storage, and retrieval—and memory can be distorted at any one of these stages.[9]

In a criminal case, encoding occurs at the time of the crime. Storage occurs between the crime and the procedure the police use to retrieve the memory. Retrieval occurs during the identification procedure (e.g., photo array or live lineup).

During the encoding phase, memory can be distorted by things such as drugs, alcohol, and lighting. Fear can also distort memory because our brains do not function as well when we are afraid. This is especially problematic in criminal cases, where victims are oftentimes afraid during the event.

The storage phase of memory is also ripe for contamination. It's important to cross-examine witnesses about the time between the crime and their interview with the police. Who did they talk to about the case, what news did they read, and were there any possible influences? Witnesses often integrate information from other sources into their memories.

And then, of course, it's important to discover potential contamination in the retrieval phase. There are many examples of the police using terrible procedures to obtain identifications. There are the ridiculously intentional suggestive procedures, such as having five people of one race and one suspect of another race. There are also more subtle suggestive procedures, such as having the suspect come into the lineup last after the non-suspects (fillers) have already been standing and waiting.

Perhaps the most important part of absorbing a memory is focus. We've all had the experience of reading a book and letting our minds drift to another thought. Maybe that's happening while you are reading this book. Maybe you're thinking about dinner or something you need to do. If so, your retention of information will be deeply impacted.

Our eyes can move left to right on the page while reading, but no memory is created without focus. We see with our brain and not our eyes, and we only see what we are focused on. The same thing happens at crime scenes. Witnesses only remember what they are focused on. In cases where guns are involved, victims focus on the guns, not the faces of the suspects. There are cases where victims can give incredible descriptions of guns used in crimes, but only vague descriptions of the suspects.[10]

FAULTY IDENTIFICATION PROCEDURES

But even when witnesses are focused, mistakes can be made, especially if identification procedures are not done well.

In 1984, Jennifer Thompson was living in Burlington, North Carolina, when she awoke to find a man in her bedroom. He jumped on her, covered her mouth with his hand, and held a knife to her throat. When she tried to scream, he told her to "shut up," or he would cut her. He then proceeded to violently rape her.

While the attack was going on, Jennifer focused as clearly as possible on the rapist. She said in a 2009 *60 Minutes* interview, "I was trying to pay attention to details so if I survived, and that was my plan, I could help the police find him."

Jennifer identified Ronald Cotton in a photo array and later identified him in a live lineup. Police told her not to feel compelled to make an identification. However, she has since explained that merely being asked to choose led her to believe that the police believed her attacker was in the group. She also explained how the fear of her attacker going free influenced the process: "I assumed they must have had the suspect. Why would they want me to drive all this way if they didn't? All I had to do was pick him out. And if I failed to do that, would he go free? Would he find me?"[11]

Another issue with the identification process is that even when a witness is unsure about an identification, the jury rarely gets to see that lack of confidence. A victim may ponder at length with uncertainty over photos or at a live lineup, but the jury will only see the victim confidently point out the suspect in court.

A witness's initial uncertainty will often disappear after the police confirm that the witness has correctly picked out the suspect in their custody. This type of confirmation happened after Jennifer picked Ronald Cotton out of the photo array and was told, "You did great, Ms. Thompson."[12] And, after she selected him at the live lineup, a police officer told her, "We thought that might be the guy. It's the same person you picked from the photos."[13]

Jennifer identified Ronald Cotton in court, and he spent more than ten years in prison until DNA proved a man named Bobby Poole was the actual attacker. As a result of faulty identification procedures, Ronald suffered ten years of imprisonment, and Jennifer suffered what she has described as "crippling guilt." Victims like Jennifer Thompson aren't looking to wrongfully convict innocent people. They want the person who committed the crime to be caught and off the streets. But, due to the shortcomings of human memory, faulty identification procedures, and improper confirmation by the police, Ronald Cotton went to prison for a crime he did not commit.

Remarkably, Jennifer and Ronald ultimately became friends and have been two of the most powerful voices in the push to reform eyewitness identification procedures.

One difficulty in reforming these procedures is that the mistakes are often unconscious. Perhaps an officer holds up the photo of the suspect two seconds longer than the other photos without realizing it. Or, an officer tells a witness like Jennifer Thompson, "Good job," without thinking that comment will give undeserved confidence to the in-court identification.

These are reasons why perhaps the most critical reform in identification procedures is to make the procedures "double-blind." Neither the witness nor those conducting the identification procedure should know who the suspect is in the lineup. Double-blind procedures are a staple in scientific studies to avoid bias that influences the study's outcome. For example, when testing a new pharmaceutical drug, it's important to give some patients placebos and others the medication to assess the true efficacy. But it's also essential that the doctors who give out the medication and placebos to the test patients do not know who got the medication and who got the placebo. That knowledge could cause a well-intentioned doctor to treat the two groups differently, which could throw off the study because it will be unclear whether the medication or different treatment caused the difference in outcomes.

Well-intentioned mistakes by the police during the identification process led to those identifications being thrown out of court until the US Supreme Court's 1977 decision in *Manson v. Braithwaite*.[14] In that case, the Supreme Court ruled that even when police obtained an identification by using "unnecessarily suggestive" procedures, the identification could be admitted at trial if the judge believed it was still reliable.

The police investigation in *Manson v. Braithwaite* was conducted by an undercover state police officer, Glover, who purchased heroin from a seller through the open doorway of an apartment. For two or three minutes, Glover stood within two feet of the seller in a hallway illuminated by natural light. A few minutes later, Glover described the seller to another officer as being "a colored man, approximately five feet eleven inches tall, dark complexion, black hair, short Afro style, and having high cheekbones, and of heavy build."[15] The other officer, suspecting from the description that a man he knew named Braithwaite might be the seller, left a photograph of Brathwaite in Glover's office. Glover viewed it two days later and identified Brathwaite as the seller.

The US Supreme Court ruled that even though the procedure was sug-gestive (since the officer was only shown one photo, not an array of pho-tos), and the procedure was unnecessary (because there was plenty of time to do a proper procedure), the identification was still admissible. The Court reasoned that the witness was a trained police officer with an oppor-tunity to see the suspect and accurately describe him, so the identification was reliable. Further, the Court found that reliability is the "lynchpin" of admissibility and, thus, courts should consider the totality of the circum-stances and admit identifications even where the procedures are unneces-sarily suggestive if they are deemed reliable.[16]

Justices Thurgood Marshall and William Brennan dissented in the case, recognizing a "high incidence of miscarriage of justice" resulting from the admission of mistaken eyewitness identification evidence at criminal trials. They argued that if a procedure was unnecessarily sugges-tive, then, by definition, it was likely to result in a misidentification.[17]

These prophetic words are well documented, as there is a high rate of bad identifications among the exonerated.

EVEN MULTIPLE VICTIMS CAN MAKE MISTAKEN IDENTIFICATIONS

When multiple victims make an identification, the evidence to convict is compelling, but that still doesn't mean it's accurate. In the Luis Vargas case, not one, not two, but three separate women identified our client Luis as the man who raped them. On December 7, 1999, just before being sentenced to fifty-five-years-to-life for three crimes he didn't commit, Luis addressed the Los Angeles Superior Court, stating, "I will pray for God's mercy on all of you . . . but as far as I'm concerned, the individual who really did these crimes might really be raping someone out there."[18]

Luis was right. The victims who testified that they had been raped by Luis had in fact been attacked by a man who came to be known as the "Teardrop Rapist." That man continued to rape women long after Luis went to prison. The Teardrop Rapist got his moniker because many of his more than thirty victims described him as having one or two teardrop tattoos under his eye. His attacks had a particular modus operandi as

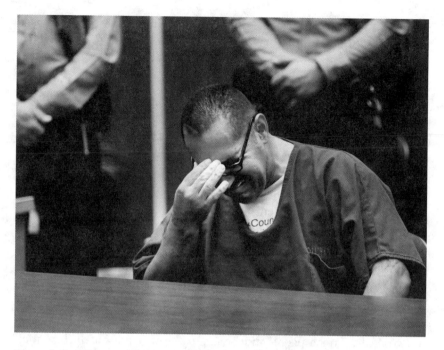

Figure 6. Luis Vargas at the moment the judge rules he will be freed after sixteen years of wrongful incarceration. Photographed by the California Innocence Project.

described in the following FBI bulletin: "The suspect typically approaches women who are alone and on their way to school or work, or are waiting at a bus stop, between the hours of 5:15 AM and 8:00 AM. The suspect converses with the victim, then threatens to kill the victim with a handgun or a knife. The suspect then forces the victim from the sidewalk to a secondary location, where he sexually assaults her."[19]

The Teardrop Rapist's attacks all happened within 1.6 miles of the attacks that sent Luis to prison and had the same modus operandi. One attack even occurred when Luis was in jail and on trial, but that information wasn't given to Luis's defense attorney. It could have been used to prove Luis innocent. CIP staff attorney Raquel Cohen was able to link the cases together using DNA from the crime scenes, and Luis was freed after spending seventeen years in prison for crimes he did not commit (see fig. 6).

Multiple victim identifications like those in the Luis Vargas case are hard to overcome, particularly when a parade of witnesses testify in court and point to the same person. In 1895, in London, a woman accused Adolf Beck of defrauding her out of property worth £30 (about $36). Soon after, a procession of women came forward who had been defrauded in the same manner as the first woman. Each of these women identified Adolf as the con man out of a lineup, and each woman was more positive than the last. Overall, twelve women identified Adolf, and he was convicted of ten counts of theft and false pretenses. Adolf was released from prison in 1901, and three years later, another woman reported the same story of fraud to Scotland Yard. The officers arrested Adolf, and, again, he was picked out of the lineup. Later, more women came forward reporting similar stories, and each identified Adolf. Again, he was convicted on all counts against him.

Ten days after the second conviction, while Adolf was locked up, the same fraudulent actions were committed against a new group of female victims. A man named John Smith was arrested, and it was discovered that he was the perpetrator of each of the cons for which Adolf was convicted. On July 19, 1904, Adolf was freed and pardoned. Over the course of two trials, sixteen people independently swore under oath that Adolf had defrauded them.[20]

FIXING THE PROBLEM

Although human memory may be faulty and unreliable, legislative reforms can improve identification procedures. These reforms make it less likely innocent people will be wrongfully convicted, and more likely guilty people will be rightfully convicted.

To make identification procedures valid and scientific, they must follow strict protocols. As discussed, the first protocol used should be double-blind procedures. To avoid situations where a police officer influences the witness due to the officer's knowledge of who the suspect is, neither the witnesses nor the officers conducting the procedure should have this information.

It also should be made clear to the witness that the suspect may not be in the lineup. Jennifer Thompson assumed the police had her attacker in custody and in the lineup, or as she said, "Why would they want me to drive all this way if they didn't?" When the witness assumes the suspect is in the lineup, they will simply choose the person who looks most like the person who committed the crime. When witnesses are led to believe the suspect is in the lineup, and the identification is the culmination of the investigation, there is likely to be a misidentification when the actual perpetrator is not in the lineup.

The officers conducting the lineup should also tell witnesses that the investigation will continue regardless of whether they make an identification. Additionally, they should not confirm or give feedback to the witness about their choice (e.g., "Good work, you got it right").

When creating the photo or live lineup, every effort should be made to make the fillers match the description of the suspect given by the witness or witnesses. In cases like Uriah Courtney's, where he was the only one who matched the victim's description, the witness is obviously going to pick him. Similarly, in Guy Miles's case, he was also selected because he was the only person in the lineup who matched the description given by the witnesses.

Each witness should also give a statement about how confident they are in the identification at the time of the procedure. Too often, witnesses aren't sure at all about an identification, but their confidence is boosted between the procedure and trial by police, prosecutors, and other influences. By the time of trial, they take the stand and say, "I'm 100 percent sure that's the person who committed the crime." The jury has no idea how much less confidence the witness actually had in the identification. That information is critical to the jury in assessing how much weight to give the evidence.

Identification procedures should always be video recorded so the defense attorney, judge, and jury can assess any possible influences or inadequacies in the process. Even honest police officers, doing their best to create a fair procedure, may unknowingly make mistakes that can lead to a bad identification.

Finally, jurors should be educated as to the problems with memory and identification procedures. They should hear from experts, and their instructions should explain how an identification can be faulty. Jurors need to understand that identifications are often not the powerful evidence prosecutors and police officers claim them to be.

During the last decade, the battle to make these reforms throughout the United States has resulted in approximately half the states adopting some or all of them. Los Angeles County, the nation's most populous county, resisted reform, even after their procedures were proven faulty time and time again. The county also paid out tens of millions of dollars in lawsuits to people wrongfully convicted based on faulty identification procedures. Finally, in 2018, after years of advocacy, Los Angeles and every county in California that had resisted change were forced to modify their procedures when Governor Brown signed into law a package of identification procedure reforms.

Bad identifications that lead to wrongful convictions are a global problem. All humans have problems with memory, and all identification procedures have the potential for failure. Police departments should voluntarily make reforms if they want to get the right person off the street, but if not, they should be forced to make the changes through legislative processes.

We all look like other people in the world. When those people commit crimes, we are all at risk of being wrongfully convicted.

5 You Get Confused When You Are Tired and Hungry, and People Yell at You

"How many of you think you'd never confess to a crime you didn't commit?"

I stared out at some confused, some thoughtful, and some disinterested faces in the sea of San Diego State undergraduate students I was teaching about wrongful convictions. About ten hands went up out of the approximately one hundred students in the lecture hall. It wasn't an accurate measure of how many actually believed this, because they'd all been in an educational setting long enough to know raising their hands might lead to an unwanted public interaction. I noticed all the raised hands were men.

I pointed to one of them. "Why do you think you'd never confess?"

"I just don't think I would."

"Yes, but why?"

He shrugged. "I just don't think I would."

That really was the extent of it. The ten students, like many people, just didn't think they'd confess to something they hadn't done. They had no basis to believe this. They had never been kept up all night while being screamed at by homicide detectives. They had never been told they better go along with a police officer's version of what happened, or they'll spend the rest of their lives in prison. They had never been lied to about evidence implicating them in a crime.

"How many of you don't believe innocent people confess to crimes they didn't commit?"

The same hands went up. They wouldn't falsely confess, so why would any innocent person?

Anyone who read *The Crucible* in high school understands why people confess when subjected to torture. Even after more than thirty years working in our deeply flawed criminal legal system, I'm grateful I was born in the late twentieth century. Just think back to the Salem Witch Trials, where birthmarks could be deemed a sign of the devil and get you killed in a brutal fashion.

The so-called *third degree* (a term with Shakespearean and Masonic ceremonial roots meaning intense interrogation) continued unregulated in the United States until the 1936 case of *Brown v. Mississippi*.[1] In that case, police officers beat three Black men until they confessed. The United States Supreme Court ruled, in a landmark decision that now seems obvious, that convicting people based on confessions obtained through beatings was unconstitutional. There's no doubt these beatings continue to this day in the United States and around the world, but they are not the normal course of obtaining confessions in our legal system. Instead, police obtain confessions through psychological warfare. As a result, the public finds it difficult to understand why an innocent person would confess when subjected to less violent interrogation techniques.

AMANDA KNOX

I first met Amanda Knox in April 2014 at the Innocence Network Conference in Portland, Oregon. The conference is an annual event, held at a different location every year. At these conferences, post-conviction lawyers and staff members from innocence organizations around the world join exonerees for three days of conversation and training. Additionally, the conference is an opportunity for those of us who work in isolation to connect and commiserate with our colleagues. For the exonerated, the conference allows them to bond with the only people in the world who can truly understand their experiences and feelings.

Amanda was a twenty-year-old student living in Italy when she was charged with murdering her housemate, Meredith Kercher. The case became a global news story, filled with false incriminating facts linking Amanda to the crime and a character assassination geared toward creating a fictitious person capable of participating in the brutal murder of a friend.

Greg Hampikian, director of the Idaho Innocence Project and one of the DNA experts in Amanda's case, introduced me to her. Instead of the arrogant, cold-blooded killer portrayed in much of the media, I met a friendly, intelligent young woman who seemed grateful to be included in the event. Like I've heard other exonerees express over the years, she was both comforted and saddened to be around so many people who'd suffered the same misfortune she had.

Amanda's case was unique in that she was the youngest person I've ever met to be convicted, serve substantial prison time (almost four years), and ultimately be exonerated. Her case was also unique in that it had become an international news story. But the way her case went off the tracks, with fatal flaws in both the investigation and prosecution, was very similar to the more than one hundred exonerees who also attended the conference that year. It was also similar to the cases discussed in this book.

First, like Bill Richards and Kim Long, Amanda came home to the crime scene after Meredith had been murdered and before anyone had yet discovered the body. So, just like Bill and Kim, authorities could place her at the scene.

Second, just as in Bill Richards's case, the police and prosecutors found her behavior suspicious because her response to the murder of her roommate was not what they expected. As Amanda says in her book, *Waiting to Be Heard:* "I'd never sobbed openly. I'd never cried publicly . . . I bottled up my feelings. It was an unfortunate trait in a country where emotion is not just commonplace, but expected."[2]

Finally, just like Bill and Kim, and pretty much every innocent client I've ever represented, the police focused on Amanda and then built the case around her. They ignored facts that contradicted her guilt and embraced and exaggerated flimsy, circumstantial, and often blatantly false evidence that fit their narrative. They didn't go into her interrogation with the purpose of finding out what she knew or didn't know about Meredith's murder. They went in convinced Amanda had played a role in the murder, and they sought confirmation. Amanda's description of her mental state during the interrogation is illustrative of why interrogation techniques are often unreliable.

> Sitting in that airless interrogation room in the *Questura*, surrounded by people shouting at me during forty-three hours of questioning over five days, I got to the point in the middle of the night where I was no longer sure what truth was. I started believing the story the police were telling me. They took me into a state where I was so fatigued and stressed that I started to wonder if I *had* witnessed Meredith's murder and just didn't remember it. I began questioning my own memory.[3]

Amanda's description of her feelings during the interrogation is consistent with the research by Richard Ofshe and Richard Leo, explained in their article "The Decision to Confess Falsely: Rational Choice and Irrational Action."

> An innocent suspect is likely to experience considerable shock and disorientation during the interrogation because he is wholly unprepared for the confrontation and accusations that are at the core of the process and will not understand how the investigator could possibly suspect him. An innocent individual may become progressively more distressed, confused, and desperate as he is told of evidence that incriminates him.[4]

It's important to remember that improper interrogations don't just harm suspects, they compromise investigations. Disorientated suspects often lead the police further away from the truth by going along with the false narrative the police have created. That makes it less likely the investigators will solve the crime and more likely these same investigators will falsely implicate innocent people.

In the Meredith Kercher investigation, Italian police poorly translated an English text from Amanda saying, "see you later" (where she was simply saying, "Goodbye"). Police hatched a theory that she had met up with her employer Patrick Lumumba, and he committed the murder. In the pressure of the interrogation room, Amanda ultimately went along with this false narrative and implicated Lumumba. Prosecutors charged Lumumba, Amanda, and her boyfriend Raffaele Sollecito, based on this false narrative. Even when authorities discovered the true murderer—Rudy Guede, whose DNA was all over the crime scene—they created a new, wild-sex-party-turned-to-murder narrative to keep Amanda and Raffaele implicated in the crime.

Fortunately, the truth ultimately came out in Amanda's case, but not before she spent more than four years in prison for a crime she did not commit.

BRENDAN DASSEY

Like Amanda's case, in the Brendan Dassey case (made famous in the Netflix docuseries *Making a Murderer*), the police created evidence consistent with their narrative. The police interrogated sixteen-year-old Brendan four times over forty-eight hours. They went into the interrogation believing both Steven and Brendan had been involved in the murder, and they were looking for confirmation. The interrogators used what Professor Laura Nirider, co-director of the Center on Wrongful Convictions at Northwestern University School of Law (and one of Brendan's longtime lawyers), called a "guessing game" interrogation technique. In 2020, Professor Nirider described the interrogation: "Brendan was simply guessing during his interrogation. When asked to describe how Ms. Halbach was killed, he guessed—incorrectly—that she had been stabbed and strangled; as police continued pressuring him, he even guessed that her hair had been cut. Finally, frustrated detectives had to tell him that she had been shot."[5]

Brendan's confession was complete fiction, based largely on information the police fed him and the plot of a movie he'd seen. This led to the police actually fabricating evidence to make the crime scene consistent with the story Brendan had told them.

THE FAIRBANKS FOUR

Unfortunately, police taking advantage of a vulnerable teenager to obtain a confession is not limited to Brendan Dassey's case. In 1997, a teenager named William Holmes and his friends brutally beat and killed a man named John Hartman on a street corner in Fairbanks, Alaska. Police arrested a teenage Alaska Native named Eugene Vent, who eyewitnesses saw stumbling drunk in the street, about four blocks from the crime scene. Instead of waiting for Eugene to sober up before questioning him and/or contacting his parents to be present, a detective embarked on hours of intensive interrogation, including lying to Eugene that police had found his footprint in the blood on the crime scene. Although Eugene repeatedly denied he had anything to do with the killing, the detective eventually convinced him that he couldn't trust his own memory, and Eugene confessed to the murder.[6] Eugene's confession ultimately implicated three of his friends (George Frees, Marvin Roberts, and Kevin Pease). A jury convicted these four teenagers, who became known as the "Fairbanks Four." They spent eighteen years in prison until Bill Oberly and his team at the Alaska Innocence Project proved another group of teenage boys committed the crime.

THE TRUTH ABOUT POLICE AND INTERROGATIONS

Despite what crime shows and movies portray, there are two fundamental truths about police interrogations:

1. Police officers do not have superpowers to tell if people are telling the truth;[7] and
2. Police officers do not focus interrogations on getting to the truth. Instead, officers focus on getting the suspect to agree with the theory the police often have already developed.

In their article "The Problem of False Confessions in the Post-DNA World," Steven Drizin, who co-directs the Center on Wrongful Convictions with Laura Nirider, and Richard Leo, a longtime scholar on false confessions, distinguish interviews from interrogations.

Interrogation is different than interviewing: whereas the goal of interviewing is to obtain the truth through non-accusatorial, open ended questioning in order to gather general information in the early stages of a criminal investigation, the goal of interrogation is to elicit incriminating statements, admissions and/or confessions through the use of psychological methods that are explicitly confrontational, manipulative, and suggestive. The purpose of interrogation is not to determine whether a suspect is guilty; rather, police are trained to interrogate only those suspects whose guilt they presume or believe they have already established.[8]

The most common technique for obtaining confessions over the past fifty years has been the Reid Technique. A psychologist and former police officer, John Reid, developed this "system" for interrogation around 1955. It is the technique police used to obtain Brendan Dassey's false confession.

The Reid Technique involves isolating a suspect away from lawyers, family, and friends in a small interrogation room where interrogating officers use the following nine steps to obtain a confession:

Step 1. Tell the suspect there is overwhelming evidence of their guilt. This may involve the interrogator lying about evidence implicating the suspect (e.g., "We've got a video of you committing the murder").

Step 2. Shift the blame away from the suspect to some other person or set of circumstances that prompted the suspect to commit the crime (e.g., "I can understand why you would kill him. He was disrespecting you").

Step 3. Never allow the suspect to deny guilt (e.g., "There is no point in saying you didn't do it. You did. All the facts tell us that").

Step 4. When the suspect gives reasons why he or she did not or could not commit the crime, build them into the guilty narrative (e.g., "I wouldn't kill her. I loved her"; answer: "Sure, you loved her. That's why when she was interested in other men you got so angry").

Step 5. Keep the focus of the suspect on the investigator's guilt narrative. Look them in the eye, pose questions, interact. Keep the suspect from thinking about their punishment.

Step 6. Look for non-verbal signs (e.g., crying, head nodding) that you are getting closer to moving the suspect toward a confession. Be sympathetic and urge suspect to tell the truth.

Step 7. Pose the "alternative question." (e.g., Don't ask, "Did you kill your wife?" Ask, "Did you decide to kill your wife a long time ago or was the decision spontaneous?")

Step 8. Once you have an admission of guilt, get the suspect to give details. Do it in front of other witnesses, so the suspect knows more than one person has heard the confession.

Step 9. Document the suspect's admissions and have them sign the confession.[9]

Note that none of these steps are focused on getting the suspect to tell the truth. They are all focused on getting the suspect to agree with the interrogators.

In their research, Leo and Ofshe explain why innocent people subjected to this technique often confess: "Investigators elicit the decision to confess from the innocent in one of two ways: either by leading them to believe their situation, though unjust, is hopeless and will only be improved by confessing; or by persuading them they probably committed a crime about which they have no memory, and that confessing is the optimal course of action."[10]

Over the past few years, the Reid Technique has decreased in popularity as it has become apparent that it often leads to false confessions. In a study of the first 325 DNA exonerations in the United States (1989–2014), innocent defendants falsely confessed or made admissions in 27 percent of those cases.[11]

LEGAL PROTECTIONS DURING INTERROGATIONS

Just as many jurors don't believe innocent people confess, even when subjected to the psychological pressure of interrogation (what Leo refers to as the myth of psychological interrogation), there is also a general belief that the law has evolved in the United States to protect people against interrogations.[12] Anyone who has watched a crime show or movie that takes place in the United States over the past fifty years can probably recite the warnings police typically give before an interrogation. Those warnings come from the 1966 US Supreme Court decision in the case of *Miranda v. Arizona:* "You have the right to remain silent. Anything you say can and will be used against you in a court of law. You have the right to an attorney.

If you cannot afford an attorney, one will be provided for you. Do you understand the rights I have just read to you? With these rights in mind, do you wish to speak to me?"[13]

In *Miranda* (and the case of *Escobedo v. Illinois*[14] two years earlier), the Court attempted to address the precarious situation suspects are in after arrest and before their first court appearance. Typically, until the first court appearance (unless there has been an indictment), a defendant doesn't have a right to a lawyer. Therefore, the police could question a suspect prior to these decisions without worrying about an annoying defense attorney interrupting their process.

The *Miranda* decision recognized that "without proper safeguards, the process of in-custody interrogation of persons suspected or accused of a crime contains inherently compelling pressures which work to undermine the individual's will to resist and to compel him to speak where he would not otherwise do so freely."[15]

Thus, the Court ruled, "In order to combat these pressures and to permit a full opportunity to exercise the privilege against self-incrimination, the accused must be adequately and effectively apprised of his rights, and the exercise of those rights must be fully honored."[16]

All that sounds great in theory, but the reality is that there are many ways around the *Miranda* rule, and they often lead to false confessions in the middle of the night before the arraignment courts open.

First, the *Miranda* rule only applies to a "custodial interrogation," meaning it only applies to people who have a reasonable belief that they are not free to leave and are being subject to "words or actions reasonably likely to elicit an incriminating response."[17] Often, police will tell a suspect they are free to leave before they begin interrogating to get around *Miranda*.

The Court has also found that *Miranda* only applies in a "police dominated atmosphere."[18] Therefore, *Miranda* doesn't apply if a suspect is questioned by an undercover police officer, even if that officer is pretending to be a suspect's cellmate. The Court has endorsed these kinds of shenanigans and has specifically said the police can lie to get a confession. Sometimes, the simple lie of the police having prosecutorial, judicial, and juror powers to decide charges and sentencing can cause a person to falsely confess if the deal seems too good to pass on.

Perhaps the most significant reason *Miranda* doesn't stop innocent people from falsely confessing is the remedy for a *Miranda* violation and the Court's rejection of the "cat out of the bag" argument.

The result of a *Miranda* violation is that any statement obtained in a custodial interrogation without a waiver of *Miranda* rights can't be used during trial. However, that doesn't stop the police from going through all the steps of the Reid Technique without advising a suspect of their *Miranda* rights. Once a confession is obtained, the police can then obtain a waiver and get a second confession. The court may toss out the first confession—made by the suspect prior to the *Miranda* waiver—but will admit the confession obtained after the *Miranda* waiver. And one confession, true or false, is enough to gain a conviction.

The "cat out of the bag" expression refers to evidence that was hidden and then later revealed. There are multiple theories for the origin of the expression, including the nineteenth-century "Pig in a Poke" scam, where pig sellers put cats in bags and sold them as pigs, only to be revealed as cats when the purchaser got home and opened the bag.

The "cat out of the bag" argument, in relation to the second confession after the *Miranda* waiver, is that, in the suspect's mind, it's pointless to assert their right to silence and demand a lawyer be present for the questioning after confessing. The cat is already out of the bag.

The Supreme Court specifically rejected this argument in *Oregon v. Elstad.* In that case, an eighteen-year-old suspect was questioned in his family's living room about a burglary without the benefit of *Miranda* warnings. The suspect confessed, and the police arrested him. The police then gave the suspect his *Miranda* warnings. After that, the suspect waived his rights and gave a second confession at the police station. At trial, the court admitted the second confession into evidence.[19] Not surprisingly, the prosecution at trial only needed one confession to get a conviction, so the pre-*Miranda* waiver statements become unimportant when police secure a post-*Miranda* waiver confession.

Furthermore, many suspects simply waive their rights after the police tell them it's a "mere formality" and an "opportunity to get their side of the story on the record," or that "only guilty people with something to hide refuse to waive their rights and talk."

Based on their research, Ofshe and Leo explain as follows:

Neither an innocent nor a guilty party is likely to appreciate the full signifi-
cance of Miranda warnings. An innocent person will likely believe that he is
not in any jeopardy by waiving his *Miranda* rights and answering questions
because police have sought out his help in solving the crime, and after all, he
is innocent. He also may believe that the *Miranda* warnings are merely a
bureaucratic formality that are significant only for the guilty. The guilty person will likely risk waiving his rights because he doesn't believe the police
have decided to arrest him, wants to find out what evidence they have, and
hopes to direct their attention elsewhere.[20]

Since the Supreme Court handed down the decision in *Miranda,* police
officers have been figuring out ways to operate in formal compliance with
the rules, but in profound contrast with the spirit of the safeguards. Chuck
Weisselberg, a professor at University of California, Berkeley, and a former
federal defender, wrote in his article "Mourning Miranda" that after
reviewing the various police techniques to get around the rules of
Miranda, he concluded that "little is left of *Miranda*'s vaunted safeguards
and what is left is not worth retaining."[21]

Miranda has also had a negative effect on the law as it relates to the
definition of a "voluntary" confession. As long ago as 1897, in the case of
Bram v. United States,[22] the Supreme Court discussed the principle that
involuntarily obtained confessions violated the Fifth Amendment. In
1968, in the case of *Greenwald v. Wisconsin,*[23] the Court held that when
police obtain a confession from a suspect after they had deprived him of
food, sleep, and medication, the confession was inadmissible because,
when looking at the "totality of the circumstances" in how the confession
was obtained, it was involuntary. More recently, however, we've seen
courts ignore strong indicators that a confession is involuntary where the
police obtained a waiver of *Miranda* rights.[24]

Finally, *Miranda* only protects defendants if the police are willing to
play by the rules. When they don't, it will likely be the word of a criminal
defendant calling foul play versus a police officer claiming everything was
by the book.

When I first met Marilyn Mulero, she told me she repeatedly told the
police she didn't want to talk and she wanted a lawyer when they interrogated her. The request of a lawyer during an interrogation is supposed
to end the interrogation.[25] Instead, the detectives kept her up all night,

telling her she was going to be executed if she didn't confess, and that her codefendant had turned on her. In the early morning hours, before her arraignment when the court appointed her a lawyer, the police got their confession. They later denied Marilyn had invoked her *Miranda* rights, and the tough-on-crime judge, who was a former homicide detective, believed the police and not Marilyn.

NEW AND QUESTIONABLE INTERROGATION TECHNIQUES

As the Reid Technique has started to fall out of favor, other questionable interrogation techniques have begun to fill the void.

Scientific Content Analysis (SCAN) is a system where suspects write answers to questions that police officers then "analyze" for their truthfulness. According to the creators' website, "SCAN transforms the investigator from an ordinary collector of information into a walking polygraph."[26] It breaks down the investigative process into three easy steps:

1. Give the subject a pen and paper.
2. Ask the subject to write down his/her version of what happened.
3. Analyze the statement and solve the crime![27]

Does this seem too good to be true? Probably because it is. According to the Laboratory for Scientific Interrogation website, where the SCAN method is promoted, "it is based on the idea that every person expresses themselves with a different 'linguistic code,' and those who take the SCAN training will learn how to interpret the code." They further claim, "SCAN changes the process of obtaining information from an art to a science." And "every word in the subject's statement—the pronouns and connections, the subjective time, the changes in language—will 'talk' to you and show you the answer." And, "while others are out searching for physical evidence, you have already solved the case—using only the subject's own words."[28]

Based on this "technique," authorities could believe a suspect is lying if they express themselves in weird or awkward ways, or just suffer from poor grammar. According to Ken Armstrong, who wrote the article "Why

Are Cops around the World Using This Outlandish Mind-Reading Tool?,"[29] there is no scientific support to suggest the SCAN method works. It hasn't been challenged sufficiently because the courts haven't admitted the results as evidence. Thus, the technique hasn't been cross-examined.

Professor Drizin is quoted in the same article, saying that "SCAN and assorted other lie-detection tools suffer from 'over-claim syndrome'—big claims made without scientific grounding." Asked why police would trust such tools, Drizin said: "A lot has to do with hubris—a belief on the part of police officers that they can tell when someone is lying to them with a high degree of accuracy. These tools play into that belief and confirm that belief."[30]

Several new interrogation techniques have also emerged focused on "opening up" the suspect to as much conversation as possible. One technique came from the HIG (High-Value Detainee Interrogation Group), a joint effort of the CIA, FBI, and Pentagon intended to be used in potential terrorist investigations, but now being used by local law enforcement. A second one is the "cognitive interview" used by Canadian police. A third is the Planning and preparation, Engage and explain, obtain an Account, Closure, and Evaluation (PEACE) technique used by British police. Unlike the Reid training, these techniques don't rely on small, isolated rooms and lying to suspects. They focus on building rapport and getting as much information out of a suspect as possible that can then be verified or proved to be false against other evidence.[31] While these techniques appear to be less coercive, it is still not clear that they do not sometimes create false confessions.

Perhaps most shocking is that hypnosis is still used by investigators to obtain confessions. In the 2021 case of *Charles Don Flores v. Texas*, the US Supreme Court refused to review a case where witness testimony was obtained through "investigative hypnosis." Charles was sentenced to death for the murder of Elizabeth Black. Initially, Elizabeth's neighbor couldn't identify Charles in a photo array, yet after hypnosis, and by the time of trial, she identified him.[32]

This type of manipulation of memories is highly suspect. Just like eyewitness identifications, confessions suffer from the frailties of human beings' abilities to provide good information based on reconstructed memories. And, just like eyewitness identifications, the processes we use to extrapolate confessions can lead to bad evidence and a wrongful conviction. Party tricks should not be the basis of prosecutions.

INTERROGATION REFORMS

On the good news front, some recent improvements may reduce the chances you'll go to prison after confessing to a crime you didn't commit. More than 170 years after Édouard-Léon Scott de Martinville invented sound recording in Paris, some jurisdictions are finally mandating the recording of interrogations. Arguments against recording have lost any merit they once might have had, particularly the argument that it's too expensive. That might have been a decent argument a few decades ago in the pre-digital age, but now that every officer is carrying a sophisticated recording device in their pocket (i.e., a cell phone) it's tough to make the expense argument. However, this reform has not taken root in most of the world, and as of this writing, only twenty-five US states have recording requirements.[33]

We must go further in our reforms. We should eliminate all processes that manipulate witnesses in such a way that they are likely to create false confessions. This is critical because we know that juries will convict based solely on a single confession, true or false, even in cases where there is powerful evidence countering that confession.

The case of Jeffrey Deskovic is a clear example of this reality. He was sixteen years old when investigators subjected him to multiple questioning and interrogation sessions inquiring into the rape and murder of a classmate. Those sessions led to a confession and prosecution. Even though DNA evidence from semen in the rape kit excluded Jeffrey, the jury still convicted him based on his confession. Jeffrey spent more than fifteen years in prison before the Innocence Project in New York fully exonerated him. He went on to attend and graduate from law school to help others in similar situations.[34]

In 2018, California became the first state to mandate that children under the age of sixteen must be allowed to talk to a lawyer before waiving their *Miranda* rights.[35] This occurred after it was reported that 42 percent of exonerees, who were juveniles at the time of their arrest, falsely confessed.[36] In 2021, Illinois became the first state to ban lying to minors during interrogations. One of the co-sponsors of the law was Illinois House Minority Leader Jim Durkin, a Republican and former Chicago prosecutor, who said, "I'll never be accused of being soft on crime, but I'm more interested in seeking the truth than a conviction. We should never tolerate, under any circumstance, the use of deception to seek a statement or an admission by any defendant, let alone a juvenile."[37] Durkin recognizes that lies by the police during interrogations are not the best path to the truth from those they are interrogating. Oregon followed Illinois in passing a similar law. I'm proud of the fact that California also passed a similar law in 2022 based on advocacy from my office and other California innocence organizations. All other states should follow and expand this rule to the interrogations of adults.

Critics of reforming interrogation techniques to eliminate manipulation, lying, and even sometimes torture, often talk about the truth and solving crimes as being more important than protecting the people who are interrogated. However, truth can often get lost in the process.

I once heard Paul McCartney talk about how he'd recently watched footage of the Beatles recording *Let It Be*, the final album the band released. He said he was surprised to see how much he was laughing with John Lennon and enjoying his company because, in the fifty years since they recorded the album, he'd bought into the media narrative that the two of them were angry with each other throughout the recording sessions.

McCartney adopted an outside narrative of his own life even though he was obviously the better firsthand witness. His memories had been manipulated.

Anyone can be a victim of their own imperfect memory and their own misspoken words. In a worst-case scenario, they can lead to a wrongful conviction.

6 You Have or Care for a Sick Child

I sat on the dirty, damp concrete floor in my black suit, knowing a trip to the dry cleaners was in my immediate future. It was the only way I could look Ken Marsh in the eyes while I talked to him through the small opening in the steel wall separating us.

"The district attorney is offering time served if you plea to manslaughter."

He shook his head.

"We can walk you out of here tomorrow," I offered.

He looked at me with an intensity I rarely see outside prison walls. "I'm not taking any deal."

It seemed ridiculous for me to explain the risk of not pleading to him. It wasn't as if I was talking to someone in county jail who had only spent a month or two locked up and had no idea what it was like to spend a lifetime in prison. I've never spent a night in a jail cell, and at that moment, Ken had already been locked up for more than twenty years. He knew what he was up against far better than me. Still, I tried to talk through the decision with him over the next hour, assessing the strengths and weaknesses of our case.

"I'm going to come back tomorrow and ask you the same question," I said as I got up.

"What question?" he asked, as if there was any other question in the world that he should have been thinking about at that moment.

"Whether you want to plead."

"Don't bother. You have your answer, Justin. I will never say I killed that baby. I will die in here before I lie about that. The baby fell off the couch."

HEIDI

I met my wife Heidi at a barbecue on May 15, 1988. She was twenty-one, and I was twenty-two. I was in my first year of law school, and the barbecue took place in the Washington, DC, backyard of my law school friend Jeff Chinn. Typically, first-year law students populated the barbecues, and we had the same conversations about law school every weekend. One of Jeff's housemates met a group of European au pairs and invited them along, thinking they would liven up the event. My future wife, Heidi, was one of the European au pairs.

Heidi and I were the only vegetarians at the barbecue. It would be years before the veggie burger was perfected, so we had little to eat and an immediate cause for bonding. We also had something else in common. Heidi came from Derby, in the Midlands of England. My mother was a Scouser, having grown up in Liverpool, seventy-two miles north of Derby. We were both raised by British mums who instilled common values we still recognize today.

When I met Heidi, she'd only been in the United States for a few months. She was living with a family in the suburbs of DC and caring for twin one-year-olds and a three-year-old. Before she came to the United States, she'd spent a year as a nanny working for part of the Italian royal family in Milan. She was, and still is, an incredible caregiver, but she told me that many of her au pair friends had nothing more than two days of training in New York City before they were sent around the country to live with families and care for their children. Very little of the training focused on actual childcare, with much of it dealing with the idiosyncrasies of Americans (including our preference for showers over baths).

Eight months into our relationship, Heidi's visa expired, and it was time for her to return to the United Kingdom. I was madly in love with her, so I applied to take a law program in London and followed her back. She got work as a secretary, and I worked as a busker (street musician), playing my guitar and harmonica, and singing in the London Underground. It was a simple existence until one day I came home, and she was holding a pregnancy test strip in her hand. We moved up our wedding date and headed back to the United States in preparation for our baby. I planned to finish law school and hopefully get a job that paid more than a guitar case full of change.

Throughout the rest of law school and into my career as a lawyer, Heidi cared for our son, Alec. She also cared for other children to supplement my meager salary as a public interest lawyer. We even started a family day-care business in our home, where three or four children would come over every day, and Heidi would care for them while their parents worked. If I knew then what I know now, I'd have never been involved in any childcare beyond our own family, and I would have told Heidi the night I met her at that barbecue to quit immediately.

LOUISE WOODWARD

In 1997, I was glued to the television watching the trial of nineteen-year-old English au pair Louise Woodward. Barry Scheck, who cofounded the Innocence Project at Cardozo Law School in New York, was her defense attorney. My interest in the case went far beyond my usual interest in criminal proceedings. Looking at Louise, I saw Heidi and how easily she could have been in the same circumstance.

Watching the trial was the first time I heard the term "subdural hematoma" (bleeding on the brain), which is one of the symptoms doctors are trained to look for in child abuse cases. So-called "Shaken Baby Syndrome" was diagnosed whenever a baby had the symptoms of subdural hematomas, along with brain swelling and retinal hemorrhaging. They were known as the "triad" of symptoms indicating abuse.

Louise cared for eight-month-old Matthew Eappen in Newton, Massachusetts, when he fell into a coma and died. Dr. Patrick Barnes, who would later become one of the great critics of the shaken baby diagnosis, testified for the prosecution that he was certain the triad of symptoms existed in the case and, thus, Matthew died from abuse. The symptoms simply could not have been caused by anything else.

It was gut-wrenching watching the trial. Louise was a teenager without much experience caring for children, making her an easy target. Like many of the British women in my life, she smiled and laughed nervously at inappropriate times, making an odd impression on American jurors. Like Amanda Knox, she suffered from misunderstood cultural interpretations of her behavior.

Barry put on clear and detailed expert testimony and evidence that the injuries that killed Matthew must have occurred weeks before the alleged shaking by Louise. I vividly remember him waving a blown-up brain scan photo to the jury and shouting, "This is reasonable doubt; this is the end of the case!"

Nonetheless, Louise was convicted of second-degree murder and sentenced to life in prison. When the jury read the verdict, a worldwide audience watched her break down. Between sobs, she said, "Why did they do this? I didn't do anything."

The trial judge later reduced Louise's conviction to involuntary manslaughter and sentenced her to time served while incarcerated during the proceedings. He stated, "I am morally certain that allowing this defendant on this evidence to remain convicted of second-degree murder would be a miscarriage of justice."[1] Dr. Barnes later changed his mind about the evidence and told the *New York Times* that Matthew's symptoms weren't necessarily the result of abuse and "could have been accidental."[2]

Seven years after the Louise Woodward trial, I found myself sitting on the floor in a prison talking to my client about a similar tragedy.

KEN MARSH

Ken Marsh lived in San Diego with his girlfriend Brenda and her two children, Jessica (almost two years old) and Phillip (almost three years old). Ken worked nights at a bottling plant, and Brenda worked days at a wholesale flower market. They rotated childcare for the children.

On April 27, 1983, Brenda was at work while Ken watched the children. While the children happily played, Ken went to pick up a toy from behind the couch and noticed some trash. He decided to clean up the area and left the room to get a vacuum cleaner. While Ken was out of the room, Phillip pulled himself up on the arm of the couch and reached for a glass ashtray on the fireplace mantle. He knocked the ashtray off the mantle, and it smashed into pieces. He lost his balance, fell, and smashed his head on the brick hearth.

Ken ran back into the living room, where he saw Phillip laying on the side of the fireplace, barely breathing, with blood on the back of his head. Ken slowly picked him up, carried him to the dining room, laid him down on a towel, and called 911.

When the emergency medical technicians arrived, Phillip was pale in color and lying motionless on the ground. He didn't appear to be breathing, but he did have a pulse. The EMTs attempted mouth-to-mouth resuscitation, and Phillip made a few gasps. He had blood hemorrhaging from a soft spot on the back of his head.

The paramedics arrived on the scene five minutes later. They saw Phillip's eyes were fixed and dilated but reported no bruising nor injuries to the front of Phillip's head. At some point, Phillip went into respiratory arrest and may have had a seizure. The paramedics tried opening Phillip's airways, but he wasn't getting enough air. They decided to put sandbags on both sides of his head to stabilize it and safely transport him to the nearest hospital emergency room.

When admitted to the hospital, Phillip was unconscious, his skin was pale and cool, and he was not moving at all. X-rays were taken of his neck and cervical spine. The primary concern was potential brain swelling, so Phillip was transferred to San Diego Children's Hospital for further treatment.

During the transfer, Phillip was administered eight grams of mannitol by intravenous push into his jugular vein. This was done to give him the maximum amount of medication in the shortest amount of time to decrease the brain swelling. However, his blood pressure began to drop dramatically, his heartbeat slowed profusely, and he died within twenty-four hours.

Before the fall that led to his death, Phillip had been a very sick child. Brenda had repeatedly taken him to the doctor for vomiting, a distended stomach, hair loss, stomach pains, and severe bruising. He had also been diagnosed with mononucleosis. Phillip's autopsy documented three small lacerations on his neck and bruises on his forehead, cheek, chin, and ear. There was also brain swelling and brain and retinal bleeding.

San Diego Children's Hospital was unique. It had a team of doctors, led by Dr. David Chadwick, that analyzed cases of suspected child abuse and reported those cases to the police and District Attorney's Office. Dr. Chadwick became one of the leading proponents of Shaken Baby Syndrome in the country, and the team evolved into what is now called The Chadwick Center for Children & Families. They offer "programs and services that provide for the prevention, identification and treatment of abused and traumatized children."[3]

Dr. Chadwick's team was suspicious of Phillip's death. They believed the swelling and internal bleeding was too excessive based on a short fall, and the lacerations appeared to be "slash" injuries that couldn't have been caused by falling against a brick fireplace hearth where his body was found. The doctors ruled out the possibility that the broken glass from the ashtray could have caused the slashes because the glass wasn't bloodstained. They called the police, and Ken was arrested and charged with murder.

Ken maintained his innocence throughout the investigation and refused to accept any plea offers. At trial, a team of experts testified that they believed Phillip's injuries resulted from abuse. Dr. Chadwick testified that Phillip's bruising couldn't have resulted from a short fall and that such bruising would have required a fall from at least thirty feet. Ken was convicted and sentenced to fifteen-years-to-life.

Twenty years later, in 2003, I first met Brenda, along with Tracy Emblem, a San Diego defense attorney who'd worked on Ken's case for several years. Through tears, Brenda told me how she'd always believed Ken was innocent.

Since Ken's conviction, we've learned a great deal about baby death cases. First, doctors testified that Phillip couldn't have sustained his fatal injuries in a short fall. For decades, experts regularly testified that children could not die from short falls. Every day, millions of children worldwide fall, and while almost all of them are either fine or have minor injuries, we now know that there are occasions when short falls lead to fatal injuries. These short falls can also lead to the triad of symptoms doctors have been trained to recognize as indicators of abuse.

In 2018, pediatricians with expertise in child abuse published a study examining eight falls by children, each witnessed by an average of four people, all of which resulted in subdural and retinal hemorrhages.[4] The American Association of Pediatricians—an organization of sixty-seven thousand pediatricians in the United States—no longer advises doctors that short falls cannot result in death or in the injuries that have long been diagnosed as indicating abuse.[5]

We've also learned that the triad of symptoms can be caused by diseases such as encephalitis, meningitis, and Brittle Bone Syndrome.[6] They can also be caused by reactions to vaccines, vitamin deficiencies, and even the pressure from a normal vaginal delivery.[7]

Often, these symptoms are not discovered at birth because there will be no X-rays or CT scans if the baby is otherwise healthy. The baby is sent home, and usually, the swelling and bruising will go away. But perhaps the child suffers a short fall off the couch or changing table that leads to death. The autopsy will then reveal these symptoms, which can result in a misdiagnosis of abuse.

One study revealed that approximately 30 percent of children studied were born with subdural hematomas and retinal hemorrhages after a normal vaginal delivery. This number was even higher in assisted vaginal deliveries and significantly lower in scheduled Caesarian deliveries.[8] These babies are regularly deemed healthy and sent home.

In Ken's case, we were lucky Bonnie Dumanis had recently been elected as the San Diego County District Attorney. I'd developed a good relationship with Bonnie after she took office, and we decided to present Ken's case to her before pursuing further litigation. Bonnie agreed that the case should be reviewed, so we secured a few neutral experts to examine the evidence. Those experts concluded that Phillip had an undiagnosed blood disorder (resulting from the mononucleosis) which explained the extensive bruising. The injuries were consistent with a short fall onto a brick hearth.

Even with this evidence, there was no way to be sure we could win Ken's freedom with a petition to reopen the case based on new evidence. Every state in the United States has its own standard for reopening cases with new evidence, and, at the time, California had the toughest standard in the country. I know this because I researched every one of them along with Alex Simpson and Northern California Innocence Project attorney Paige Kaneb. We wrote a law review article documenting that it wasn't conservative southern states that made it nearly impossible to obtain judicial review of convictions where there was strong evidence of innocence. Instead, it was good old hippie, liberal California.[9]

In most states, the standard to introduce new evidence and get a conviction reversed is whether the new evidence would have changed the result of the trial. In California, the courts required new evidence that completely undermined the prosecution's case and pointed unerringly toward innocence.[10] In other words, even if we could provide scientific evidence to show it was highly likely Phillip died from an accidental fall, a judge could still find our claims didn't "unerringly point to innocence." The jury had found him guilty when the prosecution had the burden to prove guilt. When we got the case, we had the burden to prove innocence.

After we got the results from the experts, Bonnie proposed a resolution—Ken pleads guilty to manslaughter. He would get resentenced to time served for the more than twenty years he'd already been in prison and go home without litigation. That led to the scene that began this chapter with Ken vehemently refusing.

I knew the risks, and I explained them to him. Bonnie could walk away from the negotiation. We would then have to petition the court for a hearing, and even if we got one, there was no assurance we would win. I worried Ken was gambling with the rest of his life because he felt he'd be letting down his girlfriend Brenda, his other attorney Tracy Emblem, and everyone who'd fought for his innocence. I always worry about that when presenting a plea offer.

When we informed Bonnie that Ken wouldn't accept the plea, we held our collective breath. Bonnie eventually agreed to join us in a motion to reverse the conviction and then dropped all charges against him. Maybe Ken's refusal to take a deal finally convinced her of his innocence. I don't know.

Bonnie's decision to dismiss the case was bold and refreshing in a conservative city like San Diego. I heard through the grapevine she got a lot of grief from her staff. Baby death cases are the most emotional homicide cases, and they get a lot of publicity. The public doesn't understand the science, and the dismissal of the case was a repudiation of the testimony from well-respected doctors in the community.

Ken's release was also extremely emotional. There were only a few hours between filing the motion for his release and all of us standing behind him on the courtroom steps facing a large group of reporters and cameras.

Ken was stunned. He teared up while he squeezed Brenda's hand and tried to find the words to express how he was feeling. He talked about how he maintained his innocence from the day of his arrest, throughout his trial, appeals, and parole hearings, where he might have been released had he said he was guilty. "I am innocent, and I wasn't going to settle for anything less than exoneration," he told the reporters.[11]

A few days after Ken's release, we had an event at the law school to welcome him home. Bonnie stopped by and met with him in my office. He told her how grateful he was to finally be free and thanked her for agreeing to the reversal of his conviction. She asked about his plans and encouraged him to put the past behind him and create a new life.

Watching the most powerful prosecutor in the county having this friendly conversation with a man who just a few days before was condemned to die in prison gave me hope. It was possible to free innocent people without the usual wars between prosecutors and defense attorneys.

SUZANNE JOHNSON

Suzanne Johnson is another San Diegan convicted in a baby death case. She worked in a YMCA-sponsored day-care program, and on June 24, 1997, she was caring for a child named Jasmine, who fell out of her high chair. Jasmine appeared to be fine, but approximately thirty minutes later, she began throwing up and had difficulty breathing. Suzanne called 911 and administered CPR until the ambulance arrived and took Jasmine to the hospital. Within an hour, Jasmine was pronounced dead.

During the autopsy, similar injuries to those suffered by Phillip were discovered: skull fracture, bleeding in her brain, and retinal hemorrhaging. The doctor also found a previous subdural hematoma that Jasmine suffered two to four weeks before her death. Like Ken Marsh's trial, experts testified that Jasmine couldn't have sustained such injuries from a short fall, and Jasmine's head injuries were equivalent to those sustained by an infant who fell from a third-story window or from being unrestrained in a car accident.

Prosecutors argued that Suzanne caused the injuries by abuse, and it wasn't possible Jasmine would appear normal after suffering such injuries. So, at the very least, they argued, Suzanne's negligence was the cause of death because she didn't immediately call 911 after the alleged fall. On April 30, 1999, Suzanne was convicted of assault on a child causing death and sentenced to twenty-five-years-to-life in prison.

As discussed, we now know babies can die from short falls. Looking back at the childhoods of both my children, Alec and Zach, I'm glad it doesn't commonly happen because they fell a great deal. I remember a particular incident when I was a very young dad. I put Alec in his high chair and turned around to get his baby food out of the refrigerator. I heard a crash, and when I turned back around, he was crying loudly from the floor. I'd failed to strap him in correctly, and he'd slid under the tray and off the chair onto the floor. He was fine, but since the first moment I read Suzanne's case file, I've flashed back to that moment and realized I could've been in the same situation.

A decade after Suzanne's trial, the world learned about the possibility of appearing fine after a head injury (i.e., experiencing a "lucid interval") before death. In 2009, actress Natasha Richardson was skiing in Quebec, Canada. She fell and hit her head on a beginner's slope but appeared okay. In an interview, her husband, actor Liam Neeson, said she brushed off the idea of any serious injury and simply said, "Oh honey, I've taken a tumble in the snow." Hours later, her condition worsened, and she was evacuated to a hospital. X-rays were taken of her head, and after her husband saw them, he described her brain as being "squashed against the side of her skull." Soon after, Natasha was pronounced brain dead and was on life support until she died.[12]

Jasmine's fate was similar. She suffered head injuries from the fall that ultimately killed her, but for a period of time, she experienced a lucid interval where she appeared unharmed.

During my prison visits with Suzanne, it was impossible to see the merit in locking her away. She was an elderly, gentle woman with snow-white hair who talked about things like decorating the prison dorms for the holidays. The subject she'd talk about most was how much she wanted to visit with her grandchildren, but California law made that impossible. She was incarcerated for a crime against a child, so under the law, she was banned from visiting with any children under the age of eighteen, even her own grandchildren.[13]

With new medical science that countered her guilt, we presented Suzanne's case to the San Diego District Attorney's Office. We hoped to get the same cooperation we got in the Ken Marsh case, but Jasmine's family still believed Suzanne was guilty, and I was never able to convince Bonnie Dumanis to join us in reversing the conviction. With clemency as a final option, Suzanne was one of the twelve petitions we walked from San Diego to Sacramento and presented to Governor Jerry Brown. He didn't grant her clemency during his term, but in the 2020 push to free those trapped in the COVID-plagued prisons who didn't belong there, Governor Gavin Newsom granted her clemency.

On April 3, 2020, Suzanne walked out of Central California Women's Facility as a free woman into the loving arms of her family. She'd spent twenty-one years in prison for a crime she didn't commit.

AUDREY EDMUNDS

As I discussed in chapter 3, where the person who finds a dead body can become a primary suspect, the same is often true in baby death cases. Even if the deadly injury happened earlier, the person caring for the baby at the time of death can often be wrongfully convicted. That's what happened to a childcare provider named Audrey Edmunds.

Audrey babysat neighborhood children in her home in Waunakee, Wisconsin. On October 16, 1995, she was caring for seven-month-old Natalie Beard. Natalie was fussy that morning, and her mother Cindy explained when she dropped her off that she had an ear infection. Audrey gave Natalie a bottle of formula and left her alone in the living room. When Audrey returned, Natalie was lifeless, with formula dripping from her nose.

Audrey described the scene in her autobiography: "My heart hammered and I knew something was dreadfully wrong. Had she choked on her formula? Adrenaline pulsed through me as I raced through the house, the garage, and the front yard, with the baby in my arms screaming for help. I had never been so afraid in my life. It was obvious Natalie was in serious trouble."[14]

Audrey called 911, and Natalie was rushed to the hospital where she died that night. She'd only been in Audrey's care for one hour that day.

Like the other cases discussed in this chapter, Natalie's autopsy revealed extensive brain damage. Abuse was suspected, and after a cursory investigation, Audrey was charged with first-degree reckless manslaughter.

At trial, friends and neighbors testified that Audrey was a loving and caring childcare provider, and it was revealed that Natalie had been a very sick child prior to her death. Natalie had a long record of doctor visits, including a checkup several days before her death. It was reported she was lethargic, irritable, and vomiting—all possible signs of a brain injury. Countering this evidence, multiple experts testified for the prosecution that Natalie was a victim of Shaken Baby Syndrome. Audrey was convicted and sentenced to eighteen years in prison.

When we launched the California Innocence Project in 1999, I reached out to Keith Findley, a professor at the University of Wisconsin Law school. Keith had started the Wisconsin Innocence Project the year before, along with law professor John Pray, and I modeled much of our project on theirs. Keith, John, and I went on to work together on the Innocence Network board for many years, helping support the creation and management of innocence organizations around the country and the world.

Over the years, Keith has become a specialist in wrongful baby death convictions. He took on Audrey's case ten years after she was convicted, and he filed a motion for a new trial based on all the new science that challenged the Shaken Baby Syndrome diagnoses.

The new science had raised doubts in the mind of the doctor who conducted Natalie's autopsy. At the hearing on the motion for a new trial, he testified that he was no longer confident Natalie's death was caused by injuries she sustained that morning while in Audrey's care. Five other doctors also testified that the evidence did not support a conclusion that Audrey was responsible for Natalie's death. Dr. Patrick Barnes, who testified for the prosecution in the Louise Woodward case, testified that something as mundane as the ear infection Natalie had the morning of her death could have spread to the brain with fatal consequences.

Keith's motion was denied, but on appeal to the Wisconsin Court of Appeals, the court ruled that "newly discovered evidence, in this case, shows that there has been a shift in mainstream medical opinion since the time of Edmunds's trial as to the causes of the types of trauma Natalie exhibited." The court reversed the conviction, stating that "the record establishes that there is a reasonable probability that a jury, looking at both the new medical testimony and the old medical testimony, would have a reasonable doubt as to Edmunds's guilt."[15]

Clearly, Natalie wasn't a healthy baby. She had preexisting conditions that led to her death. Audrey had the tragic misfortune of being the caregiver when Natalie went into the distress that ultimately led to her death, causing the focus to be on her. Audrey was exonerated and released from prison in 2008 after spending more than a decade in prison for a crime she did not commit.

ALAN GIMENEZ

Wrongful convictions in baby death cases don't just involve caregivers like Ken, Suzanne, and Audrey. It is often the parents who are sent to prison.

Try to imagine anything worse. Your child tragically dies. While you're trying to cope with this life-changing tragedy, you're interrogated as a suspect. You are then arrested and charged with murdering your own child. People in your community, at your work, even in your family start to think you committed this heinous act. You then spend every penny you have on your defense while you sit in jail. And then, you are convicted as a child murderer and sent to prison, where you are the lowest of the low on the hierarchy of prisoners.

Alan Gimenez suffered this fate. His daughter, Priscilla, was a very sick child who suffered from a long, difficult, and traumatic birth. After which, she was given a spinal tap and chest X-ray that revealed retained fluids and a fractured rib. She was placed on oxygen for the first two days of her life.

Once released from the hospital, Priscilla started showing symptoms of fever and began projectile vomiting and having seizures. Alan and his wife brought her back to the hospital, but no tests were performed. She was simply released with instructions to the parents to cut down her formula, feed her upright, and burp her frequently during feedings.

Seven weeks after her birth, Priscilla vomited, had a seizure, and lost consciousness while Alan was feeding her. Alan called 911 and administered CPR. She was taken back to the hospital where doctors conducted numerous tests to determine the source of her problems. Blood tests showed Priscilla had anemia. A spinal tap revealed she had blood in her spinal column. She had an infection in her mouth and a fresh tear of the tissue under her tongue, likely caused by the seizure. She also appeared to have a clotting problem that prevented the drawing of her blood. Additionally, doctors discovered Priscilla's mother had Hepatitis A. Despite these problems, doctors could not pinpoint what was causing the projectile vomiting and seizures, and she was released from the hospital three days later.

Hours after her release, while Alan was again attempting to feed her, Priscilla vomited forcefully and had another seizure. Alan took her to the emergency room, and the hospital conducted a CT scan for the first time. The scan showed the rib fracture from birth and bleeding in Priscilla's brain (a subdural hematoma). The next day she died.

Alan was charged with murder based on Priscilla's autopsy, which revealed her brain was swollen and she suffered from retinal hemorrhages, along with the already discovered subdural hematoma. Once again, the triad of symptoms led to a determination of abuse, even though it was very likely the symptoms were the result of her traumatic birth.

Alan was convicted of second-degree murder and sentenced to fifteen-years-to-life in prison. We joined forces with Janeen D'Angelo, a dedicated pro bono lawyer who had spent years trying to free him. When I visited Alan in prison, I found a mild-mannered, gentle guy I couldn't imagine having already survived so many years in prison as a convicted baby killer. He told me how he'd hidden his charges from the people he was incarcerated with and even changed his paperwork to other charges when one of the prison leaders demanded to see it.

Several experts concluded that Priscilla would have had head and neck injuries that didn't exist if she'd been violently shaken to death, as the prosecution claimed. And there was evidence from the birth, which was not disclosed to the defense, that retinal hemorrhages were present at birth. It was very likely all three symptoms were present at birth. Even if they weren't, all the combined evidence pointed to Alan's innocence.

Nonetheless, with the very high standard of proof required to reverse a wrongful conviction and doctors still clinging to outdated science related to baby deaths, all of Alan's petitions to the court were unsuccessful. He was finally paroled in 2015 after twenty-four years in prison for a crime he did not commit.

MATT AND GRACE HUANG

The most bizarre child death case I've worked on in my career involved both parents being charged with murder based on a theory they had starved their child to death to harvest her organs. I learned about the case when we were walking across California with the clemency petitions. I got a call from Eric Volz, a man who had been wrongfully convicted of murdering his girlfriend in Nicaragua. After his release, Eric began assisting other wrongfully convicted people around the world to regain their freedom. We'd previously worked together freeing a former Peace Corps volunteer, Jason Puracal, who'd been falsely charged and convicted of drug trafficking in Nicaragua.

"Say that again, Eric," I said into my cell phone as I walked alongside a loud highway.

"They were charged with murdering their daughter to harvest her organs."

I had heard him correctly.

"Why would they starve her to death to harvest her organs? Wouldn't starvation destroy the organs and make them worthless?"

"Yep, none of it makes sense."

Matt and Grace Huang were an Asian American couple who moved to Doha, Qatar, with their three adopted children in 2012. Matt, a Stanford-trained engineer, was there to help oversee an infrastructure project related to improvements being made in preparation for the FIFA 2022 World Cup.

On January 15, 2013, the Huangs' adopted eight-year-old daughter, Gloria, died unexpectedly. There were no signs of trauma or anything to indicate Gloria died due to abuse. Nonetheless, the Qatari police were suspicious of an Asian couple having Black children. Adoption, particularly of children of a different race than the parents, is not common in Qatari culture. Under Qatari law, which is based on Islamic Sharia law, it's actually illegal to adopt Qatari children.

Qatar has a lot of laws that are startling to foreigners who are not familiar with the culture. It's illegal to bring pork, alcohol, edible seeds, or spices into the country. It's illegal for unmarried couples to live together. Flogging is still used as a punishment, and adultery is punishable by death.

Apparently, taking photos of government buildings is also illegal. Alex Simpson, my associate director, and Matt's brother were arrested for this crime during the legal proceedings when Matt's brother decided to take a photo of the courthouse. At that point, we had four clients to free, although the photo case was a little less complicated. Alex and Matt's brother were soon released after signing a confession and warning letter.

The Huang children were born in Ghana where they lived in abject poverty. There wasn't a ready supply of food, and the children developed unhealthy eating habits. Gloria regularly refused to eat, and when the Qatari police heard about that, it evolved into the bizarre theory that the Huangs were starving her to death. The couple were charged with murder and faced the death penalty, while their two other children were put into an orphanage.

When I flew to Qatar to assist with the defense of the Huangs, it was my first trip to the Middle East. The flight was filled with troops heading to Afghanistan, most of whom looked heartbreakingly young. After twenty-two hours of traveling, I was in a daze as my driver took me to my hotel, passing shiny ultra-modern glass skyscrapers jutting out of a barren desert.

The night before the trial, I helped prepare the defense witnesses with Eric and the local lawyer who Matt's company had retained. We had a great deal of trouble getting expert witnesses in Qatar to testify in the case. There seemed to be a common fear of reprisal from the government. We did find experts from outside Qatar who reviewed the evidence and determined Gloria had not starved to death. She was seen by witnesses running around the day before she died, which is impossible for someone who is starving. Starvation is a process that takes weeks, and the body slows down as energy disappears. If Gloria had died by starvation, she would have been unable to move the day before her death, let alone run around.

In the courtroom, Grace's head and body were completely covered in black fabric, and she was not allowed to talk to us. Matt was wearing Western clothes and free to speak. I couldn't imagine how they were both feeling. They'd lost their child, their two other children were in an orphanage, and they were facing the death penalty in a foreign country where they didn't speak the language or understand the culture.

The trial procedures were like nothing I'd ever seen. When we called a witness, instead of being allowed to ask questions, both the judge and prosecutor got a chance to rattle the witness by screaming questions for an extended period of time. There also appeared to be no record of the proceedings. When the judge wanted something documented, he'd yell it to a guy with a notebook who'd write it down. The surreal nature of the proceeding was enhanced by it being conducted in Arabic (a language I don't speak), and the time zone was pretty much the opposite of California, so for me, the trial was taking place in the middle of the night.

By the time we got to trial, the Huang case had become a global news story. The *New York Times* had published multiple stories about the case, and the courtroom was filled with international news agencies. The Huangs' plight also gained the attention of the US government, and the embassy sent representatives to court.

Many people think that when something like this happens overseas, the US government will come and bail them out, but it's not that simple. The United States has an important relationship with Qatar. We have a military base there, and footholds in the Middle East are strategically important. The US government wanted to let things play out in the Qatar legal system, hoping for a minimal disruption in the US/Qatari relationship, even though the case was outrageous, and the judicial processes were inadequate.

As the trial went on, it became clear the prosecution had no evidence Gloria died by criminal means. When Gloria had first arrived in the United States from Africa, she had giardia, a parasitic condition that can be difficult to eradicate and can cause severe nutritional problems that impair the body's ability to absorb nutrients from food. She later tested positive for Vitamin D deficiency and had other unusual blood work that, in retrospect, indicated a continuing malabsorption problem. It is likely Gloria died from an illness she contracted in Africa, but there was no way to prove it because the autopsy was completely inadequate and testing that should have been done was not. As soon as the police and prosecutors developed tunnel vision about the Huangs as slave traders and murderers, the investigation focused on seeking evidence that would support their baseless theory.

Slave trading was going on in Qatar. It was well documented that workers were being imported from other countries based on false promises. Some were promised well-paid office jobs, but when they arrived in Qatar their passports were confiscated, and they were put to work building skyscrapers in the desert at a fraction of the promised pay. Many had died on those jobs.[16]

Yet, as ridiculous as the idea was that the Huangs had starved their daughter to death to harvest her organs, even more ridiculous was the idea they were slave traders. They were simply a loving family. We had photos that were introduced in the trial of the family horseback riding together, taking trips to Europe, and living a great life.

On the day the judge was to announce the verdict, the Huangs had plane tickets and were ready to head back to the United States. No credible evidence had been introduced against them, and their defense was very strong. It was unthinkable there would be any verdict other than not guilty. But with all the international publicity, and the important relationship between the United States and Qatar, the Qatar government did not want the appearance that they had irrationally arrested an American couple and charged them with murder. The same pressure existed in the Amanda Knox case with the Italian officials, and in many others I've seen where US citizens are locked up overseas.

In every other case on the docket the day of the Huang decision, the judge gave detailed explanations for his verdicts and sentencing decisions. When it came to the Huangs, he simply said, "three years," without giving any explanation how this death penalty case had been reduced to a three-year sentence.

At that point, the US government knew the case was meritless. The US Department of State issued a statement that they "were surprised and disappointed by the court's decision" and "not all of the evidence was weighed by the court" and "some cultural misunderstandings may have led to an unfair trial." Matt spoke to reporters and said, "We have just been wrongfully convicted and we feel as if we are being kidnapped by the Qatar judicial system."[17]

As a result of pressure from the US government, including the specific involvement of US Secretary of State John Kerry, the Huangs' conviction was reversed, and they were allowed to return to the United States.[18]

When children die, people want answers, and they want someone to be held accountable. In every case I've discussed in this chapter, that desire has led to wrongful convictions in emotion-driven proceedings. That is why it's important to take the emotion out of these cases and conduct fact-driven investigations.

In the infamous 1980 Australian baby death case where a mother (Lindy Chamberlain) was convicted of murdering her nine-week-old daughter, it was well-known that the jury did not like the mother. Lindy was angry and resentful to be on trial for the murder of her baby when she had witnessed a dingo (wild dog) attack and carry off her child. The emotion of a baby dying and the jury's feelings toward Lindy drove the case to conviction. Decades later, it was proven that the baby was, in fact, attacked, carried off, and killed by a dingo, and Lindy was exonerated.[19]

In the United Kingdom, after several high-profile wrongful convictions for terrorist acts, the Criminal Cases Review Commission (CCRC) was created and given the power to reinvestigate cases of alleged miscarriages of justice. The commission has been criticized for taking too long to review cases and only acting in a small percentage of them. However, in the early 2000s, the CCRC began reviewing baby death convictions from across the country based on bad science. This type of investigation and review needs to happen at the front end of cases to avoid wrongful convictions and at the back end to remedy wrongful convictions.

In the US legal system, national commissions with the power to get convictions reversed are impossible to create. Each state and territory operates, under its own code of crimes and procedures, and the federal courts cannot intercede in a state criminal case unless a case presents federal constitutional issues. Even within a state, there are great inconsistencies in how the law is applied because local prosecutors hold much of the power. Those prosecutors suffer from the inherent bias to uphold the work

of their own offices. This bias often trumps solid scientific evidence proving a conviction was deeply flawed.

Cases like Ken Marsh, where the district attorney agrees to the reversal
of a baby death conviction, are rare. Again, these cases are very emotional
and get a lot of publicity. There are often grieving parents who want caregivers kept in prison as long as possible, and even some cases where
one parent falsely believes the other parent is responsible for the death of
their child.

Beyond the emotion of these cases, they are very complicated, and it is
often much easier to prove that the jury heard evidence based on bad science than it is to prove definitive innocence. In other words, we might be
able to prove that a doctor's testimony is false when he or she claims that
a child can't die from a short fall, but that doesn't necessarily negate the
theory that the child died from abuse.

Typically, when my office presents an innocence case involving a baby
death conviction to a district attorney's office, great deference is given by
the office to the prosecutor who handled the case at trial. Those prosecutors often spent months, sometimes years, learning about the evidence
and drawing conclusions. They usually know more about the facts and
evidence than any other lawyer in their office, and so their bosses often
defer to their judgment as to whether the case should be reviewed and
whether the conviction should be reversed. However, those prosecutors
are typically also the most biased people in their office, as they are reviewing their own work. The experts they used at trial also often continue to
support their own testimony because they suffer from the same bias. This
makes getting reversals of these cases through cooperation very difficult.

It's also very difficult to get reversals of these cases through litigation.
Typically, cases are sent back to the original trial judge when we have new
evidence of innocence, including new science that undermines baby death
convictions. Judges squeeze our hearings into their already busy calendars
and are never enthusiastic about a great deal of scientific evidence at those
hearings, particularly when it's contrary to evidence the judge has already
heard at a trial. Judges suffer from their own biases, just like prosecutors,
experts, and all other human beings.

Another challenge with judges is that they are often elected and rely on
support from prosecutors, police officers, and the general community to

keep their jobs. Appearing in the news as the judge who released an alleged baby killer can be contrary to that effort. Voters may remember this at election time and punish the judge at the poll booth. And while the public may have missed that news story, prosecutors, police officers, and, most importantly, their unions will be happy to remind everyone on election day.

That is why I love older judges. Give me the judge who is looking to retire every time. Sure, there are some old curmudgeons who will never give our cases a second look, but at least they aren't feeling the pressure of losing their jobs.

Baby death cases have devastating effects on the families who lose their children, and in cases of wrongful convictions, on those who are sent to prison for crimes they didn't commit. These cases also have a powerful effect on the people who work in this area. The doctors who make the diagnosis, including many who have changed their opinions on cases where they have testified and participated in putting innocent people in prison, are deeply affected. So too are the lawyers who litigate the cases. I often talk to lawyers who do this work about how nervous they are caring for their own babies, knowing how easily an accident can be spun into a crime.

Katherine Bonaguidi, a former staff attorney at the California Innocence Project, specialized in these cases. Several years ago, I was with Katherine in Washington, DC, when she got a call from her husband, Mike, in San Diego. He told her that he was in the emergency room with their nine-month-old baby, after she'd rolled off the bed and onto the floor. Mike, who is also a lawyer, said the baby appeared fine, but she'd thrown up and became sleepy after the fall. He got nervous, called 911, and the responding paramedics brought her to the hospital.

As soon as she hung up the phone, Katherine called her mother.

"Go down to the emergency room, sit next to Mike, and make sure he doesn't say anything dumb."

Even as a mother who was worried about her baby, as a lawyer who spends her days reviewing alleged child abuse cases, she knew Mike could be in jeopardy. She worried that a narrative could be spun about a mother out of town and a father stressed out about providing sole care to an infant. She wanted her mom to monitor the questions Mike was asked, and the answers he gave, knowing that they are often spun into something nefarious.

Parents and childcare providers always feel responsible when a child in their care is injured, even when it is an unavoidable accident. When caregivers say things like "I feel responsible" to doctors in emergency rooms, that can quickly morph into "I am guilty" on a police report. Fortunately, both the baby and Mike were fine, but it's easy to imagine another outcome.

The tragedy of a wrongful conviction must no longer compound the tragedy of the death of a child. Outdated scientific analysis should be eliminated from our criminal legal system and replaced with what we now know to be the truth. Without proper investigations, good science, and fair trials, all of us who care for young children are in jeopardy that we could one day be wrongfully convicted.

7 You Got a Jury That Was Blinded by "Science"

I've almost made it onto a jury twice. The first time it was a civil trial. I don't know much about the facts because I got thrown out before the trial began. I know the case involved a car accident, and I know someone was pulling a U-Haul because there was a lawyer there representing the company. During jury selection, a process known as *voir dire* (a French expression meaning "to see and say" that has many different pronunciations throughout the United States), a lawyer representing an insurance company questioned several members of the potential jury panel. The lawyer asked each of us what we thought about the McDonald's case where the company was sued for having coffee that was too hot and caused injury when a woman spilled it on herself.

"Outrageous," "stupid," and "her own damn fault for spilling the coffee on herself," were some of the answers given by my fellow potential jurors. When it was my turn to answer the question, I said, "Sometimes companies need to be punished to get them to change dangerous policies." The insurance company lawyer was summoned over to counsel table by the U-Haul lawyer. They had a brief conference.

"Have a good day, Mr. Brooks, you're excused from jury service," the insurance company lawyer said smiling.

The second time I was rejected was a criminal trial. I really wanted to get on that jury. It was a high-profile road rage case where two men got out of their cars, charged toward each other, and then one man hit the other man and killed him with a single blow. I discussed the incident at length with my criminal law class because it was a great case to analyze the distinctions between first-degree and second-degree murder, as well as manslaughter and self-defense.

Unfortunately, when I arrived in the courtroom, I knew my chances of getting on that jury were slim. I knew both the defense attorney and the prosecutor. The judge was an adjunct professor at the law school where I was teaching at the time. And, as a defense attorney myself, I knew the prosecutor wasn't going to want me anywhere near that jury. During the selection process, the prosecutor tried to portray me as biased based on my prior knowledge and experience. I kept saying I'd keep an open mind and follow the judge's instructions, but she knew the reality was that if I didn't agree with the rest of the jurors, I wasn't going to go along with their decision. I'm sure the prosecutor thought I was going to retry the case in the deliberation room. And if I couldn't get them to go my way, I was going to hang the jury.

"You're excused, Mr. Brooks," I heard for a second time.

In both cases, I was thrown off the jury because lawyers thought I was more likely to favor the position of their opponent. They sized me up based on what they knew about me from the jury selection process, applied their own inherent biases to what they perceived were my biases, and made a decision. I, too, have been in their position when selecting a jury. I've drawn conclusions about people based on very little information in deciding whether they would look favorably on my case or not.

In the Marilyn Mulero case, Marilyn was sent back to the trial court for resentencing after the Illinois Supreme Court reversed her death sentence. A panel of approximately fifty potential jurors was assembled and ready for the prosecutor and me to question them as part of the selection process.

In a death case, the prosecution gets to ask one of their favorite questions. Based on the US Supreme Court case of *Witherspoon v. Illinois*, prosecutors can ask potential jurors whether they have such strong feelings against the death penalty that they would be unwilling to impose a death sentence.[1] In Marilyn's case, when that question was asked, nearly half the jury pool raised their hands. They all were excused from service.

The reason prosecutors are allowed to *Witherspoon* the potential jurors is because they are allowed to remove anyone who will refuse to apply the law. If the death penalty is a legal sentence, potential jurors who say they will not impose that sentence can be removed. The problem is that when potential jurors who oppose the death penalty are removed from the pool, those who are left are also more likely to convict. Studies have shown that the process also removes more women and people of color from the jury pool.[2] Some prosecutors have been known to charge the death penalty in cases—even when they don't believe they can get a death verdict—just to get to *Witherspoon* the jury pool and end up with a more prosecution-friendly jury.

Applying my own bias to that same jury pool in Marilyn's case, I tried hard to keep an older, Puerto Rican man on the jury. He'd been very quiet during the selection process, and I didn't ask him any questions because I didn't want the prosecutor to focus on him. Puerto Rico doesn't have a death penalty. It isn't part of their culture. I hoped he'd see his daughter or granddaughter in Marilyn, and that would sway him from a life-ending sentence.

Unfortunately, during a break in the process, he walked by my table and said, "Justin, my son's name is Justin." I barely acknowledged him and just nodded my head, but the prosecutor argued that there was improper communication between the two of us, and he was removed.

Fortunately, we still got a good jury who didn't sentence Marilyn to death. As discussed in the first chapter, they sentenced her to the only alternative they were offered since the court wouldn't allow Marilyn to withdraw her guilty plea. She was sentenced to life without the possibility of parole, and it would be twenty-five more years until she was freed.

The US jury system has its roots in the British system. It's based on traditions brought to Britain by William the Conqueror in 1066, but dates even earlier to ancient Greece and Rome.[3] However, the right to a jury trial in state criminal proceedings, where most of the criminal cases occur in the United States, didn't exist until the 1968 case of *Duncan v. Louisiana*.[4] In that case, the US Supreme Court ruled that the Due Process Clause of the Fourteenth Amendment required states to provide juries in serious cases, later defined as those cases with a potential sentence of more than six months.[5]

Juries, however, are not a universal system for doling out justice. Former British colonies like the United States, Australia, and New Zealand, as well as more than forty other countries, use juries.[6] With the exception of Argentina, juries are not part of Latin American legal systems.[7] In most countries, juries do not exist.

When I'm lecturing about criminal law outside the United States, I often hear, "You have so many wrongful convictions in the United States because you have juries." I don't believe this to be true. In a bench trial (a trial with just a judge and not a jury), a prosecutor must simply convince the judge that an accused person is guilty. The judge is typically a former prosecutor who has probably become jaded to claims of innocence after years of prosecuting and sitting on the bench. As mentioned in the prior chapter, judges are subject to political pressure, as they are often elected and don't want to appear "soft on crime." With a jury, the prosecution must prove guilt to twelve people who are hopefully detached from such cynicism, bias, and political pressure.

But it's not that simple. There are problems with juries and significant obstacles in putting together a group of twelve diverse, focused, committed, and competent people to consider the facts of each case and apply the law as instructed. This is particularly difficult in cases with complex, scientific evidence.

First, there is a problem with people ignoring juror summonses and not showing up for juror duty. Nine percent of those summoned to jury duty in the United States ignore the summons, but that rate is as high as 50 percent in some jurisdictions.[8] A 2017 Pew Research survey found that only 67 percent of US citizens believed jury duty is part of being a good citizen. Within that number, only 61 percent of Latino citizens and 58 percent of Black citizens agreed. And those numbers are all trending downward, because only 50 percent of eighteen-to twenty-nine-year-olds believe jury duty is part of being a good citizen.[9]

Second, potential jurors can be dismissed for bias, and both the defense and the prosecution in a criminal case get a certain number of peremptory challenges that can be used to dismiss a juror without showing bias. This often leads to perfectly well-qualified jurors being dismissed based on some perceived bias or personality trait, such as being overly opinionated.

As a lawyer, I want to be the teacher of the facts and law to the jury. I don't want some smarty-pants juror teaching during jury deliberations. I assume this is why I keep getting kicked off jury panels.

Third, jurors have limited abilities to comprehend forensic science. The United States once led the world in science education, but that is no longer true. In 2018, the Pew Research Center reported that the United States ranked thirtieth in math education and nineteenth in science education out of the thirty-five so-called "developed" countries in the Organization for Economic Cooperation and Development.[10]

Fourth, the lack of science education is often replaced by popular culture misinformation, leading to unrealistic expectations of the ability of science to solve crimes. The so-called "*CSI* effect," where jurors expect to see sophisticated scientific evidence in the courtroom, has been talked about since the first version of the television show *CSI* came on the air in 2000.[11]

Fifth, jurors are expected to apply the law to facts and evidence in cases by way of juror instructions. Those instructions are brought into the jury room and discussed during deliberations outside the presence of the judge and the lawyers. Although the instructions are intended to bring clarity to complex questions, there is evidence that jurors often do not understand the instructions and misapply them.[12]

I've never watched *CSI, Law and Order,* nor most other crime shows. I don't say that to appear as an aloof law-professor type who is above watching television. In fact, I watch a great deal of it, mostly junky reality shows. I don't watch crime shows because they just make me think about my own cases when I'm trying to relax, and it's very annoying for my wife to hear me critiquing all the unrealistic premises. Although crime shows don't appeal to me, they are incredibly popular. In 2012, *CSI* was the most-watched show in the world.[13] Millions of people who watch these shows end up on juries, and they expect to see scientific evidence in every criminal case, even if that evidence has no relevance.

A 2008 survey published by the National Institute of Justice found the following:

- 46 percent of jurors expect to see some kind of scientific evidence in *every* criminal case.

- 22 percent expect to see DNA evidence in *every* criminal case.
- 36 percent expect to see fingerprint evidence in *every* criminal case.
- 32 percent expect to see ballistic or other firearms laboratory evidence in *every* criminal case.[14]

A prosecutor, who was a former student of mine, told me he had a rape case where the defendant didn't deny he had sex with the complainant; he was instead arguing consent. This argument made DNA irrelevant, but my former student introduced DNA evidence anyway simply because "jurors expect to see DNA evidence in a rape case."

Since jurors often have inadequate levels of science education beyond inaccurate television programs, they heavily rely on expert testimony when complicated scientific evidence is thrown around the courtroom. Unlike lay witnesses, where jurors scrutinize their testimony and credibility in deciding whether to believe them, jurors are often overly deferential to the testimony and conclusions of expert witnesses. Some scholars have suggested we adopt "Blue Ribbon Juries" comprised of jurors who have heightened knowledge of math and science.[15] This concept seems contrary to democratic participation in jury trials and the idea that we are tried by our "peers." Regardless of whether it is a good or bad idea, presently, the jury pool for marijuana possession cases is the same as for cases involving complicated scientific testimony.

The problem with jurors relying so heavily on expert testimony (and the science the experts are peddling) is that often there is little to no scientific basis for the testimony.

For example, in the baby death cases discussed in the prior chapter, jurors relied on experts whose testimony was based on what we now know to be deeply flawed conclusions about the triad of symptoms. In each one of those cases, the jury heard the story of a tragic death, and they heard experts point their fingers at innocent people and explain why they were guilty. There is no way to overstate the power of this type of expert testimony and the impact it has on jurors.

When jurors hear about the hefty resumes of experts who have outstanding credentials from top schools and extensive experience in their fields, and then they hear them testify with total confidence, it's difficult for the jurors to assess the quality of the science involved in the case.

Questionable sciences can be raised to the level of DNA in the jurors' minds.

As I discussed in chapter 2, Skip Sperber, the forensic odontologist, dazzled the jury with his expertise when he testified for the prosecution in Bill Richards's case. He'd been a practicing dentist for nearly fifty years. He testified in high-profile cases like Jeffrey Dahmer and Ted Bundy, identified bodies at Ground Zero after the September 11th attacks, testified in more than two hundred trials, and was the chief forensic dentist at the California Department of Justice, where he developed a Dental Identification System. In sum, he was arguably the best forensic dentist in the world.

Although forensic odontology is pretty much a guessing game, when Dr. Sperber told the jury only 1–2 percent of the population would match the dental evidence in the case, and Bill Richards matched, who was the jury to challenge that? Bill was convicted as soon as those words were uttered, and he stayed in prison until long after those words were retracted.

Ray Krone was another victim of bad forensic odontology. In 1992, he was convicted of murder, kidnapping, and sexual assault of a woman who worked at a bar he frequented. Experts testified at his trial that a bite mark found on the victim's body matched Ray's crooked teeth, earning him the nickname of "Snaggle Tooth Killer." The jury had no expertise in bite marks. They relied on the expert testimony, which was enough to get Ray convicted and sent to death row.

Ray was represented after his conviction by Christopher Plourd (now Judge Plourd), one of the best lawyers I've ever worked with. He earned the rare reputation of being a lawyer who truly understood and effectively used scientific evidence. Chris was able to blow the bite mark evidence out of the water when DNA testing led to the actual killer.

I had dinner with Ray shortly after he got out of prison in 2002, after his decade-long nightmare. He explained the process of slowly absorbing the reality of his situation in a way only someone who had been through the experience could truly understand.

> At first, I was bummed because I knew I was missing my softball game while the police were questioning me. Then, when they didn't let me go, I figured it would all get cleared up quickly, but I was worried about missing work.

When I was still in jail a month later, I was worried about not paying my rent and losing my apartment. It didn't happen quickly, but piece by piece my life disappeared until I'd lost everything, and I was sitting on death row waiting to be executed.

When Ray was released, he was famous for two reasons: (1) he was the one hundredth person in the United States released from death row after a finding of innocence; and (2) he went on Extreme Makeover, a television show devoted to physically improving the appearance of their guests. A dentist repaired his "snaggle tooth," changing Ray's bite mark forever.

ARSON

Another area of forensic science where jurors have often relied on faulty expert testimony is fire science. Like the faulty causal connection between the triad of symptoms present in baby death cases and alleged wrongful actions by caregivers, many experts have changed their analysis in recent years as to the indicators of an intentionally set fire. Just as Patrick Barnes changed his opinions on the causes of baby death after the Louise Woodward case, John Lentini, one of the leading experts in fire investigation, changed his mind about fire science in 1991. In that year, there was a massive wildfire in Oakland, California, that destroyed more than three thousand homes and created a lab for fire experts to study the causes of fire. It was clear the homes were destroyed by the fire spreading from house to house and were not intentionally started. However, when Lentini examined the homes, he found evidence that he'd always believed were signs of arson.

For example, webs of window cracks after a fire, known as crazed glass, had always been the hallmark of an arsonist using an accelerant (like gasoline) to create very hot fires. Yet, one out of four destroyed homes had signs of crazed glass. After conducting further experiments, forensic scientists discovered that "crazing" resulted from rapid cooling, not rapid heating.[16] Pipes and metal bedsprings melted throughout the homes; this was also typically associated with arson and the use of accelerants.[17]

When Lentini examined the Oakland fire, he'd come from a recent investigation in Florida where a man was facing the death penalty for setting a fire that killed his pregnant wife, his sister, and his four nieces and nephews. The man claimed his son was playing with a lighter and accidentally started the fire on the couch in the living room. Because it appeared there were multiple points of ignition in the home, as is typical in arson cases, the initial conclusion by investigators was that the fire must have been intentionally set with the arsonist pouring accelerants and starting the fire throughout the house.[18]

Fortuitously, a similar house was being torn down in the Oakland area neighborhood, so Lentini decided to do an experiment. He staged the house in the same way as the one that was burned down and placed cameras throughout the house. He then started a fire on the couch, just as the defendant claimed it had occurred. Lentini expected it would show the man was lying, but it proved the opposite.

There were V-shaped burn patterns throughout the house, the kind that had been used in the past to determine where a fire started. The phenomenon known as "flashover," where the contents of a room can suddenly and simultaneously ignite, gave the appearance of multiple points of ignition in the home when, in fact, there was only one. The combination of almost sending a man to death row based on mistaken conclusions and what he learned from the Oakland fire made Lentini question all that he had ever learned.[19]

JOANN PARKS

JoAnn Parks was a longtime client of the California Innocence Project with whom I spent many Christmas prison holiday visits as we fought for her freedom. In 1989, she woke up to a nightmare when she realized that the tiny, converted garage where she lived with her husband and three children was on fire. Her husband wasn't home, but her children were. JoAnn panicked and ran out of the house to get help from the neighbors. One neighbor tried to get into the house and rescue the children. He was unsuccessful, as were the responding police and firemen. All three children died.

Initially, it was believed the fire was accidental, but when the police discovered JoAnn had experienced a prior nonfatal fire that was also found to be accidental, they became suspicious. A former friend who was angry with JoAnn (and claimed she had stolen a traveler's check from her house) told the police JoAnn said she could have become rich if her daughter had died in the previous fire. That statement sparked a homicide investigation, even though it morphed into so many inconsistent statements that the ex-friend didn't even testify at JoAnn's trial.

When fire investigators inspected JoAnn's home, they knew about the prior potential evidence of arson. One of the investigators had actually inspected JoAnn's prior fire and believed he'd been duped out of declaring it an arson. The second time he was determined not to make the same mistake.

This is a perfect example of how many criminal forensic experts don't follow the scientific method. Good science eliminates as much bias as possible from the process. Whether it's a police officer who knows who the suspect is in a lineup, a radiologist who hears about potential abuse before looking at a child's X-ray, or a fire investigator who knows about a resident's previous fire, that's bad science. Fire investigators shouldn't have any information about suspects or suspicions before analyzing a scene. Any extraneous information can bias their analysis. That bias infects the conclusions they reach and the testimony they give in court. Jurors often don't understand these biases and rely on the expert's testimony as being scientifically precise, giving it far more weight than lay witness testimony.

Of course, this is exacerbated if the defense attorney doesn't understand the science, protocols, or bias well enough to do a competent cross-examination and reveal these problems to the jury.

One example of how powerful bias can be created by information given to analysts is a study where forty-one experienced forensic anthropologists were broken into three groups and asked to assess a medieval skeleton. Although the skeleton had some ambiguous features that made it difficult to determine the sex, it had been determined to most likely be a female. One group was told the skeleton was female, and 100 percent of the participants agreed. The second group was told that the skeleton was male, and 72 percent agreed. The third group wasn't given information about the sex of the skeleton, and 31 percent concluded it was male. This study illustrates how information biases conclusions, even by experienced experts.[20]

I once heard a stunning presentation by Bill Thompson, a professor at UC Irvine, about bias in so-called scientific testing. He showed slide after slide of police officers who had given information to crime lab technicians that led to inaccurate results. One of the slides was a note from a technician to a detective saying, "I've done the testing several times, but it keeps coming out wrong. It keeps not matching your suspect." That is not science.

Based on the same faulty arson science disproved by the Oakland fires, the biased investigators in JoAnn's case determined there were multiple points of ignition in the Parkses' house. Investigators ignored that the type of old television JoAnn owned was prone to spontaneously igniting. They ignored evidence that the path of the fire was consistent with an accidental fire. They ignored, and specifically rejected, that flashover had occurred in the fire. And when their own engineering expert disproved their initial theory that the main origin point of the fire was a sabotaged extension cord, they simply asserted that JoAnn must have started the fire in the same spot with a match.

There were also unsupported statements by the prosecution experts at trial (based on outdated science) definitively stating that there was no explanation other than JoAnn intentionally started the fire. Again, who were the jurors to question government experts? Even though JoAnn had no motive to set her own house on fire, the jury convicted her. JoAnn had no insurance policies in place. She lost her three children. She lost all her material belongings. And she was sentenced to prison for the rest of her life.

Every staff attorney in my office has an expertise beyond being a great lawyer. Alissa Bjerkhoel is our resident DNA expert. Mike Semanchik's expertise is in tool marks and bullets. Audrey McGinn's expertise is in evaluating rape and molestation cases. Alex Simpson is our policy and legislation expert. Raquel Cohen is our fire expert.

Raquel grew up in the cruel city of Las Vegas, spending most of her time in the cruel sport of gymnastics. She can be as tough and blunt as a casino dealer clearing the card table of an unlucky player's life savings. She also has a huge heart, and when she digs into a case, she's relentless.

Raquel took on the JoAnn Parks case when she had young children herself. Reading through the material, and putting the case together, was psychologically difficult. She imagined her own family perishing in such a fire.

Pulitzer Prize-winning author Ed Humes took an interest in the case. Ed has an impressive resume of nonfiction books that he's written on topics as diverse as transportation, trash, and the criminal legal system. Ed followed the investigation and litigation of JoAnn's case, which resulted in the book *Burned*. As part of his research, he spent time at Raquel's house and witnessed her explaining her work to her young children. "Prison is like a place for adults who have to go to time out," she said. "Now for some of them, it's like if you were put in time out but you didn't do anything wrong and you don't think it's fair. So, my job is to get those people out of time-out."[21]

Raquel spent years trying to free JoAnn from "time-out." When we were finally granted a hearing, both Raquel and Alex put on evidence from expert witnesses that proved the fire was accidental while discrediting all the evidence suggesting JoAnn set the fire. The prosecution stuck to their guns. They circled the wagons around the original testimony and the original experts who put JoAnn in prison. We were feeling good after the hearing. We'd put on a great case based on everything we've learned in the decades since JoAnn went to prison.

However, under the rules of post-conviction hearings that plague our lives as innocence lawyers, the judge found our evidence "not new enough" and not sufficiently contradictory to prove that the evidence the jury heard at JoAnn's trial should be deemed false. The judge treated the case as a "battle of the experts," with different experts saying different things. Not enough to free JoAnn.

After the judge's ruling, JoAnn spent three more years in prison until she was finally freed. In 2021, the clemency petition we'd carried from San Diego to Sacramento on the Innocence March was granted by Governor Newsom in the form of a sentence reduction that made her eligible for parole. The parole board granted her release, and she was free after spending twenty-nine years of her life behind bars for a horrific crime she did not commit.

When prosecutors and defense attorneys put experts on the stand in complex cases like JoAnn's, whoever has the "better" witnesses usually wins the case. "Better" doesn't necessarily mean the witness with the best science; it means the expert the jury is more likely to believe. Bias plays a tremendous role in this process based on age, gender, education, experience, manner, tone, and many other factors that can make one expert more believable—or more in sync—with a particular juror. Maybe the expert witness reminds the juror of their father or sixth-grade science teacher. Maybe they hated their father or sixth-grade science teacher.

Often, jurors are already biased against the defendant. Therefore, the expert who confirms that bias is the one who will be believed. In JoAnn's case, I'm sure there were jurors who believed she should have rescued her children before she ran to the neighbor's house. It's hard to truly put oneself in the situation JoAnn was in and understand her fear and panic. There were probably jurors who were convinced she was guilty when they heard about the prior fire. They may have never lived under such poor conditions that could lead to two separate electrical fires.

Another factor in JoAnn's conviction may have been the fact that her lawyer deferred giving an opening statement until the prosecution had put on its entire case. It's a common belief among trial lawyers that most jurors have already made up their minds by the time opening statements end and before any testimony is given.[22] In JoAnn's case, the jurors may have been too far down the road of guilt in their minds to turn back by the time they heard JoAnn's side of the story.

HAIR SCIENCE IS JUNK SCIENCE

Microscopic hair analysis is an example of a scientific procedure that is so deeply flawed there is a question as to whether it is even forensic science. It entails a forensic examiner looking at hair from a crime scene under a microscope and comparing it to hair from a suspect. Bias immediately plays a role in this process, as the examiner is looking for a "match" between the two samples, and obviously there is a reason to believe there will be a match (otherwise, why would the analyst be looking at the hair?). Without a lineup of hair being compared, the process is as inherently suggestive as a one-person lineup being used for an identification.

Regardless, microscopic hair analysis was first used in a 1934 murder trial, and by the 1970s, it became a standard practice in FBI labs. The analysts use descriptions of the hair—such as color and texture—in making their identifications. These descriptions are vague and nonquantifiable. They are based on the subjective view of the examiner. One examiner might see brownish hair. Another might see brownish/blonde hair. When the hairs are declared to be a "match," there is no statistical support for what this means, because there's no way to know the percentage of the population that also "matches" the same description.

By 2015, the science of microscopic hair analysis had been discredited. The FBI conducted a Microscopic Hair Comparison Analysis Review by analyzing trial transcripts. They concluded that at least 90 percent of the reviewed transcripts contained erroneous statements. Twenty-six of twenty-eight FBI hair analysts provided either erroneous statements or erroneous reports.[23] Thirty-three of the thirty-five death penalty cases in the study included false statements. The "science" of microscopic hair analysis was so faulty that, in at least one case, the examiner matched the DNA of human hair to what was later proven to be dog hair.[24]

SHELL CASINGS AND BULLETS

Spent shell casing analysis was a technique used to match markings on shell casings found at the 1929 Valentine's Day Massacre scene with those found at Al Capone's home.[25] The process involves firing ammunition from a suspect's gun and then examining the spent shell casing under a microscope to see if the markings match the markings from those collected at a crime scene. While this evidence can appear to jurors to be compelling and damning, there are two reasons it shouldn't be given much weight.

First, the ability to make microscopic comparisons of the marks on the casings and match them depends on the analyst's technical expertise and the quality of the machines used. Sometimes, it's a fully biased examiner using a primitive method like holding the casings up to a light bulb as opposed to a well-qualified examiner using blind testing and high-tech machinery.

Second, there's no statistical foundation to say how many other guns may leave the same markings. In the past, gunmetal was hammered out by hand, leaving an inconsistent texture inside the barrel of the gun. Theoretically, one could find unique markings on spent shell casings under such circumstances. Now, however, gunmetal is made by machines with much more consistency. If an anomaly was present in the barrel of the gun, it might also be present for the following hundred guns produced by that machine.

Even more troubling than testimony as to casings has been testimony regarding the metal composition of bullets. Comparative bullet lead analysis also has a storied history, beginning with the assassination of President Kennedy, where it was used to determine whether there was a second shooter.[26] For decades, the FBI testified they had scientific methods to analyze whether bullets had the same chemical composition. If the chemical composition matched, the FBI claimed the bullets came from the defendant's box of ammunition, and the results of these tests sent people to prison.

Imagine claiming you didn't fire a bullet, and then an FBI analyst takes the stand and testifies that the bullet from the crime scene is an exact match to ammunition found in your house. FBI analysts made these bold assertions until 2005 when the FBI announced they would no longer conduct the tests, stating: "While the FBI Laboratory still firmly supports the scientific foundation of bullet lead analysis, given the costs of maintaining the equipment, the resources necessary to do the examination, and its relative probative value, the FBI Laboratory has decided that it will no longer conduct this exam."[27]

Although the FBI still firmly supported the scientific foundation of comparative bullet lead analysis, courts have not been as generous in their assessments. In 2006, while assessing the testimony of an FBI agent who'd conducted comparative bullet lead analysis, the Kentucky Supreme Court determined her testimony was misleading. The analyst had testified that bullets from a crime scene—where a college student celebrating his twenty-first birthday was shot and killed—were "analytically indistinguishable" to bullets found in the defendant's home.

The court's conclusion was based in part on the fact that bullets are made from giant caldrons of molten metals, and millions of bullets are made from the same batch. Bullets from within that batch can be indistinguishable and, based on the tests that the FBI was conducting, the same conclusion could be drawn about bullets from other batches. Therefore, the court found no way to apply statistical importance toward two bullets with the same metallic composition.

FINGERPRINTS

Although fingerprints have much better reliability than comparative bullet lead analysis, the idea that they are infallible was rocked in 2004. Brandon Mayfield, a lawyer in Portland, Oregon, was arrested and falsely accused of participating in the Madrid bombing that killed 193 people and injured nearly 2,000 more. An FBI analyst declared there was a 100 percent match to Mayfield, even though a later determination matched the fingerprint to Algerian national Ouhnana Daoud, who was also seen on video near the scene of the crime.

Fingerprint analysis is based on the idea that there are unique patterns on fingers that can be matched to the prints we all leave every day on surfaces and objects that we touch. Traditional fingerprinting, developed by Sir Hem Chandra Bose in India in the late nineteenth century, looks at three common finger skin patterns: loops, whorls, and arches. Modern systems are based on this concept, but they break these patterns down into subsections.

The problem with fingerprint matching is that subjective bias, and the subjective ability to make the determination of a match, varies from expert to expert. Mistakes can clearly be made, as was proven by the Brandon Mayfield case.

In fact, one study used the Brandon Mayfield case to show how cognitive bias affects fingerprint experts' conclusions in the same way it impacts forensic anthropologists trying to determine the sex of a skeleton. Five fingerprint experts believed they were comparing Brandon Mayfield's fingerprint to the fingerprints that were found on the scene of the Madrid bombing, knowing those didn't match. In fact, they were given two fingerprints that they had personally found to be matches in prior cases. Four of the five changed their opinions, saying there was no match.[28]

The Automated Fingerprint Identification System has taken some of the human element out of the fingerprint identification process. However, it still requires human beings to make the ultimate decision from a handful of potential matches pulled out of the fingerprint database.

Duke law professor and director of the Wilson Center for Science and Justice, Brandon Garrett, calls for several reforms in the use of fingerprints in his book *Autopsy of a Crime Lab*. The reforms include blind verification by a second expert. He also calls for reforms in the way experts testify about the certainty of the conclusions because "once jurors hear that the expert looked at fingerprints and found some kind of connection between them, the hundred-plus years of cultural association between fingerprints and unique individuality come into play. People do not know about all of the assumptions and subjectivity in the method."[29]

Relying on fingerprinting can lead to wrongful convictions because of false positives, but it also can lead to guilty people going free as a result of false negatives. One FBI study of fingerprint examiners revealed that 85 percent of 169 examiners made at least one false-negative error.[30]

DNA

In 2009, the National Academy of Science issued a report criticizing all the questionable forensic sciences discussed in this chapter. The report considered two questions that should be asked of each forensic science as it is considered for admission in criminal trials:

1. The extent to which a particular forensic discipline is founded on a reliable scientific methodology that gives it the capacity to accurately analyze evidence and report findings; and

2. The extent to which practitioners in a particular forensic discipline rely on human interpretation that could be tainted by error, the threat of bias, or the absence of sound operational procedures and robust performance standards.[31]

DNA is the only forensic science that passes the test of scientific accuracy supported by breathtaking statistics in its ability to exclude and include a criminal defendant in their results. In terms of excluding defendants, DNA technology allows experts to say with 100 percent accuracy that a DNA sample from a crime scene doesn't come from a particular defendant; it is simply not their DNA. In terms of including a defendant as someone who could have left the DNA on the crime scene, with good samples and strong similarities, the probability that it's not the defendant can be stated in terms of one in trillions or even quintillions (i.e., significantly more than there are humans on earth). Basically, the chances it's not the defendant are the same as the chances they have an unknown, evil identical twin running around and committing crimes.

Horace Roberts

DNA has the power to both exonerate and convict, and no case tells that story more powerfully at the California Innocence Project than the case of Horace Roberts. In 1998, Horace was charged with murdering a woman he was having an affair with. When the police questioned him, Horace lied about the affair and that was twisted into a theory that he was lying about not killing her. A watch was found near the victim's body, and after hours of police interrogation, Horace began to think the watch might have been his. It took three trials, but ultimately Horace was convicted of second-degree murder and sentenced to fifteen-years-to-life.

Mike Semanchik spent years working on the case, focusing a great deal of attention on the watch and the victim's estranged husband. Horace ultimately realized the watch wasn't his—it was just similar to a watch he had—so Mike had the watch tested for DNA. Horace was excluded from a mixture of DNA from several people on the watch, but the victim's stepson's DNA was included in the mixture. Mike then had the victim's clothing and biological material from under her fingernails tested. The original investigation missed a bloodstain on the victim's pants. Testing confirmed the blood belonged to the victim's estranged husband. A DNA profile from the material under the fingernails was entered into the national DNA databank. It matched up with the estranged husband's nephew.

Police soon arrested and charged the stepson, the victim's estranged husband, and his nephew for the murder. Horace was released after spending twenty years in prison for a crime he did not commit.

In contrast to DNA evidence, Brandon Garrett states in his book *Autopsy of a Crime Lab* that "there are no population statistics for characteristics observed on bitemarks, hair, fingerprints, or other objects like firearms or toolmarks. We have no idea how common or rare the details are that the examiners rely upon for these forensics."[32]

Furthermore, even DNA evidence is still subject to human error, and it's only as good as (1) the people who gather the biological material to be tested; (2) the people who do the testing; and (3), the people who evaluate the results.

Contamination, for example, is a serious problem with DNA results. Think about what would have happened to Uriah Courtney (discussed in chapter 4) if the officer who had initially talked to sixteen-year-old Natalie had gathered the clothes she was wearing during the sexual assault, put those clothes in the back seat of his squad car, proceeded to Uriah's house, arrested him, and put him in the same squad car. Uriah's proximity to the evidence could easily result in his DNA showing up when the clothes were tested. In conjunction with Natalie's identification, our post-conviction testing would have been seen as confirming his guilt, and Uriah would still be in prison.

DNA contamination can happen anywhere along the chain of custody of evidence—from the scene of the crime, to the lab, to the courtroom. We like to believe officers are meticulous and well-trained in evidence collection, but that's often not true. In Los Angeles, there was a case where police officers smoked and threw cigarette butts on a crime scene they were investigating. Those cigarette butts were collected, and DNA tested, at a high cost to the taxpayer, just to be embarrassingly matched up to the officers.

And then there are the officers who are not merely incompetent, but instead intentionally fabricate evidence. Those corrupted officers often justify their behavior, believing they aren't fabricating evidence to convict an innocent person, but just making sure a guilty person gets convicted. This is known as "noble cause corruption," where the ends justify the means. They believe they are "framing the guilty."

Lab Fraud

For more than a decade, Fred Zain developed the reputation as the best DNA analyst in West Virginia because he always got a result from his testing. DNA testing often fails for various reasons, including insufficient or contaminated samples. The reason Zain was always successful was because he'd simply fabricate results to comport with the investigating officer's suspicions, often not even running the tests at all.

A criminal investigation of Zain's work found an astounding amount of fraud, including fabricating scientifically implausible results in both his work at the West Virginia Crime Lab as well as later work in Texas at a medical examiner's office. Although it's difficult to assess exactly how much of his work led to wrongful convictions, due to complications in unraveling his fabricated evidence from real evidence, he may have been responsible for wrongfully convicting hundreds of people.[33]

Lab fraud, unfortunately, is not limited to Fred Zain. Crime lab scandals have occurred in Chicago, Houston, San Francisco, Oklahoma City, St. Paul, Detroit, New York, Philadelphia, and the FBI lab. In the United States alone, there have been more than 130 documented crime lab scandals.[34]

More than seven thousand test results from a New Jersey crime lab were called into question in 2015 after evidence revealed a lab technician had been fabricating results.[35] In 2022, Massachusetts settled a lawsuit for $14,000,000 with more than thirty-one thousand criminal defendants whose cases were tainted by a crime lab scandal.

The combination of jurors lacking scientific knowledge, junk science, sloppy investigations, failure to follow scientific protocols, and outright fraud has led to many wrongful convictions. This is an area where reform is desperately needed.

The only way to remedy the problem of wrongful convictions occurring because of jurors being blinded by bad science is to make sure that jurors (and judges) are truly getting the full picture of the evidence at trial and assigning the appropriate weight to the evidence. This requires full disclosure of all the evidence, as well as appropriate education in the courtroom from experts in the field. Further, there must be heightened scrutiny of scientific evidence and the procedures used in obtaining results before that evidence comes into a courtroom. Some junk sciences, such as microscopic hair analysis and bullet lead analysis, should never be admitted into evidence. Other evidence, such as fingerprinting, should be presented with a full picture of all the possibilities for mistaken matches for the judge and jury to consider.

As long as we have people involved in the scientific process of creating evidence, and people involved in the judicial process of decision-making, there will be mistakes. No matter how good the science is, human error can lead to wrongful convictions. As Albert Einstein once said, "Only two things are infinite, the universe and human stupidity, and I'm not sure about the former."

8 You Work with Children or Let Them in Your House

We receive thousands of requests for help every year at the California Innocence Project. Most of them begin with a letter from an incarcerated person, handwritten with meticulous detail, stating basically the same thing: "I am innocent." These letters begin our process of deciding which cases will receive our limited resources.

The letters are opened by volunteers. Most are law students, some are college students, some are older adults, and some are even high school students. My son, Zach, and my niece, Zerina, both interned in our office when they were teenagers. We once had a volunteer who was a retired prison warden from San Quentin.

In response to the letters, the volunteers send out our intake application: ten pages of questions focused on getting as much information about the case as possible from the potential client. They also request some basic legal documents needed to complete the review and assess which legal processes have already been exhausted.

With this information in hand, a memo is written that summarizes the case, which is then reviewed by a lawyer in our office. That lawyer decides if the case moves on to further investigation or gets closed. In making that decision, two questions are asked: (1) whether the lawyer believes the case is one where an innocent person may have been wrongfully convicted; and (2) whether the lawyer believes the case could be winnable (i.e., there is a potential to discover evidence of innocence).

One of the heartbreaking parts of our work is when the answer is "yes" to the first question, but "no" to the second. Contrary to what some prosecutors believe, we don't take on those cases. It's tragic when a case appears to be one where an innocent person has been wrongfully convicted, but there's no chance for success in reversing the conviction. There might have been terrible representation at trial, bad identification processes, coercive questioning, and all the issues discussed in this book, but without new and strong evidence of innocence, the case may be hopeless. This happens overwhelmingly in sexual assault cases.

Staff Attorney Audrey McGinn, our in-house expert on sexual assault cases, grew up in a small town in the Nebraska cornfields. She comes from generations of farmers. As a child, she was the Junior National Tractor Pull Champion, and her life consisted of friends, family, farming, and church. Audrey is a talented lawyer. She is smart and funny and loud. She's that person you'd choose to go with on a long road trip because she's endlessly entertaining and filled with great stories of farm life in Nebraska.

In our office, Audrey has the unenviable task of deciding which child molestation cases we take on and which ones get a rejection letter. Everyone in our office understands the weight of rejection letters. We are typically the last line of defense, and when we say no to people with life sentences, it is likely they will die in prison.

Screening child molestation cases is very difficult. Often, the potential client has been convicted based on testimony from their own children, or children in their family who now may be willing to recant that testimony. Any court looking at the recantations will treat them as highly suspicious and likely motivated by the relationship. Often, the potential client was an upstanding citizen in the community with a good job and no prior criminal convictions. We almost always receive support letters from friends and family. They swear the potential client would never do anything like molest a child, but we know that it is the type of crime that is often hidden from all but the victims.

In screening the cases, Audrey must consider all of this. She must imagine how she could ultimately litigate the case in court and present the evidence in a way that can overcome the immense burden of proving innocence. Most cases have no chance of success, but that doesn't mean there aren't a great deal of false child molestation cases. These cases are particularly tragic, because when anyone—innocent or guilty—goes to prison for child molestation, as with baby killers, they are treated as the lowest of the low in the prison hierarchy.

JOHN STOLL

John Stoll was one of those people. I first heard about his case from our sister project, the Northern California Innocence Project (NCIP). At the time, the project was directed by Cookie Ridolfi, whose legal career began in the '70s when she defended herself after being arrested for chaining herself to a bridge in protest of the Vietnam War. Cookie and her wife, Linda Starr, a brilliant appellate lawyer who now directs NCIP, called me and asked whether we wanted to work on John's case together. They usually handle cases in Northern California, and we handle Southern California. The case was in Bakersfield, a small city in the desert 111 miles from Los Angeles. It was on our turf, but they were enthusiastic about the case and had already begun working on it, so we decided to join forces.

One of the reasons Cookie and Linda were enthusiastic about the case was that Bakersfield was a well-known hot spot for wrongful convictions. At the time, Ed Jagels was the district attorney. He was notorious for prosecuting false child molestation cases, including an alleged ring of twenty-seven cases between 1982 and 1985, twenty-five of which were later overturned.[1]

These types of false prosecutions were not limited to Bakersfield in the 1980s. The McMartin Preschool case received worldwide attention when the McMartin family members, who worked at the preschool in Manhattan Beach, were accused of sexually abusing the children in their care. Interviewers used highly suggestive techniques when interviewing the children. The interviewers gave the children information about sexual acts that the children ultimately weaved into their own stories. The stories spiraled into bizarre tales of sodomy, bestiality, satanic rituals, witches, and orgies. The children claimed abuse occurred in underground tunnels and chambers, which excavation of the property proved did not exist. The trial lasted seven years and, at the time, was the most expensive in US history. In the end, the allegations were proven to be false, and all the defendants were freed.[2]

John Stoll's case had many of the same elements as the McMartin case. It began when John had a bitter custody battle with his ex-wife over their son. Strategically, she accused John of molesting their son, which triggered an investigation.

John was one of the fortunate people in Bakersfield who had a swimming pool. In a place where the summer temperatures often exceeded one hundred degrees, it was literally a hot commodity. John had a circle of friends who brought their children over to his house to enjoy the pool on those hot days.

Acting on the accusations from John's ex-wife, police and social workers questioned John's son and five other boys John had contact with at his house. The children were between the ages of six and eight. One child was threatened with having his parents deported if he didn't cooperate.

Investigators used highly suggestive questioning techniques. Like the McMartin Preschool case, investigators suggested sexual acts to the children, and they were ultimately parroted back. Some children detailed sexual acts that would have been physically impossible.

The children ultimately accused John, and a man who rented a guest house from John, of molestation. Two of the children accused their own mother and her boyfriend of engaging in sexual orgies with John and the children. When the children began to implicate the police and prosecutors in their stories, the questioning was cut off.

With the falsified statements in hand, John, his tenant, and his friends were all arrested and put on trial. During the proceedings, the defense attempted to introduce psychological evaluations of the defendants showing they didn't have a propensity toward child molestation. The judge wouldn't admit the evidence, and they were all convicted. The court sentenced John to forty years in prison.

Four years after the trial, John's friends' convictions were reversed on the basis that the judge improperly excluded the psychological evidence regarding propensity toward child molestation. Ironically, even though John's name appeared first on the appellate papers (and this type of evidence has since become known as "Stoll Evidence"), John wasn't released because his lawyer didn't properly object to the judge's denial of the motion to introduce the evidence at trial. John's friends' lawyers had objected to the judge's ruling, so they went home. John stayed in prison.

During the years John was incarcerated, the children grew up and began to understand the implications of their false testimony. They had almost no contact with each other, except for two who were brothers. When we talked to them, they all said the same thing: they had fabricated their stories to the police and social workers. The only child who didn't recant his original trial testimony was John's son. He was the youngest of the children at the time of the alleged incidents. He refused to talk to us.

John's habeas hearing was unlike any I've ever participated in. Judge John Kelly was grouchy and seemed to enjoy yelling at our team. The case received a great deal of media attention, and the courtroom was packed every day. One day, a man wore shorts into the courtroom, violating the judge's dress code. The man refused to leave, so the judge cleared everyone else out, and had the bailiffs drag the bare-legged screaming man down the hallway and out the front door.

Judge Kelly yelled at us, blaming us for Mr. Shorts's presence. We calmly explained we had no idea who he was, and only the well-dressed law students in the audience were with us.

Our opponent in the hearing was Assistant District Attorney Lisa Green. She sat alone at her table, while ours was crowded with Cookie, Linda, Jan, Stanley Simrin (a local Bakersfield lawyer), Jill Kent (a Northern California Innocence Project staff attorney), John Stoll, and me. I sat closest to the prosecutor, who became irritated by our crowd pushing up against her space in the courtroom. At one point in the hearing, she actually made a motion asking the judge to move me further away from her. I obliged.

Our behavior in the courtroom wasn't the only thing that bothered her. In preparing to cross-examine one of the prosecutor's expert witnesses, Linda got in touch with the expert. While working on her doctorate, the expert wrote an article asserting that children don't lie about child molestation. When Linda talked to her, the witness said she thought the court was calling her to testify, not the prosecution. Apparently, she'd spent most of her career backing away from the article and didn't want to testify for the prosecution. Linda told her that Judge Kelly wasn't calling her as a witness, and neither were we. She was coming to court as a prosecution witness.

There was nothing wrong with Linda contacting this expert or telling her this information. However, when the expert told Lisa Green she wasn't testifying for the prosecution, Lisa went to the judge and accused us of witness tampering. The next morning, he gave us an earful, and there was a suggestion that criminal charges could be brought against us. Fortunately, that didn't happen.

Surrounding John's conviction and all the alleged sex crimes in Bakersfield were allegations that high level officials in the city were involved in a sex ring with young boys. A series of articles entitled "The Lords of Bakersfield" were published by the *Bakersfield Californian* newspaper claiming four of these officials were murdered by their juvenile victims.[3] In 2021, there were still lawsuits pending in cases involving these allegations.[4]

At the time of John's hearing, the boys who had accused him of molestation were in their late twenties. Except for John's son, they consistently testified that they made false statements when they were children. It was so sad to hear how the false testimony had haunted them their entire lives. Watching them tearfully apologize to John was heartbreaking on many levels. John held no bad feelings toward them, knowing they, too, were victims of the police and prosecutors who obtained the false statements.

I had the difficult task of cross-examining John's son. He marched into the courtroom with his head held high, ready to counter what he perceived were false recantations by the other boys. The prosecutor's direct examination was very short. She merely confirmed with him that he stood by his testimony from when he was six years old. I took him through that testimony, and it soon became clear that, even though he'd spent a week in a hotel room in Bakersfield waiting to testify, no one had gone over it with him.

I asked him about several of the sexual acts he testified to at trial where he allegedly engaged in sexual acts with both boys and girls before he was six years old. Here's an example from the hearing transcript:

QUESTION: Do you remember a girl named Mandy?

ANSWER: Yes, I do?

QUESTION: And what do you remember about her?

ANSWER: I just remember that was a girl that kissed me. I just remember her name because that was the same as my little sister's.

QUESTION: So, you just remember her kissing you?

ANSWER: Yes.[5]

I then read him his trial testimony where he'd claimed that Mandy had touched his penis, that he'd had sex with her, and that both she and another girl at school had "done nasty things" to him. He denied any of that happened.

After contradicting his memory several times with his prior testimony, John's son shifted to saying he remembered very little about his childhood. As I read each sexual incident he'd reported as a child, he said he couldn't remember any of them. In other words, he had no memory of any sexual abuse. His confusion about what was real and what investigators had led him to believe was sad. The police and the social workers, through improper and suggestive questioning when he was a child, had turned his childhood and adult memories into a distorted soup of lies.

At the end of the hearing, but before the judge ruled, John thanked our team and said, "I hope this goes well, because if it doesn't, when I go back to prison, I'm dead."

John lived a lie in prison, claiming he was there on other charges. The hearing had substantial news coverage, including CNN, so he could no longer hide from his conviction. At the time, I remember being happy knowing he'd be held in isolation at the county jail until the judge ruled.

Even though Judge Kelly complained about the crowded courtroom and the media, I think he secretly enjoyed all the attention. While judges sometimes send their rulings to us in the mail, he summoned us to Bakersfield so he could read his ruling from the bench.

You could hear a pin drop in the crowded courtroom as he went through every problem he had with our case. It seemed like an hour went by, but it couldn't have been more than ten minutes. Then, he turned a corner and started talking about how troubled he was by how the boys were questioned. Finally, he said the magic words. Conviction reversed.

We all burst into tears and hugs. It had been a long and draining case. Four days later, John was released from jail after the District Attorney's

Figure 7. Fighting in court to free John Stoll after twenty years of
wrongful incarceration. Photographed by the California Innocence
Project.

Office announced it would not re-prosecute the case. It was John's sixty-
first birthday. He'd spent twenty years in prison for crimes that never happened (see fig. 7).

Ed Jagels eventually retired, and Lisa Green took the helm at the Kern
County District Attorney's Office. However, Jagels came out of retirement
in 2019 to volunteer at the District Attorney's Office and figure out ways
the office could fight against sentencing reforms that were decreasing
prison sentences.[6]

Child molestation cases, like baby death cases, spark outrage due to the
vulnerability of the victims. Simply accusing someone of child molestation, without any facts to back up the allegation, can be a powerful political tool. During the 2016 presidential election a false story known as "piz-
zagate" claimed that Hillary Clinton was molesting children in the
basement of a Washington, DC, pizza restaurant.[7]

Of course, none of this is to say that children are not molested. And, as
stated in the introductory pages of this chapter, it is difficult for my
office to sort the truth from the fiction. However, when perpetrators of
such abuse are not detected for many years, this can lead to follow-up

investigations that overzealously look for child molestation where it doesn't exist.

Neither child molestation nor overzealous investigations are unique to the United States. Jimmy Savile spent more than fifty years as a celebrity in the United Kingdom before his death in 2011. He hosted major television shows like *Top of the Pops* and was known for his charity work, particularly with charities involving children. He was knighted by both the Vatican and Buckingham Palace for his altruistic endeavors.[8] After his death, an investigation was launched into allegations of child abuse going back the entire span of his career. The result was a report documenting hundreds of allegations of abuse.[9]

It was believed that Jimmy's actions were common knowledge and tolerated due to his celebrity. As often happens in the criminal legal system, like a pendulum swinging in the opposite direction with the same force, the embarrassment that came from the Jimmy Savile case led to an aggressive sweep for potential child molesters. That sweep caught some innocent people in an overly wide net.

Operation Midland began in the United Kingdom in 2014 when a man named Carl Beech claimed, in multiple reports, that he'd been molested as a child by high-profile people who were part of a pedophile ring. He also claimed he'd seen young boys sexually assaulted and then murdered. His allegations included claims against former members of parliament, former cabinet ministers, the former director of MI5, the former home secretary, and the former prime minister.[10]

In the wake of the Jimmy Savile revelations, these accusations were taken seriously and investigated. The investigation soon went public and seriously damaged the reputations of the accused. Eighteen months later, with no proof or witnesses to validate the allegations, the investigation ended with Carl Beech himself being the only one formally charged with child molestation. He was convicted on that charge, as well as the charge of "perverting justice" for misleading authorities. He was sentenced to eighteen years in prison.[11]

Bungled investigations are common in all criminal cases, but unique to child molestation cases are the problems associated with questioning children. This is a global problem. Like John Stoll's case, in the famous French case known as "The Outreau Trial" (named after the town in France where it took place), four children were questioned about suspected abuse. The children's statements led to eighteen different people being charged with abuse, including the parents of the children. Most of the accused were later acquitted. One took his life while in prison.[12]

In Australia, a governmental report estimated that one in five child sex abuse accusations are false. Given the severe consequences imposed for sex abuse crimes, false accusations in Australia are punishable by a sentence of seven years in prison.[13]

To root out false allegations, and to preserve the truth of legitimate claims, suggestive or coercive techniques must be avoided when interviewing children. The National Institute of Child Health and Human Development (NICHD) has developed protocols that increase the reliability of information collected from children.

The protocols start with guidelines on how the interviewer should introduce themselves and develop rapport with the child. They then outline how to use open-ended questions and avoid yes/no, leading, or overly suggestive questions. Most significantly, questioning should be focused on obtaining information, not giving information that can be repeated back. And, of course, under no circumstances should the child be threatened, bribed, or forced to talk.[14]

Child molestation investigations often begin based on children exhibiting behaviors that have been linked to abuse, including bedwetting, nightmares, fighting, cursing, inappropriate sexual behavior, changes in eating habits, avoiding certain people, and clinging to others. These behaviors could also be exhibited by children who have not been abused. When children aren't properly questioned about what's going on in their lives, false memories can be created, and real memories can be lost. That can lead to innocent people like John Stoll being wrongfully accused and convicted while guilty people avoid prosecution.

Life after prison wasn't easy for John. He was a man in his sixties who'd lost all his family and friends. He had no money and nowhere to go. My incredibly generous friends, Cookie and Linda, took him in and invited him to live in the small guest house behind their house that Linda had used as an office.

Eventually, John got back on his feet and started working again. The state awarded him more than $700,000 for his time in prison, and Kern

County settled a lawsuit he filed for $5,000,000. John fell in love with a former correctional nurse, and they moved into a beautiful house near the beach on the central coast. When I asked John why he was drawn to someone who worked in prisons, he said, "She was never locked up, but she can relate to where I was for twenty years."

9 Someone Lies about You

Sorting through the truths and fictions in a criminal case is not an easy task. People lie. Sometimes it's a person trying to get out from under his or her own charges who is willing to throw someone else under the bus. Sometimes it's a police officer covering up sloppy police work or using lies in an attempt to get to the truth. Sometimes, as discussed in chapter 7, it's a corrupt and/or lazy forensic examiner fabricating results. Sometimes it's an alleged victim or witness giving false testimony.

There are a million reasons people lie in life, and the consequences are usually not severe. But in the criminal legal system, lies can lead to innocent people going to prison.

SNITCHES

In John Stoll's case, the children who testified against him gave false testimony due to the suggestive questioning. Still, there was a more nefarious type of lie in his case that has become far too common in the criminal legal system. There was a snitch who had been locked up with John. He claimed John told his cellmates about the molestations.

There were three reasons we knew the snitch was lying:

First, there is no chance John was talking to anyone in jail or prison about molestation, let alone admitting that he himself was a molester. John lied about his charges for years to stay alive.

Second, the testimony the snitch gave at trial was ridiculous. He named each child by name and then detailed the acts John had allegedly admitted to doing. I'd worked on the case for a while before I could fluidly throw the children's names around and connect each allegation to the right child. Yet somehow the snitch memorized every detail and was able to spit it back verbatim to the police.

Third, the snitch's record revealed that John's case wasn't his first rodeo. He had a list of felonies that should have put him in prison for life under California's three-strikes rule. Yet, he was out on the streets. He was clearly a career snitch who had made a lot of deals in exchange for fabricated testimony.

Our investigator, Craig Woolard, found the snitch living in a trailer park in Northern California. He agreed to talk to us if we'd meet him at a bar that showed NASCAR. We found one and had quite an enlightening conversation with him. He admitted John never said a word to him about child molestation. Instead, he'd agreed to help the police, they gave him the police reports in John's case, and he read the information into a tape recorder. I'd like to say it was shocking to hear all this, but it wasn't. I was fifteen years into my criminal defense career at the time, and I'd seen and heard too much.

The next day, the snitch showed up in court to testify against John in his habeas hearing. I couldn't wait for him to take the stand so we could have the same conversation in front of the judge that we'd had the day before. Instead, the prosecutor talked to him about our meeting, and she changed her mind about putting him on the stand.

Snitching is a big problem in the wrongful conviction world. The first documented case of a wrongful conviction involving a jailhouse snitch in the United States occurred in 1819. The snitch claimed a man named Jesse Boorn had confessed to killing his brother-in-law. As a result, Jesse and his brother, Stephen, were both convicted of the murder and sentenced to die. Jesse had his sentence reduced to life in prison, but Stephen was awaiting execution when the alleged murder victim showed up alive.[1]

Rob Warden, a legendary Chicago journalist who cofounded Northwestern's Center on Wrongful Convictions, reported in 2005 that 51 of the first 111 death row exonerations involved snitches. That number made snitch testimony the leading cause of wrongful convictions in death penalty cases.[2]

In 2011, the prosecution of Scott Dekraai, a man who shot and killed eight people in California at a hair salon in Orange County, triggered an investigation into a massive snitch scandal implicating both the Orange County Sheriff's Department and the Orange County District Attorney's Office. A veteran snitch was intentionally housed in Scott's cell to obtain information. It was soon revealed that a network of snitches existed, and the government was placing them in defendants' cells to obtain information that couldn't legally be obtained through questioning.[3]

As discussed in earlier chapters, the constitutional right to counsel begins once a person has been formally charged with a crime. At that point, the police can no longer question a suspect about the crime without their lawyer being present. Jailhouse informants are not police, so casual conversations they have with other people in the jail can be used in court to obtain convictions. However, in Orange County, the snitches were not random cellmates who casually obtained information. These snitches were planted in the cells and told by police and prosecutors to obtain specific information. That made the snitches an extension of the police and prosecution who were attempting an end-run around the constitutional right to counsel.

Beyond the constitutional reasons for suppressing jailhouse snitch testimony, this type of evidence lacks reliability and has proven time and time again that it leads to convicting the innocent. When a jailhouse informant has no information to offer, they are given tremendous incentives to invent false information. Sometimes, as in the Stoll case, a snitch can avoid a third strike and a life sentence. Sometimes there are lesser incentives, such as being moved to a better correctional facility. In San Diego, there was a snitch scandal where prosecutors allowed snitches to meet up with women for sexual encounters in the prosecutor's offices.[4]

Leslie White, a self-described jailhouse snitch, demonstrated on the CBS news show *60 Minutes* how easy it is to fabricate information. With the cameras rolling, he posed as a police officer and called different government agencies, including district attorney's offices and coroner's offices, and obtained details about cases. Once he had information about a particular case, he'd arrange to be transported to or from court with the defendant in that case, so he could later claim he obtained the information from a conversation during the trip.[5]

Snitch testimony should be completely removed from courtrooms. Our rules of evidence have an overriding principle that evidence shouldn't be admitted in court when its prejudicial effect outweighs the probative value of the evidence. Snitches have extraordinary motives to lie, and this is often not understood by jurors. When snitches lie in court, it can lead to life in prison, or even the death penalty, for a potentially innocent person. That level of prejudice is too great in the balance to allow this type of testimony.

WITNESSES

As mentioned in the prior chapter, we receive thousands of letters a year at the California Innocence Project. They all have my name on them, and I think the clients and their families imagine me reading them, but if I did, I wouldn't get anything else done.

In the early days, when I was the only full-time lawyer in the office, I read all the letters. I'll never forget the one I received from Mike Hanline. Mike claimed he was set up, and it wasn't he who killed the man that led to his life sentence. Instead, it was a lawyer in Ventura (where the murder happened). Perhaps it was my own inherent bias against believing lawyers are out there committing murders and setting people up, but I was doubtful. Then I had a conversation with a well-respected lawyer in San Diego who had worked for the accused lawyer.

"I got this crazy letter from a guy who is locked up for murder who says your former boss was the real murderer," I told him.

He nodded and said, "Yeah, I could see that."

"What? Why?" I asked.

"He was dealing drugs out of the office and up to all sorts of crazy stuff. That's why I got out of there."

We dug in and began investigating. In 1978, a biker named J. T. McGarry was murdered. Mike was convicted based on the theory that he was in a love triangle with J. T. and a young woman named Mary Bischoff. The prosecution's theory as to the motive for the killing was as old as time—jealousy.

Mary was nineteen at the time she testified against Mike. Her testimony was a confusing mess. She was clearly intoxicated, and she even fell off the stand at one point. Mary was the key to Mike's conviction, so we tracked her down to where she was currently living in the Midwest and sent two law students out to interview her.

I later learned from her that she thought our very preppy law students were both hit men sent to kill her. She'd fled back to the Midwest after J. T.'s murder and evidently lived in fear ever since.

We confirmed with her that the lawyer who Mike suspected of committing the murder had manipulated her and the entire investigation. When she was brought back to California by the police, in 1978, the lawyer met her at the airport and took her out drinking before she made her statement. The lawyer sat in on her interview with the police and stopped the questioning a couple of times when Mary started to deviate from the case against Mike they were creating. By the end of the interview, the police and the prosecution had all they needed. Mike was the killer. He went to prison.

In Mike's case, the biggest challenge we had was the usually simple task of getting access to the court records. Because the trial involved biker gangs and informants, some of the police reports and trial transcripts were sealed. Alex Simpson and Mario Conte litigated on behalf of our office in federal court just to get the records from the case unsealed. When they accomplished that, we learned about reports that would have changed the outcome in the case had the defense learned about them at trial. The reports included tips given to the police that clearly pointed to other suspects, including the lawyer Mike suspected to be the killer.

In the Supreme Court case of *Brady v. Maryland*, two men (Charles Boblit and John Brady) were tried and convicted separately of murder and sentenced to death for their participation in the same killing. Boblit gave a statement to the police where he confessed to being the shooter, yet that statement wasn't turned over to Brady's lawyer. The Supreme Court ruled that the statement would not have likely changed the guilty verdict since the murder had occurred during a robbery. Thus, both men would be guilty of felony murder regardless of who the shooter was. However, the Court also found the statement might have changed Brady's sentence; since the jury had the option of a sentence of less than death, knowing Brady wasn't the shooter would have likely influenced that decision. The Court ruled that "suppression by the prosecution of evidence favorable to an accused upon request violates due process where the evidence is material either to guilt or to punishment, irrespective of the good faith or bad faith of the prosecution."[6]

Brady was a landmark decision. It made clear that police and prosecutors could no longer hide potentially exculpatory evidence, or any evidence that could reduce a sentence, from the defense. It led to decades of litigation as to what constitutes "favorable to an accused," and more than fifty years after *Brady*, I'm still surprised by police officers' and prosecutors' subjective interpretations of evidence considering this standard. It's always seemed to me that turning over everything the prosecution and police have is the best course of action to avoid a constitutional violation.

Mike's habeas hearing was a lengthy process in federal court. After we got our hands on the withheld reports, we argued they amounted to "*Brady* evidence," and thus were sufficient grounds to reverse Mike's conviction. Federal magistrate Judge Andrew Wistrich agreed, and on October 22, 2010, he issued a fifty-page report and recommendation which began with lyrics from my lifetime musical hero Bruce Springsteen and the song, "Long Walk Home."

"That flag flying over the courthouse means certain things are set in stone: Who we are, what we'll do, and what we won't."

As soon as I read those lyrics on the first page of the decision, I knew we'd won. It had indeed been a long walk home. At that point, Mike had already spent thirty-two years in prison. Judge Wistrich agreed with us that the evidence pointing to other suspects should have been disclosed to Mike's attorney at trial, and thus there was a constitutional violation. Judge Wistrich wrote as follows:

> Considering the cumulative effect of the undisclosed evidence and the arguments it would have supported at petitioner's trial, there is a reasonable likelihood of a different outcome if the evidence had been disclosed to the defense.[7]

Wistrich was particularly critical of the prosecution:

The prosecution was so successful in violating the trial court's orders and its constitutional obligation that by the time the exculpatory evidence came to light—nearly three decades later—many of the important witnesses had died or disappeared. Permitting the prosecutor to engage in this sort of gamesmanship with impunity signals that the constitutional rules established in Brady and its progeny are merely "pretend rules" that need not be taken seriously.[8]

I remember celebrating Mike's victory back in 2010. So many people had worked so hard on the case over the years. Our students and staff—particularly our program manager, Kim Hernandez—had spent endless hours investigating the evidence, looking for the truth. I wrote the original habeas petition we'd filed nearly a decade earlier, but Alex Simpson and Mario Conte carried most of the litigation from there. It was a great team victory.

Unfortunately, our celebration was short-lived. Magistrate judges, like Judge Wistrich, are appointed to assist District Court Judges. Wistrich's "Report and Recommendation" was just that, a recommendation to District Court Judge Virginia Phillips. Even though Wistrich had spent years connecting the dots through hearings and filings, and he was the judge who heard the evidence firsthand from live witnesses in his courtroom, Judge Phillips disagreed. She found the evidence presented was not "sufficient to establish by clear and convincing evidence that no reasonable factfinder would have found the Petitioner guilty."[9]

This is the stuff that makes you pull your hair out in our weird world of litigating innocence claims. We review thousands of cases that come into our office, always looking for the ones where we believe we can develop evidence of innocence. We spend years deconstructing those cases, looking for all the mistakes and lies that may have led to an innocent person being convicted. We then construct a case for innocence, putting witnesses like Mary Bischoff on the stand who admitted to all her lies, which, combined with misconduct by the government, led to Mike's conviction. A judge hears all the evidence and agrees with us. But in the end, another judge just reads through the cold record, without hearing any firsthand evidence, and disagrees.

We were devastated by Judge Phillips's decision, but not defeated. We went back to the district attorney to see if we could get cooperation on reinvestigating the case based on all we'd learned through the federal hearing process. They knew, like we did, that Mary Bischoff had lied, and that she was the key to Mike's conviction. But that wasn't enough to convince them Mike was innocent. They wanted evidentiary proof.

Before J. T. McGarry was killed, his hands were bound with tape. That tape had been held in evidence for more than three decades, and through the miracle of DNA testing, a profile had been lifted off it. After three more years of arguing and negotiating in state court, the district attorney assigned to the case told us that he'd agree to dismiss the case if neither Mike's nor his codefendant's DNA was on the tape. The testing was done. Neither Mike's nor his codefendant's DNA was on the tape. The district attorney agreed that the combination of the hidden police reports and the new DNA testing meant that his conviction should be reversed.

Four years after Judge Wistrich had recommended Mike's release, he was finally freed. Mike had spent thirty-six years in prison for a crime he didn't commit, at that time more than anyone in the history of California. Alex Simpson and I walked him out, along with his wife Sandee, who waited all those years for him to come home (see fig. 8).

As with all our exonerees, we asked Mike what he wanted for his first meal. It is one of the great joys of our work to join our clients for that meal. Mike said he'd seen Carl's Jr. ads in prison, and their food looked great. Most of our clients want steak or lobster, but Mike just wanted a fast-food burger.

Our team of lawyers and students all joined Mike at Carl's Jr., along with his wife, Sandee. We recorded him ordering his food and declaring, "That's what meat tastes like!" after the first bite of his burger. We posted the video online and it immediately went viral, gaining millions of views from around the world. We sent the video to Carl's Jr., asking them to do something nice for Mike in exchange for all the free advertising he provided. They gave him free food for a year. Check out the YouTube video. It's called *Michael Hanline Released after 36 Years [of] Wrongful Imprisonment*.[10]

Figure 8. Mike Hanline talks to the media about his thirty-six years of wrongful incarceration. Photo credit: Heidi Brooks.

POLICE OFFICERS

Sometimes it's not the snitches who are lying in court as agents of the police—sometimes, it's the police officers themselves. According to a 2020 report by the National Registry of Exonerations, 54 percent of wrongful convictions involve some form of official misconduct. The misconduct fell into five categories: witness tampering, misconduct in obtaining false confessions, fabricating evidence, concealing exculpatory evidence, and misconduct at trial. In 35 percent of the exonerations, the misconduct involved police officers. In 13 percent of the exonerations, police officers testified falsely at trial.[11] When I worked in Chicago, police officers commonly referred to their own testimony as "testilying."

In the chapter on interrogations, I talked about how interrogation techniques can lead to false confessions. One of the techniques involves lying to suspects to get them to confess. In the 1969 case of *Frazier v. Cupp,* police officers lied to a suspect, falsely telling him that his codefendant confessed. The Supreme Court validated lying to suspects, stating,

"The fact that the police misrepresented the statements that Rawls had made is, while relevant, insufficient in our view to make this otherwise voluntary confession inadmissible."[12]

During interrogations, the lies police tell are not limited to claiming codefendants have already confessed. Police also lie about polygraph results, evidence found at crime scenes implicating suspects, surveillance videos of suspects committing crimes that don't exist, and a host of other creative lies. And, of course, there is the classic lie that suspects can get lesser charges and sentences if they cooperate with the police and tell the police what they want to hear. But, of course, those decisions are made by prosecutors, and police have no authority to back up those promises.

Marty Tankleff is a New York civil rights lawyer and an adjunct professor at Georgetown University. When he was a seventeen-year-old senior in high school, he woke up to an unimaginable nightmare. His mother had been stabbed to death in her bed, and his father had been beaten so badly he was barely alive. The police interrogated Marty for hours, telling him lie after lie, culminating with a fake phone call where the police claimed Marty's own father (who had become comatose and died) told them Marty was the attacker. Believing his father would never lie, Marty started to think maybe he'd killed his parents and suffered a blackout. He made incriminating statements that led to his conviction for the murders. Marty spent seventeen years in prison before he was exonerated after an investigation by his defense team discovered twenty witnesses who confirmed that Marty's parents' murders were orchestrated by his father's business partner.[13]

Then there are situations where the police lie about what they told a suspect during an interrogation to give more credibility to a confession. For example, in the Christopher Ochoa and Richard Danziger cases, both men were convicted of rape and murder based on Christopher's spoon-fed confession. In Austin, Texas, a Pizza Hut manager was attacked, tied up with her bra, raped, and shot in the head during a robbery. The police claimed they were extremely careful not to give any facts about the crime to Christopher when interrogating him, when, in fact, they fed him all the information. They also coerced the confession with threats of the death penalty, and, of course, also lied to him by falsely claiming that Richard had already confessed and implicated both of them.

Ultimately, the real culprit came forward and admitted to the crimes, and the Wisconsin Innocence Project was successful in using DNA testing to exonerate both Christopher and Richard after they served more than a decade in prison for crimes they did not commit.[14]

I once had a student in my criminal procedure class who was a former homicide detective. He'd retired and decided to go to law school. When I was teaching about confession law, he shared with the class his favorite technique for getting confessions, which involved using a calculator attached to a microphone that he referred to as a "Fromm Meter." He'd punch random numbers into the calculator and then run the microphone all over the suspect's body. His partner would then come into the room and say, "We've got the Fromm reading from the crime scene," and then read off a piece of paper the same number that was punched into the calculator. My former student would then dramatically show the calculator to the suspect and say, "We've got your Fromms, you can deny all you want, but we know you were on the crime scene, so you're going to get convicted and go to prison. You might as well confess."

Of course, there are no such things as "Fromms." It's a brand of dog food. My student claimed his technique never led to false confessions because, "Why would an innocent person confess just because I told them some nonsense about Fromms?"

Perhaps the Fromms fraud alone wouldn't cause a false confession, but combined with other lies, or other factors—such as a suspect's alcohol-related blackout—it could lead to a false confession. And, although less common than in the past, there are still cases where police use physical violence combined with lies to get confessions.

Then, there are situations where police officers simply fabricate crimes and lie about the facts to get a conviction. Danny Larsen was a victim of this type of police corruption when he was convicted in a California court of a "third strike" and sent to prison for life. The conviction arose out of an incident where police officers approached Danny and several other people in a parking lot, and one of them threw a knife under a car. Danny matched a description given in a 911 call of a man who had a gun, so the police focused on him. When he had no gun, they arrested him, falsely claiming they saw him throw the knife.

Miraculously, a former chief of police from North Carolina happened to be in the parking lot. He and his wife saw that it wasn't Danny who threw the knife, and they told the officers it was another man. The officers weren't interested in what the couple had to say and asked them to leave. No report was made about their observations.

Danny's case was dismissed at the preliminary hearing because there was no evidence he'd concealed the knife, a necessary element of the crime. The police officers then changed their initial statements. They claimed they witnessed Danny removing the knife from a concealed place on his waistband.

Danny's defense attorney failed to call the former chief of police, his wife, or any of the other witnesses in the parking lot. Because Danny had two prior felony convictions from a decade before, he was convicted of being an "ex-felon in possession of a dirk or dagger" under California law and sentenced to twenty-seven-years-to-life.

We litigated Danny's case for several years. Even after we got his conviction reversed, Jan Stiglitz had to fight an appeal filed by the office of then Attorney General Kamala Harris. Her office claimed that, even though the court had found Danny innocent, and the court ruled that he received ineffective assistance of counsel, Danny should still stay in prison because his claim was not filed on time. You often hear the rhetoric of people "getting off on technicalities;" this was an example of someone being kept in prison on a technicality. In the end, we won the appeals and Danny was finally released after nine years of wrongful incarceration.

Despite all these stories, and even after more than three decades as a criminal defense attorney, I still believe most police officers wake up every day and try to do their best to serve their community. However, cases like Danny's cannot be treated as extremely rare and isolated incidents.

In 1998, crimes committed by police officers in the Rampart division of the Los Angeles Police Department (LAPD) came to light. Ironically, the so-called "Community Resources Against Street Hoodlums" (CRASH) unit, created to police gang violence, had been acting as a gang themselves. The members of this police gang committed serious crimes, including illegal shootings, beatings, planting evidence, dealing drugs, bank robbery, perjury, and a host of other crimes committed to cover up their criminal behavior.

The investigation into Rampart police officers began when six pounds of cocaine was stolen from the LAPD evidence room. Investigators believed Officer Perez of the CRASH unit was involved. He was arrested, charged, and put on trial for stealing the drugs and selling them on the street through his girlfriend. The jury hung eight to four in favor of conviction.

More information implicating Officer Perez in drug transactions came to light. To avoid a retrial, he cut a deal to give information about other activities of the CRASH unit in exchange for a lighter sentence. As a result, Officer Perez confessed to crimes committed by himself, his partner, and more than seventy police officers in the unit.[15]

The scandal led to the reversal of 106 convictions, and the city paid more than $100 million in civil settlements. After the scandal broke, I was invited to a meeting of lawyers and politicians hosted by legendary criminal defense attorney Johnnie Cochran. Cochran pleaded with the group to dismantle the LAPD instead of settling on individual convictions being reversed and financial remuneration. In the end, the CRASH unit was disbanded, the chief of police was fired, and the Department of Justice oversaw reforms within the LAPD. Still, thousands of officers remained on a force that allowed a shocking culture of criminality and corruption to develop. It's hard to believe other officers weren't engaged in illegal activity and were simply not caught.

These types of scandals are not limited to Los Angeles. Dozens of exonerations have resulted from the corrupt work of Detective Reynaldo Guevara in Chicago, the detective who put Marilyn Mulero behind bars.[16] And, in 2018, the Illinois state attorney's office dismissed fifteen convictions secured by a sergeant named Ronald Watts and his team. Sergeant Watts extorted money and fabricated drug charges in the housing projects on the South Side of Chicago.[17] A year later, there was another mass exoneration of eighteen people Sergeant Watts had framed.[18] To date, the state has tossed 110 convictions connected to him.[19]

In New York City, a detective named Louis Scarcella worked the streets of Brooklyn during the 1980s and '90s. More than fifty of his cases were reviewed for alleged misconduct.[20] He was accused of, among other things, framing eight men for murders they did not commit.[21] The investigation led to several exonerations.

In January 2022, Bronx District Attorney Darcel Clark announced that more than five hundred convictions had been or would be reversed because they were all linked to a former detective who was facing perjury charges. She stated in a press conference, "We did not want to dismiss or vacate out of hand all cases he was involved in; we investigated those that hinged on his testimony and sworn statements. His compromised credibility suggests a lack of due process in the prosecution of these defendants, and we cannot stand behind these convictions."[22]

Prosecutors sought similar dismissals in Philadelphia when federal investigators found that police officers were framing defendants on drug charges. Since the first officer was arrested in 2013, more than 1,100 convictions have been vacated and dismissed.[23]

It's impossible to believe these officers were the only "bad apples," or that more officers within these police departments were not committing similar criminal acts (but perhaps with more discretion). This type of corruption is also not limited to the United States. It happens everywhere in the world. I've spent a great deal of time working in Latin America over the past thirty years, and I've witnessed shocking levels of corruption.

Mexico, for example, has one of the most corrupt police forces in the world. Police officers in Mexico earn on average about twenty thousand pesos a month, around twelve thousand dollars a year. Police officers in the United States earn, on average, more than sixty-seven thousand dollars a year. Poverty can lead to criminal behavior whether you are a police officer or anyone else. And when police officers in Mexico can't support their families on their salaries, they are easily corrupted.

Two young lawyers and filmmakers, Roberto Hernández and Layda Negrete, revealed how corruption and lies lead to wrongful convictions in Mexico with their 2008 documentary *Presunto Culpable* (Presumed Guilty). The documentary was banned in Mexico, but nonetheless went on to become the most watched documentary in Mexican history.[24] Roberto and Layda's cameras follow a man named Toño throughout the judicial process.

Toño was a twenty-six-year-old street vendor and aspiring dancer/rapper. On December 12, 2005, police officers grabbed him off a Mexico City street and shoved him into a police car. He was accused of shooting and killing a young man named Juan Reyes. Toño was convicted and sent to prison for twenty years based on an eyewitness identification by Reyes's cousin that was manifested by corrupt police officers.[25]

A retrial of the case was granted when it was discovered that Toño's first attorney had a forged license to practice law. In the retrial, Toño himself, after being coached by his legal team, engages in a process known as *careos* (*face off*), where the accused person can question witnesses face to face. Through a series of questions, Toño gets the only eyewitness to admit he never saw the shooting. He also clearly shows that the witness had been coached by the investigating officers. Nonetheless, Toño is convicted again, and his freedom is only gained once an appellate court reviews the video from the retrial created by the lawyer/filmmakers.

Another filmmaker brought out similar corruption with the Argentinian film *El Rati Horror Show,* created, written, narrated, directed, and starring Enrique Piñeyro, the most interesting person I've ever met.

Enrique showed up at my office several years ago with the idea that he wanted to start an innocence organization in Argentina. He was accompanied by Manuel Garrido, a former prosecutor who had risen in the ranks to lead anti-corruption investigations in Argentina, until he asked too many questions. Enrique was a former doctor, who then became a commercial airline pilot at LAPA Airlines, and then became famous when he blew the whistle about safety concerns two months before LAPA Airlines Flight 3142 crashed and killed sixty-five people. A movie was made about the crash and Enrique's efforts to bring attention to the safety problems that led to the crash. Enrique starred in the movie as himself, and he then went on to make several films as both an actor and director.

El Rati Horror Show follows Enrique while he investigates and dissects the case of Fernando Carrera, a young businessman who was sentenced to prison after the car he was driving crashed and caused the death of three people, including a six-year-old child, and injured six more. Enrique establishes with his investigation that Fernando wasn't responsible for the accident. It was instead caused by police officers who shot Fernando, mistaking him for a suspect they were searching for, and caused him to crash. The officers then covered up their mistake by falsely accusing Fernando of firing at them. Fernando was convicted of murder and sentenced to thirty years in prison.

Enrique's investigation and film revealed the truth of what happened. That led to a long appellate process, but finally, on October 25, 2016, the Argentina Supreme Court ruled that Fernando had been wrongfully convicted and he was declared innocent.[26]

"VICTIMS"

At the age of sixteen, Brian Banks was one of the country's best high school football players and a star at Long Beach Poly High School. It was no easy task to be a standout player at Poly; the school graduated more professional athletes than any other high school in the United States. At last count, the same school that graduated Snoop Dogg and Cameron Diaz also graduated eight National Basketball Association players, twenty Major League Baseball players, and fifty-eight National Football League players. Everyone agreed, Brian would be next in line.

In the summer of 2002, Brian attended summer school. He was getting ready for his senior year and the opportunity to showcase his talents on the football field. He was receiving recruitment letters from the best college football teams in the country, but there was only one place where he truly wanted to play. The University of Southern California (USC), a traditional football powerhouse, had been his boyhood dream, and it was becoming a reality. The USC coach, Pete Carroll, had already come to his practices and talked to Brian about joining the team.

Those dreams fell apart on July 8, 2002, when Brian ran into a female schoolmate in the hallway. They flirted with each other and then decided to go to a stairwell in a building that was off-limits to students. The area was known as "the spot," and students often went there to make out.

Brian and the girl quietly snuck by open classroom doors, where classes were going on, and went into the stairwell. They began kissing and touching each other but did not have sex. When a teacher came into the stairwell above them to talk on her cell phone, Brian got nervous about getting caught and suspended from the football team, so he told the girl he had to go and left her alone in the stairwell.

It's still unknown whether she was embarrassed and angry by Brian's departure, or if she had other reasons, but after their brief encounter, the girl told a friend Brian had raped her. The friend told a teacher, the school called the police, and Brian was arrested. He was charged with rape, and he was also charged with kidnapping for allegedly dragging her to the stairwell.

Brian spent the next year in jail awaiting trial. His mother sold her house and her car to pay for a lawyer who, on the day of trial, told him he had two options. Option number one: go to trial as a "big Black teenager" in front of an all-White jury, who would likely believe the girl, and get sentenced to forty-one-years-to-life in prison. Option number two: plead no contest to the charges and likely get a sentence of supervised probation, or, at worse, he would have to spend eighteen more months locked up.

Even though he was innocent, Brian didn't want to die in prison, so he pleaded no contest. Unfortunately, the judge had other ideas about sentencing, and even after Brian received a favorable sentencing evaluation, he was sentenced to six years in prison.

At the time Brian should have been moving into his dorm at USC and starting his life in college; instead, he was navigating the brutal and deadly politics of life in the California prison system. Like child molesters and baby killers, rapists are treated as among the lowest of the low. Like John Stoll and Alan Gimenez, Brian made up a story about a phony crime. That didn't stop him from having to prove himself when individuals wanted to fight him, but it did save him from being jumped by a gang of vigilantes and stabbed to death, as often happens with rapists in prison.

Brian tried to be productive while he was incarcerated. He finished high school. He read every book he could get his hands on. He took as many classes as he could, and he focused on what he could control. But it wasn't easy learning about the successes of players he'd played with, some of whom had gone on to have the kind of professional career that was taken away from him. It was particularly hard when he learned the girl whose lie put him in prison received a settlement of $1.5 million from the school district, claiming school officials failed to protect her from the alleged attack.

The days, weeks, months, and years went by, and Brian was finally released. High school was gone, USC was gone, and he was an adult. He registered at a junior college and started playing football on their team, but that became impossible when California passed a law requiring all convicted sex offenders on parole to wear an ankle monitor. As a result, Brian's activities were severely restricted. He couldn't attend a single game out of the county. Playing football was no longer possible.

As a convicted sex offender, it wasn't easy to find work. He had to sit by an electrical outlet twice a day for an hour to charge up the ankle monitor, a tough accommodation to get from a potential employer who would already be unlikely to hire someone with Brian's undeserved criminal record. Other aspects of life outside were tough as well. A parole officer constantly monitored him, he couldn't go near parks or schools, and he was publicly listed on every sex offender website.

One day, Brian was online looking for work when he got a Facebook friend request. Shockingly, it was from the girl, now a woman in her mid-twenties, who had falsely accused him. He messaged her and asked her why she would contact him. She replied that he "looked good," and she wanted to "let bygones be bygones."

Brian knew the only way he'd ever get beyond his criminal conviction was if she admitted she'd lied about the rape. Otherwise, he'd be a convicted sex offender the rest of his life. So, risking a parole violation for having contact with her, he set up a meeting at an investigator's office and secretly videotaped her confessing that he never kidnapped nor raped her.

Brian came to the California Innocence Project with the video. We'd already turned him down twice for representation while he was in prison because, like Marilyn Mulero, his plea agreement was extremely difficult to reverse, and there was no new evidence. Even though the alleged victim had claimed Brian ejaculated, and the rape kit done on the day of the alleged rape contained none of his DNA, this was known at the time of trial. The lack of DNA would have been compelling evidence of his innocence if the case had gone to trial, but it hadn't because Brian took a plea deal. It wasn't new evidence so we couldn't use it in the post-conviction processes.

The video was new evidence, but it posed another problem. With more paparazzi than any place in the world, California has very strict rules about recording people without their permission. The secret recording was not legal, and I was pretty sure a judge wasn't going to let the video into court. And, predictably, the alleged victim recanted her recantation once she realized the county was going to come after her for the $1.5 million payout.

Figure 9. The moment Brian Banks is finally exonerated. From left: Alissa
Bjerkhoel, Brian Banks, Justin Brooks. Photo credit: Heidi Brooks.

Another problem our office faced was our limited resources. With so
many of our clients serving life sentences or sitting on death row, we had
never represented someone who was out of custody.

Regardless, Brian's case was compelling. We knew he was innocent and
was serving a form of a life sentence as a convicted sex offender. So, we
took on the case.

Alissa Bjerkhoel led the legal effort, going through Brian's extensive
record and drafting a habeas petition. Mike Semanchik dug into the investigation. I worked on a political solution, knowing that this case would
be tough without cooperation from the district attorney's office. I was
able to get the head of the post-conviction unit to sit down with Brian
and hear his story. That led to a joint investigation, and ultimately the
magic words we dream of hearing from district attorneys: "We concede"
(see fig. 9).

On the day of Brian's exoneration, there was tremendous media attention on the case (see fig. 10). Brian did dozens of interviews and always talked about his dream of playing football in the NFL. As a result, seven head coaches of NFL teams contacted him and gave him tryouts, including Pete Carroll. The former USC coach who'd recruited him had moved on to coach at the professional level for the Seattle Seahawks. Brian had only played football through his junior year in high school and a few games at the junior college level. Although every team said he had the physical ability to play at the NFL level, his football knowledge was too limited to jump to the professional level. No team picked him up.

Brian isn't a person who gives up easily. He spent the next year training and studying to try again. He lived with my family for part of that time, and it was inspiring to see his determination. I remember working out with him at the local YMCA. He needed to collect weights from all over the gym to get a good workout, whereas most of the gym patrons, including me, were fine with a small set of light dumbbells.

All that hard work paid off. Brian signed with the Atlanta Falcons, and, on August 8, 2013, he made his debut in a game against the Cincinnati Bengals. He picked up two tackles as one of the oldest rookies in the history of the NFL. Sitting in that stadium and watching him play was one of the highlights of my career.

Brian only played with Atlanta for a short time, but it was enough for him. He needed to fulfill his dream of playing in the NFL, and he accomplished that. He went on to work in the front office of the NFL in New York City, and he now works a corporate job while also supporting other people who have been wrongfully convicted.

Fake rape allegations are not limited to the United States. Darryl Gee, a teacher in the United Kingdom, was convicted of rape based on a false allegation. He was sentenced to eight years in prison and died while incarcerated. He was exonerated four years later. A former student claimed Darryl had violently raped her when she was ten years old. This same student made almost identical false allegations against another man named John Hudson. John served twelve years in prison before his conviction was overturned.[27]

Warren Blackwell, also in the United Kingdom, was falsely accused of rape by a woman who had also made false allegations against seven other men, including her father. She kept moving and changing her name, so

Figure 10. Brian Banks addressing the media about a decade of lost dreams. Photo credit: Heidi Brooks.

various police departments didn't know they were dealing with the same woman. Warren spent more than three years in prison for a crime that never happened.[28]

A study of rape investigations in Victoria, Australia, between 2000 and 2003 reported that 2.1 percent of the claims were deemed to be false.[29] There are many other studies from around the world reporting wildly different numbers of false rape claims as high as the unlikely number of 41 percent,[30] all with different protocols in gathering data, and thus making them difficult to rely on. What is clear is that, although false reports of rape may be rare, and those that go to court and lead to a conviction may be even rarer, they do happen.

When I discuss false rape allegations, I often get pushback from people arguing that the number of actual rapes that are unreported, uninvestigated, and unprosecuted is much higher than the number of false allegations. That is accurate. In the United States, one in five women have been raped, yet rape is the most unreported of all crimes.[31] Studies have shown that as many as 80 percent of rapes go unreported in the United States.[32]

One of the reasons for the lack of reporting by victims is that rape cases are often not fully investigated and prosecuted, putting the victims through additional trauma throughout the process.[33] In England and Wales, a recent study reported that while there are an estimated 128,000 victims of rape each year, only 43,000 victims report the crime to the police, 3,000 make it to prosecution, and just 2,000 result in convictions.[34]

Clearly, changes need to be made. Decades ago, a standard defense in a rape case was to claim consent and portray a victim as promiscuous by simply bringing in the victim's prior sexual history. Rape shield laws, which keep these irrelevant factors out of rape trials, have decreased the continued victimization often associated with rape prosecutions, but reporting is still far too low. At least one study has shown that creating resources for victims, such as social service agencies where they consult with social workers, increases reporting,[35] but increasing reporting will not solve the problems associated with lack of convictions.

Recognizing that there are sometimes false rape allegations is in no way inconsistent with also recognizing that rapes are often unreported, uninvestigated, and unprosecuted. All rape allegations, like any other crime, should be taken seriously and thoroughly investigated. Where the investigation casts significant doubt on the allegation, the case should be dropped. Where the cases are strong, they should be fully prosecuted.

False rape allegations are just a small slice of cases where the false testimony of "victims" can put innocent people in prison. People in all types of criminal cases may have reasons to lie. Perhaps it's for money, revenge, or any one of the many motivations and frailties of our species. The bottom line is this: sometimes people lie, and sometimes it leads to innocent people going to prison.

PROSECUTORS

In the competitive world of our adversarial court system, lawyers can sometimes create the illusion that weak evidence is actually stronger than it first appears. This happens on both sides of the courtroom. On the defense side, for example, coaching of an alibi witness might make an alibi stronger than it is. That could lead to a guilty person going free. On the prosecution side, the coaching of witnesses can lead to wrongful convictions.

Mark Godsey describes the problem of "synthesized testimony" in his book *Blind Injustice:*

> Synthesized testimony occurs when police or prosecutors take witnesses who initially provided details helpful to the suspect and, convinced because of tunnel vision that the witness *must* be wrong, ask pointed questions of the witness suggesting that his or her memory is off. Some witnesses take the cue and begin to question their memory. Sometimes they will change their statements to correspond with what is clear the police believe *must* have happened.[36]

As a prosecutor, Professor Godsey goes on to say that he was "taught by mentors not to write down parts of a witness statement" that he believed were inaccurate. This was rationalized because a "guilty criminal shouldn't get off because of some careless witness who opened his mouth and blurted something out before thinking it through."[37]

Then, there are the cases where prosecutors just blatantly fabricate evidence. These cases are rare, but even more uncommon is a resulting punishment for the unethical prosecutors who engage in this behavior. Texas prosecutor Ken Anderson fabricated evidence that led to the wrongful conviction and twenty-five-year incarceration of exoneree Michael Morton. Anderson has the distinction of being the only prosecutor in US history to be sent to jail for fabricating evidence that resulted in a wrongful conviction. Anderson's sentence was ten days, but he was released after five due to good behavior.[38]

As far as suing prosecutors when they cause wrongful convictions, that's something that doesn't happen in the US legal system. Prosecutors, like judges, have absolute immunity against being sued, except in the rarest of cases where they are treated as investigators.

In the 1983 film *The Big Chill,* Jeff Goldblum's character says, "I don't know anyone who can get through the day without two or three juicy rationalizations." Unfortunately, there's a great deal of truth in this. When prosecutors are confident they are the heroes, and they're confident they know who the villains are, dishonest behavior can be rationalized in the pursuit of "justice" and filed away as the ends justifying the means.

Although it's unlikely that lying will ever be eliminated from the criminal legal system, some measures can be taken to reduce the impact of lies. For example, as discussed, snitch testimony should be eliminated from trials via the rules against weak and prejudicial evidence. The incentive to lie is simply too great to allow this type of testimony. In terms of other witnesses' lies, as with many of the causes of wrongful conviction, the ability and resources to investigate is the key to arming attorneys in the system with the information needed to challenge the lies. For example, had the attorney in the Brian Banks case done a more thorough investigation, she would have had the information to challenge the alleged victim's statements as to what occurred that day. In terms of police and prosecutorial lies, better training and supervision and more transparency is needed. And when police and prosecutors are caught in lies, severe penalties should follow.

10 You Are Poor and/or a Person of Color

I was born in the Bronx in 1965. I was one of seven children: six boys and one girl. My parents were immigrants—my father from Australia and my mother from England. My father was a failed professional tennis player who had a new get-rich-quick scheme every week, and my mother was a schoolteacher. As each business rose and fell, my family moved. I can't ever remember going to the same school two years in a row. Third grade was in suburban Ossining, New York. Fourth grade was in a rural school in the Catskill mountains. Fifth grade was in suburban Philadelphia.

I don't remember seeing real poverty until my family moved to Puerto Rico in 1979. I was thirteen years old and, even though my parents had been unemployed off and on throughout my childhood, I'd never experienced true poverty. There were times when we had to move out in the middle of the night, use food stamps, eat government-funded school breakfasts, and other hallmarks of a poor family, but I was never hungry, and there was always a roof over our heads.

My first night in Puerto Rico, my brother Stephen and I slept on the rooftop of the Catholic school where my parents had secured jobs as English teachers. We fell asleep under a beautiful, star-filled tropical sky, only to be awoken in the middle of the night by pouring rain.

The next day we went exploring around the island on the public buses. We didn't speak a word of Spanish between us, but we found our way. I remember seeing the stunning blue of the Caribbean for the first time, palm trees with real coconuts, and houses brightly painted in colors I'd never seen before. I also remember seeing people living in makeshift aluminum structures, sleeping on the city sidewalks, and begging at the bus stops.

In New York City and Philadelphia, I'd seen homeless people and rundown buildings, but for some reason, it hadn't registered for me the way it did in Puerto Rico. Maybe it was the contrast between so much beauty and so much pain. Maybe because, as a teenager, I was starting to make sense of the world. Maybe it was because I was observing a new culture that made me notice things I hadn't noticed on my own. I still don't know exactly why.

In my first year in Puerto Rico, I attended an "American" school filled with rich kids, whose parents had great jobs at US companies with branches on the island. I worked as a janitor after school to pay the tuition, while the other kids played sports and went to country clubs. I felt like an outsider. I hadn't hung out with kids like that on the states, and it was no easier in Puerto Rico.

In my second year on the island, my parents sent me to a Puerto Rican school. As the only *gringo*, and with my limited Spanish, my outsider status was now official. It was incredibly frustrating not understanding conversations going on around me and struggling to fit in. So, every weekend, I would take buses to the tourist sections of the island where everyone spoke English. As an American teenager, hotel employees would just assume I was a tourist on vacation with my family. I'd hang out by the pools, go swimming, eat free food put out for the guests, and enjoy a nice resort day before taking a bus back inland.

My cover was blown at my favorite hotel when I brought a Puerto Rican friend from school. As soon as we sat by the pool, a security guard came over and asked to see his room key. When he didn't have one, he was asked to leave. The guard ignored me, even though we'd come in together.

I followed behind my friend, complaining that he blew it. We were teenagers, and I perceived it as just another negative interaction with an authority figure. But as I look back at that moment from more than forty years ago, I realize it was more than that. My skin color came with privileges my friend didn't have.

Anyone who believes the criminal legal system is not racist must also believe that society is not racist, because the criminal legal system is made up of the same people who make up society as a whole. And anyone who believes that poverty doesn't impact the ability to navigate the criminal legal system has simply never experienced the criminal legal system.

RACE

Some commentators declared the election of Barack Obama in 2008 as an indication we had entered a "Post-Racial America."[1] While the election of the first Black US president was a historic event, the 43 percent of White voters who voted for Obama did not prove that racism was over.[2] Racist individuals were not converted overnight.

Fourteen years after Obama's election, Lafayette City Court Judge Michelle Odinet proved this point when she was caught on video freely (and gleefully) referring to a Black suspect using the N-word and comparing him to a roach.[3] Of course, Judge Odinet is not the only racist in our society, nor in our criminal legal system. Most racists are not in high profile positions or caught on video making racist statements. Most racism is below the surface and difficult to identify and navigate. It is often more implicit than explicit, although explicit racial bias has dominated our criminal legal system since colonial times.

In 1705, the first slave code was adopted in Virginia. Though slavery was widely practiced by then, there were no laws that conferred a legal right to own people and treat people as chattel. Slave codes changed that. They took away the rights and freedoms of Blacks, identified them as commerce, restricted their conduct and movement, and conveyed the power to punish and even kill them. Slave codes had the net effect of legitimizing enslavement. More perniciously, they seeded a national consciousness defining Blacks as lesser humans for centuries to come.[4]

The 1865 adoption of the Thirteenth Amendment brought with it the end of the Civil War and, in theory, slave codes. The Thirteenth Amendment abolished all slavery and involuntary servitude, except "as a punishment for a crime." Former slave states exploited the Thirteenth Amendment exception to return Blacks to forced servitude. One way they did so was by passing so-called "Pig Laws." These laws (named after the provisions against stealing pigs) were enacted throughout the South to keep Blacks working on plantations under slave-like conditions. They mandated severe punishments for those who didn't perform under unfair labor contracts and criminalized unemployment.[5]

Explicit bias continued in so-called "Black Codes." These codes criminalized Black unemployment, loitering, tax nonpayment, and general disobedience. Black people incarcerated for these crimes were then leased out for farm labor and public work projects.[6]

"Jim Crow" laws continued the nation's trend of explicit bias through the early 1900s. Named after a blackface minstrel character played by a White actor in the 1830s, the laws mandated segregation and created other race-based crimes. Several states criminalized marriage between Blacks and Whites.[7] Virginia made it a felony to falsely register your race on your birth certificate.[8] North Carolina made it a crime for "white and colored schools" to exchange books.[9]

In 1896, the Supreme Court upheld these policies in a vote of seven to one. The Court created the "separate but equal" doctrine in the case of *Plessy v. Ferguson,* where a man in Louisiana who was "seven-eighths Caucasian and one-eighth African blood" was arrested and criminally charged with sitting in the "white section" of a train. The Court rejected the argument that the Thirteenth Amendment and the Fourteenth Amendment's Equal Protection Clause banned such segregation, stating: "A statute which implies merely a legal distinction between the white and colored races—a distinction which is founded in the color of the two races, and which must always exist so long as white men are distinguished from the other race by color—has no tendency to destroy the legal equality of the two races, or re-establish a state of involuntary servitude."[10]

The separate but equal doctrine continued to guide lawmaking in the United States until the 1954 case of *Brown v. Board of Education of Topeka* when the Supreme Court overruled *Plessy,* finding that: "We conclude that, in the field of public education, the doctrine of 'separate but equal' has no place. Separate educational facilities are inherently unequal."[11]

Brown was successfully argued by Thurgood Marshall, who went on to become the first Black justice of the Supreme Court. The case set the stage for decades of dismantling blatant, explicit discrimination in our laws. However, just as the abolition of slavery created pushback in the form of laws to control Black people (and the birth of White supremacist terrorist groups like the Ku Klux Klan), there was pushback against *Brown* too. Policies and laws that appeared to be race-neutral, when put into practice were not.

The evolution of these policies and laws can clearly be seen in the presidential campaigns of the last fifty years. Presidential candidates are the only politicians who must run truly national campaigns to get into and stay in office. Therefore, their platforms and promises both shape and are shaped by the views of most of the country.

In an interview with *Harper's Magazine* in 1994, John Ehrlichman, former advisor to President Richard Nixon and coconspirator in the Watergate scandal, admitted that the War on Drugs—which led to an explosion in our prison population—had more to do with repression than drugs.

> The Nixon campaign in 1968, and then the Nixon White House after that, had two enemies: the antiwar left and black people. Do you understand what I'm saying? We knew we couldn't make it illegal to be either against the war or blacks, but by getting the public to associate the hippies with marijuana and blacks with heroin and then criminalizing both heavily, we could disrupt those communities. We could arrest their leaders, raid their homes, break up their meetings, and vilify them night after night on the evening news. Did we know we were lying about the drugs? Of course, we did.[12]

President Ronald Reagan ramped up the War on Drugs. His wife, Nancy, became famous for her "Just Say No" campaign. Tremendous resources were poured into law enforcement agencies regulating drugs, and prison populations skyrocketed.

To truly understand the colossal shift in the criminal legal system brought on by the war on drugs, one need only look at the Anti-Drug Reform Act of 1986. Before this legislation, no federal law prescribed more than a one-year sentence for possession of any amount of any type of drug.[13]

That bears repeating in ALL CAPS with an exclamation mark: THE MAXIMUM FEDERAL PENALTY FOR POSSESSION OF ANY DRUGS WAS ONE YEAR!

Both state and federal sentencing guidelines with mandatory minimums began putting low-level drug offenders away for decades. Yet, even while federal judges were quitting due to their moral objections to the high sentences, the Supreme Court gave its stamp of approval by rejecting Eighth Amendment challenges that argued the sentences amounted to cruel and unusual punishment. The Supreme Court even found life sentences for the sale of drugs to be constitutional.[14]

There has since been legislation to adjust some of the harshest sentences, but even as recently as June of 2021, the Supreme Court upheld a fifteen-year sentence for a man who had possession of 3.9 grams of crack cocaine, or less than the weight of four paper clips.[15]

When George H. W. Bush's campaign for president against Mike Dukakis was floundering, he used criminal legal policy to right the ship. Willie Horton, a Black man in Massachusetts, had committed violent crimes while on release from prison on a furlough program. Since Mike Dukakis was the governor of Massachusetts, and thus the executive in charge of the state criminal legal system, Bush used the Willie Horton case to argue Dukakis was "soft on crime." Bush came from behind to win the White House, and both Republicans and Democrats learned that appearing soft on crime was no way to win elections.[16]

Bill Clinton heard this message loud and clear, and he brought Southern Democrats to the table with his tough-on-crime policies. In one of his last acts as governor of Arkansas, Clinton oversaw the execution of a man so mentally disabled he requested to save the pie from his last meal until after the execution. Clinton's 1994 crime bill increased federal prison sentences, granted funding to states to build more prisons, and escalated the war on drugs. And although novelist Toni Morrison referred to Clinton as "the first black President," he tapped into White Americans' fear of Black people in the 1990s.

Money from policing and corrections continued to influence the policies through the George W. Bush administration into the Obama administration, and prison populations continued to grow. President Barack Obama attempted to remedy this problem by passing the Fair Sentencing

Act, reducing the sentence disparity between crack and powder cocaine. This was a significant reform because crack cocaine, a cheap substitute for powder cocaine, was more commonly used in poor communities of color, leading to grossly disproportionate sentences than those received by more affluent White people caught with powder cocaine. Five grams of crack cocaine carried a minimum federal sentence of five years, whereas five hundred grams of powder cocaine received the same five-year sentence.[17] Obama also granted 1,715 clemencies; this was more than the prior twelve presidents combined.[18] But there were no far-reaching federal policies created to undo decades of devastation wrought by the US criminal legal policies that created the largest prison population in the world and the highest incarceration rate in the world.

The United States prison statistics are particularly staggering when you consider the United States' population is 328 million and China's population is 1.4 billion. China has a billion more people than us, but we lock up more of our citizens than they do. The United States has 5 percent of the world's population, yet we have 25 percent of the world's prison population.[19] In 1972, there were two hundred thousand people incarcerated in the United States. By 2017, there were 2.2 million.[20]

These numbers are also troubling when you consider the alleged correlation between economics and crime. The theory goes that poor countries have high crime rates because people commit crimes when they don't have legal options to make a living wage. The United States is arguably the richest country in the world based on GDP, but it also has a tremendous gap between rich and poor.[21]

Over the past several decades, the statistics for Black incarceration skyrocketed. Under President George W. Bush, the incarceration rate for Black males in the United States was more than five times the rate in apartheid South Africa.[22] Today, more than 60 percent of the prison population in the United States is made up of people of color. With one out of every twelve Black males in prison or jail on any given day, that rate is six times the rate for White males.[23] Based on current rates, the chances of a Black male being incarcerated at some point in his life is one in three.[24]

The tremendous incarceration rate for Black men, combined with the legal restrictions placed upon them after release, created what Professor

Michelle Alexander described as a new caste system in her 2010 book, *The New Jim Crow*.

> What has changed since the collapse of Jim Crow has less to do with the basic structure of our society than with the language we use to justify it. In the era of colorblindness, it is no longer socially permissible to use race, explicitly, as a justification for discrimination, exclusion, and social contempt. So, we don't. Rather than rely on race, we use our criminal justice system to label people of color "criminals" and then engage in all the practices we supposedly left behind.[25]

Although the United States still has the highest incarceration rate and total number of prisoners globally, a crashing economy led to a decrease in prison populations in 2009. The global recession left states unable to continue to fund policing and corrections at the prior levels. As a result, states had to make up huge budget shortfalls. Even against powerful lobbying by the police and correctional industry, cuts had to be made, and prison populations had to be reduced.

The global recession shifted the rhetoric from crime—particularly the fear of Black crime—to immigrants crossing the border to "take jobs away." Consider, for example, the United States Department of Justice Civil Rights Division investigation into the immigration practices of the Maricopa County Sheriff's Office (MCSO). Maricopa County sits on the US/Mexico border and is home to one of the largest Latino populations in the United States. County residents complained that, under the former leadership of disgraced sheriff Joseph Arpaio, MCSO used discriminatory policing practices to harass and disenfranchise its Latino residents.

Following a two-year investigation, the Department of Justice found that MCSO engaged in egregious racial profiling of Latinos through unlawful stops, detentions, and arrests.[26] They also found that MCSO jail employees referred to Latinos as "wetbacks," "Mexican bitches," and "stupid Mexicans." Supervisors widely distributed an email that included a photograph of a Chihuahua dog dressed in swimming gear with the caption "A Rare Photo of a Mexican Navy Seal."[27]

In the 2016 presidential campaign, immigration was at the center of many debates. Both the Democrats and the Republicans called for bringing jobs back to the United States from Latin America. Donald Trump, the man who took out a full-page ad in the *New York Times* calling for the execution of the Central Park Five in 1989,[28] young men who were later exonerated and renamed the Exonerated Five, referred to Mexicans as rapists and murderers and called for a wall to be built on the two-thousand-mile Mexican border with the United States.[29]

As nightly news shows flashed images of detention facilities filled with families living in horrendous conditions, many believed oppressive immigration policies began with Trump. However, his hateful rhetoric simply brought on more scrutiny of practices that had been going on for a long time. Quietly, with the reduction of prison needs after the downturn of prison populations in 2009, the corrections industry had shifted to building immigration detention facilities.

Latinos have suffered a long history of discrimination in the United States. And, like the discrimination against Native people on land they once exclusively occupied, discrimination against Latinos has continued to occur on land they once occupied in the Spanish colonies that preexisted the Anglo-American communities.

In 1848, at the end of the Mexican American War, Mexico gave up more than half its land to the United States. That included land in what is now in the states of Arizona, California, New Mexico, Texas, Colorado, Nevada, and Utah. Just as Black labor was used in the South after abolishing slavery, Mexican labor was used to develop the West. Discrimination flourished. Mexicans were banned from entering certain businesses and segregated into poor housing. During the gold rush, violence against Mexicans increased to stop them from benefitting from mining. The Anglo-American population used mobs and violent policing tactics to dominate both the Native and Mexican American populations. Thousands were killed in conflicts, and between 1848 and 1926, at least 597 Mexican Americans were lynched, including a fourteen-year-old boy.[30] An armed conflict with the Dakota Tribe led to thirty-eight simultaneous hangings, the largest mass execution in US history.[31]

The Great Depression of the 1920s heightened violence and discrimination against Latinos. Jobs were in short supply, and even though Mexican Americans were seeking jobs on land that was once Mexico, they were seen as the foreigners by the Anglo-American population. When Donald Trump spoke about Mexicans in his run for president, he said,

"They're taking our manufacturing jobs. They're taking our money. They're killing us."[32] That rhetoric was nothing new. It was at least one hundred years old.

And just as with Black Americans, legalized discrimination against Latinos is part of our history. Separate schools, for example, with horrendous and inadequate conditions, were mandated for Latino children until *Brown v. Board of Education of Topeka.*

This history is important in order to understand how race plays a large role in wrongful convictions. Race can be removed from the text of laws, but the implicit bias rooted in our society is much more difficult to identify and eliminate.

Implicit bias is unconscious bias. It is the bias that every one of us carries with us based on our life experiences. It infects all human-made processes, including the creation and enforcement of laws.

Lawmakers carry unconscious biases even as they do their best to propose and pass legislation they believe will help their communities. Their "good ideas" are based on their own biases and fears stemming from their own life experiences. Judges and jurors bring their biases into the courtroom, where witnesses who look and sound like the people they love and trust in their lives will appear more believable. Police officers act on their biases in a myriad of ways, such as the long history of racial profiling making it more likely that people of color will be singled out for stops and arrests.[33] People of color also suffer a greater amount of police brutality.[34]

In 1991, a video captured the images of Los Angeles police officers brutally beating a Black man named Rodney King. Twenty-nine years later, another video documented the murder of George Floyd. In both situations, other officers stood by and did nothing. The killing of a young Black teenager named Trayvon Martin by a neighborhood watch member named George Zimmerman in 2012 sparked the Black Lives Matter movement, but the killing of George Floyd turned it into a global protest, with millions of young people taking to the streets and demanding change.

Demands for better hiring, training, and supervision to ferret out blatantly racist practices in police forces are certainly changes that need to be made. The more difficult challenge, however, has to do with implicit bias. That bias plays out in how police treat suspects, and it permeates the entire criminal legal system.

Consider another DOJ investigation, this time into the Ferguson Police Department (FPD) in Ferguson, Missouri. In 2014, FPD Officer Darren Wilson shot and killed Michael Brown, an unarmed Black teen. The city erupted in unrest amid claims that Brown was FPD's latest casualty in a long history of disparate policing and excessive force. The Department of Justice Civil Rights Division subsequently investigated the Department. It found overwhelming evidence that Blacks experienced "disparate impact in nearly every aspect of Ferguson's law enforcement system."[35]

A study of how the human brain reacts to watching the suffering of others revealed that the reaction is different when one observes people of their own race suffering versus someone from another race. Black and White participants in the study were shown images of Black and White people in situations where they were suffering. The participants' brains were monitored while they looked at the images, and there were different neural responses when the race of the person in the situation changed. The study concluded that people show more empathy for people within their own racial group.[36]

USC law professor Jody Armour discusses this and other studies indicating similar results in his book *N*gga Theory*. Professor Armour posits the differing levels of empathy toward people of different races changes the analysis by judges and jurors in their decision-making.[37] In other words, a White judge or juror assessing whether a White man who shot a Black man during an altercation was reasonable will likely come to different conclusions than a Black judge or juror assessing the same scenario.

A 2018 study by the National Bureau of Economic Research used virtual reality to illustrate implicit bias. The participants in the study (law students, economic students, practicing lawyers, and judges) watched trials using virtual reality headsets. The technology made it possible to make everything the same in each trial except the defendant's race, which was changed for different participants. The participants were then asked to make findings of guilt or innocence and assign sentences if they found the defendant guilty. The study concluded that people of color were more likely to get convicted and get longer sentences.[38]

Studies looking at real cases confirm this bias. For example, an ABC News nationwide analysis of eight hundred jurisdictions in the United States concluded that Black people were five times more likely to be arrested than White people.[39] In addition, a 2019 study of more than one million appellate court opinions from both state and federal courts found "strong and consistent evidence of implicit racial bias."[40]

A 2017 study by the United States Sentencing Commission reviewed and categorized sentences based on race of the people convicted for similar crimes between 2012 and 2016. The study concluded that Black males received sentences that were, on average, more than 19.1 percent longer than White males sentenced for the same crimes.[41]

I witnessed this type of discriminatory sentencing firsthand when I practiced in Washington, DC. Most of the DC prison residents were Black, and I saw judges hesitate to incarcerate White people based on the perception that it was a greater punishment to be White in the facility than Black. Of course, that further increased the racial disparity in the prison.

Brian Banks talks about witnessing a similar phenomenon decades later in the Sylmar Juvenile Hall in California:

> In those first few months, the only kids I saw who got out of Sylmar without a heavy sentence were the white kids. No joke. That's not an exaggeration. They were the only ones. The difference in sentencing was like day and night. Every white kid who came through was released.
>
> I could hardly believe it. I mean, I knew that white privilege existed. I saw it here and there with my white friends. But I never saw it like I did in the juvenile justice system. One of my best friends in the world was white. I had no animosity toward anyone because of the color of their skin. But in here? It wasn't personal. It was automatic. It was given. Blacks and Hispanics were treated one way, whites were treated another way. No one denied it. No one tried to hide it. It was just the way it was—the way it always was and still is.[42]

Even after sentencing, there is racial disparity in whether people get out of prison and/or get their records cleared based on pardons. A Pro Publica study of pardons granted by the president between 2000 and 2011 revealed that White people were four times more likely to get a pardon than people of color. Black people, in particular, had the lowest statistical chances of receiving a pardon.[43]

One example of a wrongful conviction case that was deeply impacted by race was the case of Louis Taylor and the Pioneer Hotel fire.

The Pioneer Hotel was built in 1929 in downtown Tucson, Arizona. It was an eleven-story hotel frequented by wealthy guests. Five days before Christmas in 1970, fire spread through the hotel. Guests on the higher floors were trapped. Trucks with ladders tall enough to reach them did not arrive in time and many jumped from the building to their deaths. Ultimately, twenty-eight people died in the fire and one person died months later from smoke inhalation.[44]

Although he was praised as a hero the night of the fire for helping guests escape, ultimately the police investigating the fire focused on sixteen-year-old Louis Taylor. Their focus was based on a hotel employee stating that a suspicious Black boy was at the hotel on the night of the fire. Louis was convicted by an all-White jury of twenty-eight counts of murder. He was sentenced to twenty-eight life sentences.

The Arizona Justice Project is directed by Lindsay Herf. Lindsay was a student of mine in both my criminal procedure class and the California Innocence Project. As a student, she distinguished herself with her energy, enthusiasm, and sense of humor. She was always that student you could look at and be assured the material was sinking into at least one brain. As a lawyer, she's made me prouder than she will ever know. What could be better than seeing a former student make freeing innocent people her life's work?

Before Lindsay arrived at the Arizona Justice Project, it had a long and distinguished history of taking on tough cases and winning them. Larry Hammond, a former Watergate special prosecutor, founded the project in 1998 as one of the first innocence organizations in the United States. Larry was a man of many talents, and he handled a great deal of high-profile criminal and civil cases in his career. One of his talents was that he was known as a legal expert on arson cases.

With modern advances in arson science, Larry and his team at the Arizona Justice Project began investigating the Louis Taylor case in 2002. Arson expert John Lentini was part of the investigation and he, along with four other fire science investigators, issued a report which concluded that the evidence used to convict Louis was not supported by science and there was no reason to believe the fire was intentionally set.

The Tucson Fire Department similarly re-reviewed the 1970 arson investigation and concluded that due to the lack of determining an exact point of origin and lack of elimination of all accidental fire causes, a fire cause determination was not possible.

At the 1972 trial, the prosecution pressured a juvenile to testify that, while in juvenile detention, Louis had told him that an accelerant was used. However, chemical analysis conducted by an independent lab in 1971 showed no presence of accelerant on any of the burn materials. That lab report was never disclosed to Taylor's defense team and the jury was left believing that there was evidence of an intentionally set fire.[45]

The entire prosecution—from investigation through trial—is peppered with derogatory racial references. Numerous witnesses and lawyers refer to Louis as "the black teenager," the "Negro," the "Negro youth," the "Negro boy," the "colored boy," and the "boy." Further, the state's "fire expert," Cy Holmes, admitted that before his investigation even began, he was told by police that the fire was likely an arson committed by a Black boy, and that he believed arson fit the profile of Black youths. Forty years later, during a deposition in the post-conviction litigation, Mr. Holmes further evidenced his racist views by opining, "If they [Black people] get mad at somebody, the first thing they do is use something they're comfortable with. Fire was one of them." In 2017, this investigator still stood by this testimony.[46]

Considering the lack of any evidence that the hotel fire was intentionally started, let alone that it was Louis who started the fire, why was he convicted? In 2019, Ninth Circuit Court of Appeals Judge Mary Schroeder concluded that the conviction was based on "little more than proximity and trial evidence that 'black boys' like to set fires."[47]

In 2013, Louis's conviction was reversed. Sadly, like Guy Miles, he was forced to plead no contest to the charges in a plea agreement to avoid a new trial and more years in prison hoping for a different verdict. He was freed after forty-two years in prison, one of the longest wrongful incarcerations in US history.

Studies that look at the race of victims similarly prove the impact of racial bias in the criminal legal system. *Missing White Woman Syndrome* and *Missing White Girl Syndrome* are terms used by social scientists to describe the disproportionate response from society when White females go missing. These incidents often receive intense media coverage, particularly when the women and girls are murdered. There is widespread community outrage, prosecutors seek maximum sentences, and new laws are often named after the deceased victims—seeking even greater sentences for future defendants.[48]

On the other hand, when Black people are victims, there are clear disparities in the way cases are treated. According to a study released by the Marshall Project in 2017, cases of White people killing Black people are found to be justifiable killings eight times as often as other racial combinations.[49]

The race of victims plays a dramatic role in death penalty statistics. While Black people are only 13 percent of the US population, they are grossly overrepresented in the percentage of people sentenced to death: 34 percent of people sentenced to death in the United States are Black. An even greater disparity exists when you look at the race of the victims of capital crimes: 75.7 percent of the victims in cases where a death sentence was imposed were White people. And in the case of interracial murders, 297 of the executions since 1976 were for Black people killing White people, and only 21 were for White people killing Black people.[50]

In cases like Louis Taylor's, it's easy to identify racism impacting an innocence case. It's also easy to see how cross-racial identification discussed in the misidentification chapter leads to wrongful convictions. But, in most cases, racism is based on implicit bias, making it virtually impossible to argue in court to obtain a client's freedom.

I often wonder how much implicit bias impacts my own work and the work of innocence organizations around the world. Most of the law students and lawyers who work in our organizations are White, and we aren't immune to implicit bias. We evaluate the cases that come into our offices and choose the cases where we will offer representation. Of the first thirty-five people my office has freed, fifteen were Black, six were Hispanic/Latino, ten were White, two were Asian, one was Indian, and one was Native American. At a national level, of the first 2,775 people exonerated in the United States since 1989, 327 were Hispanic/Latino, 1001 were White, 1380 were Black, and 63 were other races.[51]

It's hard to draw any real conclusions about how bias may have impacted the selection of these cases for post-conviction representation, or ultimately the decisions by courts to reverse the convictions. However, it's clear that there is disproportionate representation of people of color who are exonerated, just as there is a disproportionate representation of people of color in the criminal legal system.

All the issues discussed in this chapter make people of color more likely to be stopped, arrested, convicted, and receive more severe penalties. Innocent or guilty, if you are a person of color in the United States, it's more likely you will end up in prison.

POVERTY

Aristotle said, "poverty is the parent of revolution and crime," and it is certainly true that poverty can lead to criminal behavior (particularly theft crimes, as poor people often commit those crimes in the fight for economic survival).[52] But poverty also creates a situation where poor people cannot escape the criminal legal system in ways that people with resources can.

Poverty can lead people into the criminal legal system early in life. Lack of quality childcare in poor neighborhoods can set children behind academically before they even enter the school system.[53] Those setbacks can lead to lack of success in school and diminished long-term opportunities for employment. Fewer educational and employment opportunities often mean that both parents must work in low paying jobs for the family to survive, and thus there is less parental supervision. Lack of parental supervision, combined with diminished community resources in poor neighborhoods to keep children active in positive after-school programs, can lead children into criminal behavior, sometimes including joining gangs. Gang membership significantly increases the chances a child will get caught up in the criminal legal system, and it will increase their sentence if he or she commits crimes. In California, if a gang member commits a felony, at least two years and up to twenty-five-years-to-life can be added to their sentence.[54]

Justice is expensive, and when poor people enter the criminal legal system, they are trapped in a paradigm where the same poverty that led them into the criminal legal system makes it more difficult to escape its clutches.

For example, poor people have trouble paying fines. Failure to pay fines can lead to increased fines, poor credit, more financial problems, and increased chances of incarceration. Sometimes judges give the choice of fines or jail time at sentencing. Poor people who can't pay the fines are forced to choose jail.

Poor people cannot afford bail. This means they will more likely sit in jail awaiting trial than people with resources. There is a movement away from bail systems, but bail reform is still needed in most states. Nearly half of the incarcerated people in the United States are low-level drug offenders, those who have been arrested for failing to pay fees or fines for minor infractions, and those who cannot afford bail.[55]

Sixteen-year-old Kalief Browder spent three years in New York's notorious Rikers Island prison complex awaiting trial for allegedly stealing a backpack. He was beaten by guards and spent almost two years of his time there in solitary confinement while awaiting trial. The charges were eventually dismissed, but the damage had been done. Kalief took his own life at the age of twenty-two.[56]

Poor people must rely on government-provided legal services. As discussed in chapter 1, public defenders are often unfairly maligned even though they can be a much better option than private counsel. However, people with resources can hire high-priced lawyers, investigators, and expert witnesses, and pay for enough of their time to get superior services.

Also, public defenders are not available in every jurisdiction. Only twenty-three states properly fund their public defender services.[57] In jurisdictions that don't have public defenders, poor people must rely on often underpaid court-appointed lawyers. As also discussed in chapter 1, the payment system may impact how good the service is. This is not a problem that is limited to the United States. In Scotland, when the system for paying lawyers went from an hourly system to a flat fee system, plea bargains increased.[58]

In the United States, free legal services terminate after trial and one initial appeal. That appeal is limited to issues that can be found within the trial transcript. In other words, once convicted, there is no right to legal assistance in obtaining evidence to prove innocence. Those with resources can hire lawyers, investigators, and expert witnesses to continue the fight for their freedom, but that is a fraction of the prison population. In 2014, the median annual income prior to arrest for incarcerated people in the

United States was $19,185,[59] hardly the type of household that could pay thousands of dollars to an appellate attorney to investigate.

The economic difficulty in obtaining appellate lawyers is compounded by the fact that having a family member in prison drains a family of its resources. Not only does the income that was provided by the incarcerated person disappear, but the family must also cope with new expenses. Most of the prison population comes from cities, but prisons are often put in rural areas where land is cheap, hundreds of miles from the cities. Prison visits can be expensive and are often cost-prohibitive when poor families cannot afford to travel a substantial distance to visit their loved ones.

The 1983 Supreme Court case of *Olim v. Wakinekona* made clear that incarcerated people have no right to be incarcerated in the state of their conviction and can thus be transferred thousands of miles to other states, even as far as from Hawaii to the mainland.[60] That has led to private prisons contracting to bring incarcerated people from out of state to fill their prison beds. Such transfers led to riots when one hundred incarcerated people from Puerto Rico were transferred to a private prison in Minnesota in 1993. They were thousands of miles from their families and their lawyers, and in a totally foreign culture where they didn't even speak the language.[61]

The families of incarcerated people also have unique expenses that others never think about. For example, prisons are the last place the phone companies can charge outrageous rates for collect phone calls. While most of us enjoy unlimited calls, and even free international phone service via the internet, incarcerated people and their families often have huge phone bills they cannot afford. Additionally, families bear the burden of buying toiletries, socks, shoes, and underwear.

On the heels of decades of tough-on-crime policies, prisons are not designed to improve people's chances of pulling themselves out of poverty upon release. Prison education and training programs are often the victims of budget cuts based on a "they don't deserve it" philosophy. Thus, formerly incarcerated people are often uneducated, untrained, and burdened with a criminal record, making it extremely difficult to find honest employment. This decreases their chances of leading successful crime-free lives upon release.

All these factors combine to make poverty both a cause and effect of crime. This paradigm can particularly impact innocent people because proving innocence requires significant resources.

For example, the cases discussed in chapter 3 (Bill Richards and Kimberly Long) were homicide cases where experts retained by the state supported the convictions. It was only through deconstructing the facts of the cases, searching for new lay witnesses, and obtaining our own expert witnesses to analyze the evidence that we were able to build the case for innocence. These cases required substantial resources that our clients didn't have.

In the wrongful conviction cases based on bad identifications discussed in chapter 4, the trial attorneys had an uphill battle confronting the positive identifications made by the witnesses. When jurors hear a witness say, "I'm 100% sure that's the person who committed the crime," they are likely to convict. It requires investigation to undermine this type of testimony and often requires an expert witness to explain the problems with identification procedures and memory. This type of expert testimony is something a trial judge might not approve payment for, or it may be a resource not readily available in some jurisdictions.

In Uriah Courtney's case, we needed experts to review the identification procedures to show they were faulty. We needed money to get DNA testing done on the victim's clothing. Ultimately, we needed to get access to the DNA databank to find the true attacker. Fortunately, we had cooperation from the district attorney's office to get these things done. But it all costs time and money.

In Guy Miles's case, even though there were witnesses who put him in Las Vegas at the time of the crime, that wasn't enough to avoid a conviction. We needed an expert to explain the problems with the identification procedures, and then we needed years of investigation to hunt down the actual perpetrators and bring them to court. Even after we had the evidence, it took multiple habeas hearings and appeals to get his conviction reversed.

In the Luis Vargas case, we had to disprove the testimony of three separate women who identified him as a rapist. We were only able to do that through DNA testing, expert testimony, and investigating thirty other rapes that occurred with similar modus operandi in the same area.

Like undermining identifications, it is very challenging to undermine confessions. As discussed in chapter 5, when jurors hear a person confessed, they are likely to convict on that alone. Discrediting those confessions is very difficult and often requires both expert testimony and proof of police misconduct. In the Marilyn Mulero case, it took decades of investigation to ultimately reveal that the detective who allegedly obtained her confession was involved in dozens of cases of false confessions.

Defending murder prosecutions when a baby is involved, like the cases in chapter 6, requires tremendous resources. The state always has a team of experts with impressive resumes ready to testify that the only reasonable conclusion is that the child was intentionally killed, and the suspect is the killer. Even with the cooperation of the district attorney, we had to retain multiple experts in the Ken Marsh case to undermine the case at trial. Every one of these cases needed an exhaustive investigation. They are incredibly time-consuming, complicated, and expensive. Even absurd prosecutions based on nothing, like the Huang case in Qatar, took tremendous resources to unravel.

It goes without saying that all the cases in chapter 7 (You Got a Jury That Was Blinded by "Science") require a great deal of resources to defend. When the prosecution has experts testifying to scientific proof of a person's guilt, the defense must have experts testifying to scientific proof of innocence. The JoAnn Parks case, for example, required an incredible amount of fire investigation and the best experts in the field to find the truth. And even after we had that evidence, we couldn't get a court to reverse her conviction. Instead, we had to rely on the governor to grant her clemency to get her released after twenty-nine years of wrongful incarceration.

It might appear that child molestation cases, such as the ones discussed in chapter 8, are simply the children's testimony versus the defendant's credibility, but that isn't the best way to approach those cases. To defend them effectively, it requires experts to review the interviewing techniques, and it often requires experts to review medical reports to look for consistency, or lack of consistency, with the statements of the alleged victims. Even with all the recantations from the children in the John Stoll case, it was an expensive battle that involved multiple experts to achieve his exoneration.

Lies, as discussed in chapter 9, are often tough to undermine. To effectively combat lies—whether they be from snitches, the police, or an alleged victim, as in the Brian Banks case—it takes investigation. Snitches must be outed based on their prior snitching, their motives for lying, and the inconsistencies in their statements. It is even more difficult to undermine false police testimony. They are professional witnesses and good at covering their tracks. With alleged victims like the one in Brian Banks's case, the defense must search for witnesses and evidence that can pull apart the lies. All of this takes time and money.

When former NFL star O. J. Simpson was acquitted in 1995, I was asked by a reporter whether the case proved that people were able to get away with murder in the United States. Setting aside the question of his guilt or innocence, I answered, "No, the case proves the number of resources it takes to successfully take on the government."

O. J. spent millions on his defense. He had a dozen of some of the best defense attorneys in the country representing him, and he was able to retain some of the best experts. His case is the exception that proves the rule. The overwhelming number of people charged with crimes in the United States are poor, only have the limited resources provided by the state, and their cases will likely end in plea bargains without any serious investigation or analysis of the evidence by experts.

Poor people are at a huge disadvantage when they are up against the resources of the state or federal government. The idea that the defense has an advantage because the government has the burden of proof is a false narrative. The government has police forces at their disposal as their investigators. They have crime labs and experts at their disposal to do testing and testify. They have highly trained prosecutors, who are generally paid more than public defenders. The Equal Defense Act, initially sponsored by then-Senator Kamala Harris, is working its way through Congress as of this writing. The bill intends to more fairly compensate public defenders and bring their pay more in line with that of the prosecutors they face in court.[62] The fact that this bill is needed proves that prosecutor offices have an unfair advantage in seeking, supporting, and retaining high quality attorneys.

All these inequities contribute to poor, innocent people being convicted. The inequities get even worse after conviction, when the government continues to have all the resources, but no longer has the burden of proof. We have the burden of proof, and our clients and their families typically have no money. Whatever they had left after the trial disappeared during the years in prison while their families struggled to survive.

Our work isn't cheap. Even though our project, like most of the innocence organizations in the world, is staffed by law students, and we have a team of volunteer lawyers, we still must pay some full-time staff and all the investigation and litigation costs of our cases. This includes expenses as basic as gas money to drive around the state looking for witnesses and visiting clients, getting copies of transcripts and crime scene photos, forensic expert expenses, phone and mailing costs, and all the usual expenses involved in running a law firm.

When we started the California Innocence Project, we had very few resources. We raised money from bake sales, fun runs, dodgeball tournaments, and bar nights. We were fortunate to get a large donation from Southern California legendary guitarist Joe Walsh and his band, The Eagles. Joe and the band put on a concert for us and raised enough money to keep us going for the first couple of years. Without that boost, I'm not sure we would have made it through that time.

It's absurd to think that we take on the California government—funded by the fifth largest economy in the world, with every resource at their disposal—from our little office in San Diego funded by donations and bake sales. This is the challenge facing every innocence organization in the world. Find one close to you and support them if you can.[63]

Conclusion

The idea you might go to prison for a crime you didn't commit is a frightening one. It's something none of us want to think about, but it's a disturbing possibility. I've seen it happen so many times that I've even formulated a plan in my head if it ever happens to me.

Day one on the prison yard, I'll approach the gang leaders and tell them I'll be their personal lawyer. I'll promise to spend every day in the prison law library working on their cases if they protect me. Hopefully, that never comes to pass, but after more than three decades working in the criminal legal system, I know it's a possibility.

If I'm charged with a crime I didn't commit, I won't make the mistakes I write about in chapter 1. Although I may suffer the wrath of prosecutors who I've aggravated over the years, the relationships I've made with defense attorneys will assure I'll get good counsel. And, of course, I'll have the ability to assist in my own defense. I'll also have the benefit of being a White person with resources, and so I'm unlikely to suffer many of the inequities described in chapter 10.

However, I'll be unable to avoid all the facts and circumstances described in the eight chapters in between. Just like anyone else, I could find myself in the wrong place at the wrong time, or suffer from bad police practices, faulty science, lies, and everything else described in this book. The bottom line is that anyone can be wrongfully convicted.

So, what should we do about it? As I wrote in the introduction, it's our collective criminal legal system. It acts on our behalf. It protects our families, our homes, and our lives. We have a collective responsibility to constantly strive to improve it. And, when an innocent person goes to prison, we have a responsibility to get them out and address the problem that led to the wrongful conviction.

To address the problems associated with poor defense lawyering described in chapter 1, we must commit to providing excellent representation to people charged with crimes. It was nearly two hundred years after the United States Constitution established the right to counsel in federal court that the right was mandated in state courts. The challenge today is to make sure the representation is excellent in all cases, not just the ones where defendants are lucky enough to be appointed a great lawyer or have the resources to pay for one.

It's not enough to provide lawyers in criminal cases. The lawyers must have particular skills and training. And even with skills and training, excessive caseloads, apathy, cynicism about a client's claim of innocence, failure to investigate, lack of resources, and lack of experience can all lead to inadequate representation. Considering the twenty-five-year odyssey of Marilyn Mulero's case, it's clear our laws do not sufficiently protect people who receive inadequate representation. The standard of "reasonable representation" is too vague and proving that competent counsel would have made a difference at trial is too difficult. There should be specific standards, and if they are not met, an automatic retrial.

As to the issues addressed in chapter 2—where I describe the likelihood of wrongful convictions in both rural areas and inner cities—recognition, training, and resources are the path to improvement. There should be no difference in the quality of lawyers, police officers, judges, and forensic analysts based on locality, and their practices should be uniform.

Of course, this is difficult to achieve. The criminal legal system is largely funded at the county level in the United States. Different counties have different resources and funding priorities. The only way to increase the quality is by setting national standards and providing remedies (such as reversal of convictions) when those standards are not met.

Finding your partner's dead body, as described in chapter 3, should not be enough to convict a person of murder. Again, training is a remedy for this problem. Police officers, and ultimately prosecutors, often have blinders on once a suspect has solidified in their minds. People like Kim Long and Bill Richards suffered due to that blindness.

Ultimately, judges and jurors must be a check on these prosecutions. They must demand more than opportunity and motive for a conviction. No one should go to prison for murder on flimsy and circumstantial evidence.

The bad identification and false confessions described in chapters 4 and 5 require a great deal of focus and reform. We must recognize that human memory is faulty, and procedures used to extract those memories can distort the truth.

All identification procedures should be double-blind. Neither the witness, nor those conducting the photo arrays and live lineups, should know who the suspects are and who the fillers are. It should be made clear to the witnesses that the suspect may not be in a lineup. Everyone in the lineup should closely resemble the description given by the witness. The lineup procedure should be documented, preferably with a video recording, so the defense can later review the procedure and determine whether intentional or inadvertent contamination of the process occurred.

Finally, the witness should give a statement as to how confident they are in the identification. That statement should be shared with the defense to combat confidence that morphs from "number three kind of looks like the guy" to "I'm 100% sure number three is the guy" in the time between the identification procedure and trial.

All interrogation tactics that lead to false confessions should be abolished. Coercion and deception should not be accepted practices. Unreliable procedures like hypnosis should not be part of modern police techniques. Unduly long interrogation sessions without the benefit of counsel should become a thing of the past. One study revealed that 84 percent of false confessions occur after interrogations of more than six hours.[1] Suspects get worn down and confused, or sometimes they just get angry and falsely confess to "get it over with." Simply shortening the acceptable amount of time interrogations may proceed would decrease the number of wrongful convictions.

Reforming identification and confession procedures are in all our best interest. Fewer innocent people would be convicted, and more guilty people would be convicted. It's that simple. It's time to listen to the experts and adopt best practices.

The same goes for the factors that lead to wrongful baby death convictions described in chapter 6, the faulty sciences described in chapter 7, and the investigations that lead to wrongful convictions for child molestation in chapter 8. No one should go to prison because jurors believed one expert over another in a disputed area of science. And where there is dispute, the benefit of the doubt should go to the person who is facing a life in prison or the death penalty. We must strive to get the best scientific information into our criminal legal system, whether we are talking about new data about baby deaths, fingerprinting, bite marks, arson, hair analysis, shell casings, DNA, lead bullet analysis, child interviewing techniques, or any forensic science that is used to convict and exonerate.

In terms of the lies described in chapter 9, the reality is that people will always lie. Our criminal legal system must do the best it can to discover those lies. We must deeply scrutinize motivations and reveal them in court so that judges and juries have the complete picture. We must investigate cases of corruption and eliminate those who lie from our system as best we can. We must provide resources and processes so that every criminal case is thoroughly investigated and people don't go to prison simply based on untruths.

Similarly, eliminating bias, inequity, and discrimination in the system based on race and poverty, as described in chapter 10, is extraordinarily difficult and may never be achieved. As discussed, explicit bias in the letter of the law is much easier to identify and reform than the implicit biases that permeate our system and our society. We must look to the statistical evidence to recognize racial inequities and begin to address them through training and policy reform.

Economic inequities also lead to unequal application of the law. We should examine all inequities in the criminal legal system, from bail reform to trial resources for the poor, to sentences that have unequal impact based on economics. The path to deal with these inequities is long and challenging.

Every year in San Diego, there's a large event where all the criminal defense attorneys get together and reflect upon the victories and challenges of the prior year. Several years ago, the California Innocence Project was honored at this event with an award based on a great year of victories. I looked around the room at my colleagues, including some of the best criminal defense attorneys in the United States, and said, "I know what you all are thinking. If you got to choose the cases you took on like we do, you'd be up here receiving this award instead of us!"

Innocence cases get a great deal of attention, and most lawyers don't have the luxury of picking their own cases. However, it's often not easy for us to set aside cases where we believe the potential client is guilty but has suffered unfair processes, inadequate representation, vindictive prosecutions, and/or outrageous sentencing.

Two examples of that are the cases of Kenneth Corley and Sergio Ayala. Both were sent to prison for life under California's harsh Three Strikes Law. Most people believed that when the law was created, it only applied to violent offenders. That's not true. The law currently applies to anyone who commits three serious or violent offenses, and prior to a 2012 reform, the third strike didn't even have to be serious or violent.

Kenneth had prior drug offenses. The third offense was "possession of drug paraphernalia." That put him in prison for life. Sergio had prior burglary charges, and when he stole a $150 leaf blower out of the back of a truck, that put him in prison for life.

Both these cases made me crazy. When the Three Strikes Law was reformed to require the third strike be serious or violent, I assigned the cases to Mike Semanchik and Audrey McGinn, who took them to court and won both men their freedom. Kenneth was the first person in California released under the new law, and Sergio was the second. Hundreds more followed. Men and women sentenced to die in prison for minor offenses.

You won't find Kenneth's or Sergio's stories on our website. We didn't even file their petitions under the name of our organization. Our mission stays the same: to free the innocent. But in those cases, it seemed impossible to look away from the injustice.

Separating out the so-called "good people" in prison from the "bad people" based on innocence alone has been a criticism of our movement. Although I have devoted most of my career to freeing innocent people from prison, I recognize that focusing empathy on the innocent may lead to a lack of empathy for the guilty, and that's something that troubles me. Jody Armour criticizes the innocence movement in his book *N*gga Theory*, for that reason. He states: "The excessive blame and punishment of guilty black offenders, especially the violent and serious ones who most inflame the urge for retaliation and revenge, is a much more pervasive and pernicious problem, running throughout every phase of the criminal justice system, than the problem of wrongful convictions or executions of innocent blacks."[2]

I appreciate this criticism, although I do believe innocence work does go beyond the individual problems of a wrongly convicted innocent person facing a prison sentence or execution. For example, as states are increasingly moving away from the death penalty, one of the leading reasons cited is the risk of executing an innocent person.[3] I believe this is a result of the publicity associated with the freeing of nearly two hundred innocent people from US death rows. There have also been many reforms to the criminal justice system associated with the innocence movement that make the system better for everyone. We often use our cases as a direct springboard for policy reforms. As I mentioned in the introduction, Jasmin Harris leads CIP's policy efforts. Both she and Alex Simpson constantly go door to door in Sacramento, telling our state representatives the stories of our innocent clients and the reforms needed to stop the same thing from happening again. As a result, we've been involved in writing or rewriting more than a dozen California laws related to criminal justice.

However, I still substantially agree with Professor Armour's position. There is a great deal of work to do beyond reforming the system to protect the innocent.

Dismantling the criminal legal system to solve these systemic problems is particularly difficult due to a combination of politics and money. Politicians, from those running for local city council to those running for the United States presidency, continually make campaign promises that they'll keep us safe using policies that make great sound bites but have little social science to support them. And they always look for short-term solutions, like putting more police on the street, because they need to show short-term results to get reelected.

The truth is we need long-term solutions to decrease crime and scale down our criminal legal system. We need to invest more in education from preschool on, increase opportunities for young people, transform prisons from places that warehouse huge numbers of our citizens with a revolving door, to places where people learn and train for life outside the walls. We need to decriminalize activities that create no real harm to society and decrease sentences to increase the number of available resources in the criminal legal system. Those resources should be used to improve all aspects of the system, from policing to trial procedures to corrections. The best solutions might not show results for years—long past the next election—so they are difficult to get on political agendas. Still, they are necessary and could become a reality if the public understood their need and demanded change.

Money has also infiltrated our criminal legal system. It has derailed the best policies for our society toward ones in the best interest of businesses who provide services to the system and the politicians they financially support. In the 2016 presidential election, the figure of 80 billion dollars a year was thrown around as the amount we spend annually in the United States on mass incarceration.[4] More recently, it's been revealed that the actual number is more like 180 billion dollars, because the money spent to lock people up goes far beyond correctional facility expenses. The larger figure includes the costs of policing, prosecuting, indigent defense, health care, food, contracting with private prisons, and staffing costs throughout the system. It also includes costs that families absorb, such as 1.4 billion dollars in bail fees, 1.6 billion dollars paid into prison commissary accounts, and 1.3 billion dollars paid for prison phone calls.[5] With all the money involved in the system, combined with policies in the United States that do not effectively keep money out of the political process, we've created a monster that requires constant feeding at the cost of tremendous human suffering.

How can innocence organizations do anything to improve the system against such powerful forces? We do policy work, but the heart of our work is bringing innocent people home. I often tell my lawyers and students, "Don't focus on the problems of the entire system and how many people are desperate for help, because it's too overwhelming. Focus on today and what you can do to help one person get home."

The impact of each person we bring home goes far beyond that person and their family and friends. Each exoneration is a lesson about a failing of the system. That lesson might change the way police, defense attorneys, prosecutors, forensic experts, and judges involved in the case handle future cases. People in the general public who hear about the case may think twice about weak evidence when they serve on a jury and may think twice about electing tough-on-crime politicians.

Innocence organizations also impact the system in a broader sense through their education and training missions. The law students who go through the programs go on to become ethical, justice-driven advocates who can make big differences. Excellent lawyers who demand fairness and change, both on the prosecution and defense sides, are key to improving the system for everyone.

Another impact of innocence work has been the response of prosecutor's offices around the country. The publicity of innocent people walking out of prison, arm in arm with the lawyers who have freed them, has forced prosecutors to examine their work. "Conviction Review Units" or "Conviction Integrity Units" have been formed around the country in prosecutor's offices. Some have largely been publicity stunts, so prosecutors look like they are doing the right thing, but many others have been earnest efforts to work with innocence organizations, find innocent people in prison, and get them out. Improving the quality of prosecutorial work makes the system better for everyone.

Although this book is filled with grim tales of wrongful convictions and a failing criminal legal system, I'm actually somewhat optimistic about the future. People are waking up to the high cost of decades of tough-on-crime policies and demanding change. Progressive prosecutors like George Gascón in Los Angeles and Larry Krasner in Philadelphia are being elected and bringing real change to their offices. We are also seeing an increase in the use of clemency at both the state and federal levels.[6]

Feature films, documentaries, podcasts, and books continue to bring the stories of innocence to the public and influence the conversation about innocence. I was proud to help bring the Brian Banks story to the big screen with the feature film *Brian Banks*. It also gave me an opportunity to flex my acting chops, something every trial lawyer strives to do, in my three second role as a bartender in the film.

Young people also give me hope—from my own law students at the California Innocence Project aggressively investigating innocence cases, to the millions of young people who have taken to the streets in recent years to protest for justice. You all make me believe change is coming.

The alums of the California Innocence Project give me hope. I love dropping by "The Local," a San Diego bar where public defenders hang out after work. I can always find at least one of my former students there and I enjoy hearing about the great work they are doing.

I'm also proud of my former students who have become ethical prosecutors. Chris Lawson, one of my former students who is now a senior attorney at the San Diego District Attorney's Office, recently told me, "The California Innocence Project helped mold the lens through which I see the system." I was thrilled to hear he thought like that fifteen years after graduating from our program.

And, of course, my team and my fellow freedom fighters working in innocence organizations around the world give me hope. Over the past two decades I've seen our group grow from a handful to hundreds. You have all enriched my life and I thank you for that.

Although there are many different origins for the idea going back to ancient Greece, Benjamin Franklin is often quoted as saying, "Justice will not be served until those who are unaffected are as outraged as those who are."

Most people are not outraged about wrongful convictions until it impacts them directly, but as this book makes clear, anyone can be wrongfully convicted. Don't wait to be outraged until you, or someone you love, wakes up in a cell suffering the surrealistic nightmare of being innocent in prison. We must all be outraged and act on our outrage to put justice into the criminal legal system.

Acknowledgments

Thanks to all my colleagues, family, and friends whose comments and edits greatly improved this book. Thank you Alissa Bjerkhoel, Katherine Bonaguidi, Zach Brooks, Heidi Brooks, Richard Brooks, Jeff Chinn, Raquel Cohen, Jeremy Deconcini, Steve Drizin, Keith Findley, Brandon Garrett, Mark Godsey, Meryl Goldsmith, Lindsay Herf, Louise Hewitt, Ed Humes, Maya Knee, Amanda Knox, Richard Leo, Audrey McGinn, Claire McGourlay, Marcy Mistrett, Bill Oberly, Jocelyn Perez, Catherine Pugh, Ashley Ratliff, Claudia Salinas, Lee Sarokin, Barry Scheck, Mike Semanchik, Alex Simpson, Andrea Tennant, Jennifer Thompson, Des Walsh, and Rob Warden. Special thanks to my research assistant Janey Peterson and my editor Maura Roessner.

Notes

INTRODUCTION

1. Marion v. State, 20 Neb. 233 (1886).

2. Meghan Barrett Cousino, "William Jackson Marion," National Registry of Exonerations, Pre-1989, https://www.law.umich.edu/special/exoneration/Pages /casedetailpre1989.aspx?caseid=212 (accessed April 3, 2021).

3. National Registry of Exonerations, https://www.law.umich.edu/special /exoneration/Pages/about.aspx (accessed April 3, 2021).

CHAPTER 1. YOU HIRED THE WRONG LAWYER

1. Powell v. Alabama, 287 U.S. 45 (1932).

2. Gideon v. Wainwright, 372 U.S. 335 (1963).

3. Furman v. Georgia, 408 U.S. 238 (1972).

4. Gregg v. Georgia, 428 U.S. 153 (1976).

5. Ibid., 220–24.

6. Samuel Gross, "Rate of False Conviction of Criminal Defendants Who Are Sentenced to Death," *PNAS*, April 28, 2014, https://www.pnas.org/content/111 /20/7230.

7. Death Penalty Information Center, "State and Federal Info, Illinois," https:// deathpenaltyinfo.org/state-and-federal-info/state-by-state/illinois (accessed April 15, 2021).

8. Strickland v. Washington, 446 U.S. 668 (1984).

9. Mark Godsey, *Blind Injustice: A Former Prosecutor Exposes the Psychology and Politics of Wrongful Convictions* (Oakland: University of California Press, 2017), 76.

CHAPTER 2. YOU LIVE IN THE COUNTRY
OR THE CITY

1. Documents relating to the William Richards case on file with author.

2. "Explaining the Urban-Rural Political Divide," *Niskanen Center,* July 17, 2019, https://www.niskanencenter.org/explaining-the-urban-rural-political -divide/.

3. US Census Bureau, https://www.census.gov/quickfacts/fact/table /adacityoklahoma/PST040221 (accessed April 21, 2021).

4. Clifton Adcock, "Judge Orders Second Man in Ada's 'Innocent Man' Case Freed, State to Appeal," December 21, 2020, https://www.readfrontier.org/stories /judge-orders-second-man-in-adas-innocent-man-case-freed-state-to-appeal/; "Oklahoma Innocence Project Takes on First Case," Innocence Project, July 31, 2013, https://innocenceproject.org/oklahoma-innocence-project-takes-on-first-case/; "Ron Williamson," Innocence Project, https://innocenceproject.org/cases /ron-williamson/ (accessed April 21, 2021); "Dennis Fritz," Innocence Project, https://innocenceproject.org/cases/dennis-fritz/ (accessed April 21, 2021).

5. Kim Parker, "What Unites and Divides Urban, Suburban and Rural Communities," May 22, 2018, https://www.pewresearch.org/social-trends /2018/05/22/demographic-and-economic-trends-in-urban-suburban-and-rural -communities/.

6. Ralph A. Weisheit, L. Edward Wells, and David N. Falcone, "Crime and Policing in Rural and Small-Town America: An Overview of the Issues," September 1995, https://www.ncjrs.gov/txtfiles/crimepol.txt.

7. Ralph Ioimo et al., "Comparing Urban and Rural Police Views of Bias-Based Policing," *Professional Issues in Criminal Justice* 6(1,2) (2011): 53–81, https:// www.academia.edu/2830656/Comparing_Urban_and_Rural_Police_Views_of_ Bias_based_Policing?auto=download.

8. Ibid.

9. Ibid.

10. Jennifer L. Mnookin, "How Preconceptions and Bias May Have Led to Wrongful Convictions of West Memphis Three," August 23, 2011, https://death-penaltyinfo.org/news/how-preconceptions-and-bias-may-have-led-to-wrongful -convictions-of-west-memphis-three.

11. Jack Healy, "A Rural County Owes $28 Million for Wrongful Convictions. It Doesn't Want to Pay," *New York Times,* April 1, 2019, https://www.nytimes. com/2019/04/01/us/beatrice-six-nebraska.html.

12. See Christina Buchanan, "Geographical Disparities in Wrongful Conviction Cases" (master's thesis, University of Central Oklahoma, July 2014), https://shareok.org/bitstream/handle/11244/325190/BuchananC2014.pdf?sequence=1&isAllowed=y.

13. G. H. W. Bush, "Address to the Nation on the National Drug Control Strategy," George H. W. Bush Presidential Library and Museum, September 5, 1989, https://bush41library.tamu.edu/archives/public-papers/863.

14. California v. Hodari D., 499 U.S. 621 (1991).

15. Rod K. Brunson, "Protests Focus on Over-Policing. But Under-Policing Is Also Deadly," *Washington Post*, June 12, 2020, https://www.washingtonpost.com/outlook/underpolicing-cities-violent-crime/2020/06/12/b5d1fd26-ac0c-11ea-9063-e69bd6520940_story.html.

16. Evan Hill et al., "How George Floyd Was Killed in Police Custody" *New York Times*, May 31, 2020, https://www.nytimes.com/2020/05/31/us/george-floyd-investigation.html.

17. Ray Sanchez and Eric Levenson, "Derek Chauvin Sentenced to 22.5 Years in Death of George Floyd," CNN, June 25, 2021, https://www.cnn.com/2021/06/25/us/derek-chauvin-sentencing-george-floyd/index.html.

18. US Department of Justice Civil Rights Division, US Attorney's Office District of New Jersey, "Investigation of the Newark Police Department," July 22, 2014, https://www.justice.gov/sites/default/files/crt/legacy/2014/07/22/newark_findings_7-22-14.pdf.

19. Ibid.

20. Gabriel L. Schwartz and Jaquelyn L. Jahn, "Mapping Fatal Police Violence across U.S. Metropolitan Areas: Overall Rates and Racial/Ethnic Inequalities, 2013–2017," *PLOS*, June 24, 2020, https://journals.plos.org/plosone/article?id=10.1371/journal.pone.0229686.

21. "Principals of Good Policing: Avoiding Violence Between Police and Citizens," U.S. Department of Justice, revised September 2003, https://www.justice.gov/archive/crs/pubs/principlesofgoodpolicingfinal092003.htm.

22. Samuel Sinyangwe, "Police Are Killing Fewer People in Big Cities, but More in Suburban and Rural America," *FiveThirtyEight*, June 1, 2020, https://fivethirtyeight.com/features/police-are-killing-fewer-people-in-big-cities-but-more-in-suburban-and-rural-america/.

CHAPTER 3. YOU ARE IN A RELATIONSHIP AND LIVE
WITH SOMEONE WHO IS MURDERED

1. Emiko Petrosky et al., "Racial and Ethnic Differences in Homicides of Adult Women and the Role of Intimate Partner Violence—United States, 2003–2014," *Morbidity and Mortality Weekly Report*, July 21, 2017, https://www.ncbi.nlm.nih.gov/pmc/articles/PMC5657947/.

CHAPTER 4. YOU (KIND OF) LOOK LIKE OTHER
PEOPLE IN THE WORLD

1. This name was changed due to the victim being a minor at the time of the incident.

2. Mark Godsey, *Blind Injustice: A Former Prosecutor Exposes the Psychology and Politics of Wrongful Convictions* (Oakland: University of California Press, 2017), 12.

3. Gary L. Wells, Amina Memon, Steven D. Penrod, "Eyewitness Evidence, Improving Its Probative Value," *Psychological Science in the Public Interest* 7(2) (2006): 45, 48. See also Donald A. Dripps, "Miscarriages of Justice and the Constitution," *Buffalo Criminal Law Review* 2(2) (1999): 635, 638–39 ("A Department of Justice study found that, out of a sample of more than 21,000 cases, DNA testing exonerated the suspect in 23 percent of the cases"). Since DNA evidence was first introduced into the criminal justice system, it has exonerated more than 144 people who were wrongfully convicted of crimes. Samuel R. Gross et al., "Exonerations in the United States, 1989 through 2003," *Journal of Criminal Law and Criminology* 95(2) (2005): 523, 524. "In 64% percent of these exonerations (219/340) at least one eyewitness misidentified the defendant"(Gross et al., 542). Eighty-eight percent of the rape exonerations involved eyewitness misidentification (Gross et al., 530). See also Gary L. Wells and Elizabeth A. Olson, "Eyewitness Testimony," *Annual Review of Psychology* 54 (2003): 277, 278 (stating that more than one hundred convicted felons have been exonerated by DNA evidence).

4. "Guy Miles Released from Prison," https://www.youtube.com/watch?v=oo8fvgIiR-w&t=22s&ab_channel=CaliforniaWesternSchoolofLaw.

5. "Most Learning Happens in the First 3 Years," Centre for Educational Neuroscience, http://www.educationalneuroscience.org.uk/resources/neuromyth-or-neurofact/most-learning-happens-in-the-first-3-years/ (accessed April 20, 2021).

6. Max McClure, "Infants Process Faces Long before They Recognize Other Objects, Stanford Vision Researchers Find," *Stanford News*, December 11, 2012, https://news.stanford.edu/news/2012/december/infants-process-faces-121112.html.

7. Kathy Pezdek, I. Blandon-Gitlin, and C. Moore, "Children's Face Recognition Memory: More Evidence for the Cross-race Effect," *Journal of Applied Psychology* 88(4) (2003): 760–63, https://doi.org/10.1037/0021-9010.88.4.760.

8. Marta Zaraska, "The Sense of Smell in Humans Is More Powerful Than We Think," *Discover Magazine*, October 11, 2017, https://www.discovermagazine.com/mind/the-sense-of-smell-in-humans-is-more-powerful-than-we-think.

9. Arthur W. Melton, "Implications of Short-term Memory for a General Theory of Memory," *Journal of Verbal Learning and Verbal Behavior* (July 1963), https://www.sciencedirect.com/science/article/abs/pii/S0022537163800638.

10. Vaijghn Tooley et al., "Facial Recognition: Weapon Effect and Attentional Focus," *Journal of Applied Social Psychology* (July 2006), https://www.researchgate.net/publication/229861854_Facial_Recognition_Weapon_Effect_and_Attentional_Focus1.

11. Jennifer Thompson-Cannino and Ronald Cotton with Erin Torneo, *Picking Cotton: Our Memoir of Injustice and Redemption* (New York: St. Martin's Griffin, 2009), 32–33.

12. Ibid.

13. Ibid., 37.

14. *Manson v Brathwaite*, 432 U.S. 98 (1977).

15. Ibid., 101.

16. Ibid., 115.

17. Ibid., 119.

18. Vargas sentencing hearing, pp. 10–11. On file with author.

19. "Unknown Suspect," FBI Most Wanted, https://www.fbi.gov/wanted/seeking-info/unknown-subject/view (accessed January 26, 2022).

20. Paula C. Dicks, *The Strange Case of Adolf Beck: Press Influence and Criminal Justice Reform in Edwardian England*, 2007, *Dissertations* (1962–2010), https://epublications.marquette.edu/dissertations/AAI3277080/.

CHAPTER 5. YOU GET CONFUSED WHEN YOU ARE TIRED AND HUNGRY, AND PEOPLE YELL AT YOU

1. Brown v. Mississippi, 297 U.S. 278 (1936).

2. Amanda Knox, *Waiting to Be Heard* (New York: Harper Collins, 2013), 74.

3. Ibid., 400.

4. Richard A. Leo and Richard J. Ofshe, "The Decision to Confess Falsely: Rational Choice and Irrational Action," *Denver University Law Review* 74(4) (1997): 989, https://papers.ssrn.com/sol3/papers.cfm?abstract_id=1134046.

5. Laura Nirider, "13 Years after Disproven Confession, Dassey Must Be Freed," *OnMilwaukee*, May 2, 2020, https://onmilwaukee.com/articles/dassey-clemency-nirider.

6. Marcelle McDaniel, "False Confessions and the Lessons of the Fairbanks Four," *Anchorage Daily News*, January 3, 2016, https://www.adn.com/commentary/article/false-confessions-and-lessons-fairbanks-four/2016/01/04/.

7. Lucy Akehurst et al., "Lay Persons' and Police Officers' Beliefs Regarding Deceptive Behaviour," *Applied Cognitive Psychology* 10(6) (1996), https://doi.org/10.1002/(SICI)1099-0720(199612)10:6<461::AID-ACP413>3.0.CO;2-2.

8. Steven A. Drizin and Richard A. Leo, "The Problem of False Confessions in the Post-DNA World," *North Carolina Law Review* (May 2008): 911, https://scholarship.law.unc.edu/nclr/vol82/iss3/3/.

9. Aldert Vrij, "Interrogation and Interviewing," *Encyclopedia of Applied Psychology* (2004), https://www.sciencedirect.com/topics/psychology/reid -technique.

10. Leo and Ofshe, "The Decision to Confess Falsely," 986.

11. Emily West and Vanessa Meterko, "Innocence Project: DNA Exonerations, 1989–2014: Review of Data and Findings from the First 25 Years," *Albany Law Review* 79(3) (2016): 717, https://www.iadclaw.org/assets/1/7/22.1-_Pucher-_ Meterko_Innocence_Project_DNA_Exonerations_First_25_Years.pdf.

12. Richard A. Leo, "False Confessions: Causes, Consequences, and Implications," *Journal of the American Academy of Psychiatry and the Law* (September 2009), http://jaapl.org/content/37/3/332.

13. Miranda v. Arizona, 384 U.S. 436 (1966).

14. Escobedo v. Illinois, 378 U.S. 478 (1964).

15. Miranda v. Arizona, 384 U.S. 436 (1966).

16. Ibid.

17. Rhode Island v. Innis, 446 U.S. 291 (1980).

18. Illinois v. Perkins, 496 U.S. 292 (1990).

19. Oregon v. Elstad, 470 U.S. 298 (1985).

20. Leo and Ofshe, "The Decision to Confess Falsely," 989.

21. Charles D. Weisselberg, "Mourning Miranda," *California Law Review* 96(6) (2008): 1519, 1524.

22. Bram v. United States, 168 U.S. 532 (1897).

23. Greenwald v. Wisconsin, 390 U.S. 519 (1968).

24. Paul Marcus, "It's Not Just about Miranda: Determining the Voluntariness of Confessions in Criminal Prosecutions," *Valparaiso University Law Review* (Summer 2006), https://scholar.valpo.edu/cgi/viewcontent.cgi?article =1223&context=vulr.

25. Miranda v. Arizona, 384 U.S. 436, 474 (1966).

26. "SCAN Gets the Truth!" LSI Laboratory for Scientific Interrogation, Inc., https://www.lsiscan.com/id17.htm (accessed January 25, 2022).

27. Nicky Smith, *Reading between the Lines: An Evaluation of the Scientific Content Analysis Technique (SCAN),* Home Office, Policing and Reducing Crime Unit, Police Research Series, Paper 35, http://megaplan.co.za/An% 20evaluation%20of%20the%20SCAN%20tecnique%20Nicky%20Smith%20 Police%20Research%20Series%20UK.pdf.

28. "SCAN Gets the Truth!"

29. Ken Armstrong and Christian Sheckler, "Why Are Cops around the World Using This Outlandish Mind-Reading Tool?" *ProPublica,* December 7, 2019, https://www.propublica.org/article/why-are-cops-around-the-world-using-this -outlandish-mindreading-tool.

30. Ibid.

31. Robert Kolker, "Nothing but the Truth," Marshall Project, May 24, 2016, https://www.themarshallproject.org/2016/05/24/nothing-but-the-truth.

32. Sarah Kimball Stephenson, "US Supreme Court Turns Down Texas Death Row Case Concerning Police Hypnosis," *Jurist,* January 27, 2021, https://www.jurist.org/news/2021/01/us-supreme-court-turns-down-texas-death-row-case-concerning-police-hypnosis/.

33. "Oklahoma Becomes 25th State to Require Recording of Interrogations," Innocence Project, May 14, 2019, https://innocenceproject.org/governor-signs-landmark-laws-for-preventing-wrongful-convictions/.

34. "Wrongly Convicted Man Graduates with Law Degree, Plans to Keep Helping Others the Justice System Failed," *CBSNewYork,* May 13, 2019, https://newyork.cbslocal.com/2019/05/13/wrongly-convicted-jeffrey-deskovic-graduates-pace-law-school/.

35. "California: New Law Protects Children in Police Custody," Human Rights Watch, September 30, 2020, https://www.hrw.org/news/2020/09/30/california-new-law-protects-children-police-custody.

36. Samuel Gross and Michael Shaffer, "Exonerations in the United States, 1989–2012: Report by the National Registry of Exonerations," University of Michigan Law School Scholarship Repository (2012), 60, https://repository.law.umich.edu/other/92/.

37. "Illinois Becomes First State to Pass Bill Banning Cops from Deceiving Youth Suspects," Associated Press, May 31, 2021, https://www.huffpost.com/entry/illinois-first-state-bill-banning-cops-deceiving-youth_n_60b51298e4b01de8b78609da.

CHAPTER 6. YOU HAVE OR CARE FOR A SICK CHILD

1. "Judge Zobel's Order, a Summary," *BBC News,* November 10, 1997, http://news.bbc.co.uk/2/hi/special_report/louise_woodward_case/29250.stm.

2. Clyde Haberman, "Shaken Baby Syndrome: A Diagnosis That Divides the Medical World," *New York Times,* September 13, 2015, https://www.nytimes.com/2015/09/14/us/shaken-baby-syndrome-a-diagnosis-that-divides-the-medical-world.html.

3. Chadwick Center for Children & Families, July 17, 2019, https://www.rchsd.org/programs-services/chadwick-center/.

4. Norell Atkinson, Rick van Rijn, and Suzanne Starling, "Childhood Falls with Occipital Impacts," *Pediatric Emergency Care* 34(12) (2018), https://journals.lww.com/pec-online/Abstract/2018/12000/Childhood_Falls_With_Occipital_Impacts.3.aspx.

5. Randall C. Alexander, "Shaken Baby Syndrome: Rotational Cranial Injuries-Technical Report," *American Academy of Pediatrics* 108(1) (2001): 206–10, https://

pubmed.ncbi.nlm.nih.gov/11433079/#:~:text=Shaken%20baby%20syndrome%
20is%20a,recognizable%20by%20others%20as%20dangerous.

6. Tina Joyce, William Gossman, and Martin R. Huecker, "Pediatric Abusive Head Trauma," StatPearls [Internet] (Treasure Island, FL: StatPearls, January 2022), https://www.ncbi.nlm.nih.gov/books/NBK499836/.

7. Ibid.

8. Niels Lynew et al., "Insufficient Evidence for 'Shaken Baby Syndrome'—a Systematic Review," *Acta Paediatrica* 106(7) (January 27, 2017), https://onlinelibrary .wiley.com/doi/full/10.1111/apa.13760.

9. Justin Brooks, Alexander Simpson, and Paige Kaneb, "If Hindsight Is 20/20, Our Justice System Should Not Be Blind to New Evidence of Innocence: A Survey of Post-Conviction New Evidence Statutes and a Proposed Model," *Albany Law Review* 79(3) (Fall 2016): 1045–90.

10. SB 694 Senate Bill, http://www.leginfo.ca.gov/pub/15-16/bill/sen/sb_ 0651-0700/sb_694_cfa_20150824_145242_asm_comm.html.

11. Kate Morrissey, "Man Serves 20 Years after Wrongful Conviction in Toddler's Death," *San Diego Union-Tribune*, May 13, 2016, https://www .sandiegouniontribune.com/news/data-watch/sdut-exoneree-marsh-2016may13 -htmlstory.html.

12. Ale Russian, "Natasha Richardson Would Have Turned 55 Today— How Liam Neeson Coped Since Her Shocking Death," *People.com*, May 11, 2018, https://people.com/movies/natasha-richardson-55-today-how-liam-neeson -coped/.

13. Cal. Code Regs. Tit. 15 § 3173.1 Visiting Restrictions with Minors.

14. Audrey Ann Edmunds and Jill Wellington, *It Happened to Audrey: A Terrifying Journey from Loving Mom to Accused Baby Killer* (Green Bay, WI: Title Town Publishing, 2012), 7.

15. State v. Edmunds, 746 N.W.2d 590 (2008).

16. Jonathan Liew, "World Cup 2022: Qatar's Workers Are Not Workers, They Are Slaves and They Are Building Mausoleums, Not Stadiums," *Independent*, October 3, 2017, https://www.independent.co.uk/sport/football/international/world -cup-2022-qatar-s-workers-slaves-building-mausoleums-stadiums-modern-slavery -kafala-a7980816.html.

17. Shabina S. Khatri and Alan Cowell, "Qatar Finds U.S. Couple Guilty in Daughter's Death," *New York Times*, March 27, 2014, https://www.nytimes .com/2014/03/28/world/middleeast/american-couple-in-qatar-sentenced-to-three -years-jail.html.

18. Rick Gladstone, "Matthew and Grace Huang, Cleared in Daughter's Death, Are Set to Leave Qatar," *New York Times*, December 2, 2014, https://www.nytimes .com/2014/12/03/world/matthew-and-grace-huang-cleared-in-daughters-death -are-set-to-leave-qatar.html.

19. Malcom Brown, "Dingo Baby Ruling Ends 32 Years of Torment for Lindy Chamberlain," *The Guardian*, June 12, 2012, https://www.theguardian.com /world/2012/jun/12/dingo-baby-azaria-lindy-chamberlain.

CHAPTER 7. YOU GOT A JURY THAT WAS BLINDED BY "SCIENCE"

1. Witherspoon v. Illinois, 391 US 510 (1968).

2. Mona Lynch and Craig Haney, "Death Qualification in Black and White: Racialized Decision Making and Death Qualified Juries," *Law & Policy*, February 2018.

3. "The Historic Origin of Trial by Jury," *University of Pennsylvania Law Review* (November 1921), https://scholarship.law.upenn.edu/cgi/viewcontent .cgi?article=7842&context=penn_law_review.

4. Duncan v. Louisiana, 391 U.S. 145 (1968).

5. Baldwin v. New York, 399 U.S. 66, 76.

6. Valerie P. Hans, "Jury Systems around the World," *Cornell Law Faculty Publications*, January 1, 2008, https://scholarship.law.cornell.edu/cgi/viewcontent .cgi?article=1378&context=facpub.

7. Natali Daiana Chizik, "The Implementation of Trial by Jury in Argentina: The Analysis of a Legal Transplant as a Method of Reform," Thesis, University of British Columbia, January 2020, https://open.library.ubc.ca/cIRcle/collections /ubctheses/24/items/1.0388528.

8. Maxine Bernstein, "Judges Cracking Down on People Who Snub Jury Duty," *AP*, May 21, 2017, https://apnews.com/article/62b279c38615469fb9bee 505c9c66ff5.

9. John Gramlich, "Jury Duty Is Rare, but Most Americans See It as Part of Good Citizenship," *Pew Research Center*, August 24, 2017, https://www .pewresearch.org/fact-tank/2017/08/24/jury-duty-is-rare-but-most-americans -see-it-as-part-of-good-citizenship/.

10. A. W. Geiger, "6 Facts about America's Students," *Pew Research Center*, September 7, 2018, https://www.pewresearch.org/fact-tank/2018/09/07/6 -facts-about-americas-students/.

11. "CSI Effect," Cornell Law School, June 2021, https://www.law.cornell.edu /wex/csi_effect.

12. Geoffrey P. Kramer and Dorean M. Koenig, "Do Jurors Understand Criminal Jury Instructions? Analyzing the Results of the Michigan Juror Comprehension Project," *University of Michigan Journal of Law Reform* 23 (1990), https://repository.law.umich.edu/cgi/viewcontent.cgi?article=1779&context =mjlr.

13. "Most-Watched TV Show in the World Is 'CSI: Crime Scene Investiga-tion,'" *Huffington Post*, June 14, 2012, https://www.huffpost.com/entry /most-watched-tv-show-in-the-world-csi_n_1597968.

14. Hon. Donald E. Shelton, "The 'CSI Effect': Does It Really Exist?" National Institute of Justice, March 16, 2008, https://nij.ojp.gov/topics/articles /csi-effect-does-it-really-exist.

15. Eugene Morgulis, "Juror Reactions to Scientific Testimony: Unique Chal-lenges in Complex Mass Torts," *Boston University Journal of Science and Tech-nology Law* (May 2009), http://www.bu.edu/law/journals-archive/scitech/vol-ume152/documents/morgulis_web.pdf.

16. John J. Lentini, "Behavior of Glass at Elevated Temperatures," *Journal of Forensic Sciences* 37(5) (1992), https://www.astm.org/DIGITAL_LIBRARY /JOURNALS/FORENSIC/PAGES/JFS13325J.htm; John J. Lentini, David M. Smith, and Richard W. Henderson, "Unconventional Wisdom: The Lessons of Oakland," *Fire and Arson Investigator* 43(4) (June 1993), http://assocfire.com /unconventional-wisdom-the-lessons-of-oakland/.

17. John J. Lentini, "The Mythology of Arson Investigation" (Boca Raton, FL: CRC Press, 2006).

18. John J. Lentini, "Fire Expert: How I Nearly Sent an Innocent Man to the Electric Chair," ABC, May 5, 2010, https://abcnews.go.com/2020/john-lentinis-fire-arson-investigation/story?id=10562869#.Tw3XCnLgfjM.

19. Ibid.

20. Sherry Nakhaeizadeh, Itiel E. Dror, and Ruth M. Morgan, "Cognitive Bias in Forensic Anthropology: Visual Assessment of Skeletal Remains Is Sus-ceptible to Confirmation Bias," *Science & Justice* 54(3) (May 2014), https://www .sciencedirect.com/science/article/pii/S1355030613001202.

21. Edward Humes, *Burned: A Story of Murder and the Crime That Wasn't* (New York: Dutton, 2019), 88.

22. Hans Zeisel, "A Jury Hoax: The Superpower of the Opening Statement," University of Chicago Law School, Chicago Unbound, Journal Articles, 1987, https://chicagounbound.uchicago.edu/cgi/viewcontent.cgi?referer=https://www .google.com/&httpsredir=1&article=12000&context=journal_articles.

23. "FBI Testimony on Microscopic Hair Analysis Contained Errors in at Least 90 Percent of Cases in Ongoing Review," FBI Press Release, April 20, 2015, https://www.fbi.gov/news/pressrel/press-releases/fbi-testimony-on -microscopic-hair-analysis-contained-errors-in-at-least-90-percent-of-cases-in -ongoing-review.

24. Spencer S. Hsu, "Santae Tribble, Whose Wrongful Conviction Revealed FBI Forensic Hair Match Flaws, Dies at 59," *Washington Post*, July 5, 2020, https://www.washingtonpost.com/local/legal-issues/santae-tribble-whose -wrongful-conviction-revealed-fbi-forensic-hair-match-flaws-dies-at-59/2020/07 /04/eb953b40-bbbf-11ea-bdaf-a129f921026f_story.html.

25. Paul C. Giannelli, "Daubert Challenges to Firearms ('Ballistics') Identifications," Case Western Reserve University, Faculty Publications, 2007, https://scholarlycommons.law.case.edu/cgi/viewcontent.cgi?referer=https://scholar.google.com/&httpsredir=1&article=1153&context=faculty_publications.

26. Cliff Spiegelman, "Chemical and Forensic Analysis of JFK Assassination Bullet Lots: Is a Second Shooter Possible?," Institute of Mathematical Statistics, December 13, 2007, https://arxiv.org/pdf/0712.2150.pdf.

27. "FBI Laboratory Announces Discontinuation of Bullet Lead Examinations," FBI Press Release, September 1, 2005, https://archives.fbi.gov/archives/news/pressrel/press-releases/fbi-laboratory-announces-discontinuation-of-bullet-lead-examinations.

28. Itiel E. Dror, David Charlton, and Ailsa E. Péron, "Contextual Information Renders Experts Vulnerable to Making Erroneous Identifications," *Forensic Science International* 156(1) (2006), https://www.sciencedirect.com/science/article/abs/pii/S0379073805005876.

29. Brandon L. Garrett, *Autopsy of a Crime Lab* (Oakland: University of California Press, 2021), 28.

30. Garrett, *Autopsy of a Crime Lab*, 69, citing Bradford T. Ulery et al., "Accuracy and Reliability of Forensic Latent Fingerprint Decisions," *Proceedings of the National Academy of Sciences* 118 (2011): 7733.

31. Committee on Identifying the Needs of the Forensic Sciences Community, National Research Council, *Strengthening Forensic Science in the United States: A Path Forward* (Washington, DC: National Research Council of the National Academies, National Academic Press, 2009), 87.

32. Garrett, *Autopsy of a Crime Lab*, 28.

33. "A Trail of Misconduct and the Need for Reform," Innocence Project, May 7, 2010, https://innocenceproject.org/a-trail-of-misconduct-and-the-need-for-reform/.

34. Garrett, *Autopsy of a Crime Lab*, 141.

35. S. P. Sullivan, "State Police Lab Scandal Led to Major Overhaul in How N.J. Tests Drug Evidence. It Was All Based on a Lie, Lawsuit Claims," NJ Advance Media, February 4, 2019, https://www.nj.com/politics/2019/02/state-police-lab-scandal-led-to-major-overhaul-in-how-nj-tests-drug-evidence-it-was-all-based-on-a-lie-lawsuit-claims.html.

CHAPTER 8. YOU WORK WITH CHILDREN OR LET THEM IN YOUR HOUSE

1. Justin Brooks and Zachary Brooks, "Wrongfully Convicted in California: Are There Connections between Exonerations, Prosecutorial and Police Procedures, and Justice Reforms," *Hofstra Law Review* 45(2) (December 1, 2016),

https://scholarlycommons.law.hofstra.edu/cgi/viewcontent.cgi?article=2948&
context=hlr.

2. Nadja Schreiber et al., "Suggestive Interviewing in the McMartin Preschool
and Kelly Michaels Daycare Abuse Cases: A Case Study," *Social Influence* 1(1)
(2006): 16–47, https://scholarworks.utep.edu/cgi/viewcontent.cgi?article=
1014&context=james_wood.

3. Brian Melley, "Newspaper's Report on Ring of Closeted Gay Men Roils
California City," Associated Press, March 18, 2003, https://www.seattlepi
.com/national/article/Newspaper-s-report-on-ring-of-closeted-gay-men-1110027
.php.

4. Robert Price, "Lords of Bakersfield: The Lawsuit Is the Next Act in a Sala-
cious, 40-year-old Drama," *KGET.com*, November 7, 2021, https://www.kget
.com/news/crime-watch/lords-of-bakersfield-the-lawsuit-is-the-next-act-in-a-
salacious-40-year-old-drama/.

5. *In Re Stoll, Hearing on Writ of Habeas Corpus*, Reporter's Transcript, vol. 7,
p. 990, February 25, 2004.

6. Jason Kotowski, "Former DA Ed Jagels Returning to Work to Analyze and
Lobby for Change in State Laws Impacting Crime," *Bakersfield Californian*,
January 14, 2019, https://www.bakersfield.com/news/former-da-ed-jagels-
returning-to-work-to-analyze-and-lobby-for-change-in-state/article_ded89f22-
1851-11e9-b1d2-1bbf3e21a46d.html.

7. Amanda Robb, "Anatomy of a Fake News Scandal," *Rolling Stone*, November 16, 2017, https://www.rollingstone.com/feature/anatomy-of-a-fake-news-
scandal-125877/.

8. Chris Greer and Eugene McLaughlin, "The Return of the Repressed:
Secrets, Lies, Denial and 'Historical' Institutional Child Sexual Abuse Scandals,"
in D. Whyte, ed., *How Corrupt Is Britain?* (London: Pluto, 2015), https://
www.academia.edu/23605102/_The_Return_of_the_Repressed_Secrets_Lies_
Denial_and_Historical_Institutional_Child_Sexual_Abuse_Scandals_in_D_
Whyte_ed_How_Corrupt_is_Britain_London_Pluto.

9. Chris Greer and Eugene McLaughlin, "The Celebrity Icon Mask: The Multi-
Institutional Masking of Sir Jimmy Savile," British Sociological Association, February 6, 2021, https://journals.sagepub.com/doi/full/10.1177/1749975520985385.

10. Simon Murphy, "Operation Midland: Top Public Figures Falsely Accused
by 'Nick,'" *The Guardian*, July 22, 2019, https://www.theguardian.com
/uk-news/2019/jul/22/operation-midland-four-top-public-figures-falsely-accused-
by-nick.

11. "Carl Beech: VIP Abuse Ring Fantasist Loses Jail Term Cut Bid," *BBC
News*, November 2, 2020, https://www.bbc.com/news/uk-54795942.

12. "Six Cleared Over French Child Sex," *BBC News*, December 1, 2005, http://
news.bbc.co.uk/2/hi/europe/4490088.stm.

13. Amy Sarcevic and Ugur Nedim, "False Accusations Are a Crime in New South Wales," Law Business Research, October 2, 2019, https://www.lexology .com/library/detail.aspx?g=387605e5-89c5-4e35-8d9b-6331b3805014.

14. Michael Lamb et al., "Structured Forensic Interview Protocols Improve the Quality and Informativeness of Investigative Interviews with Children: A Review of Research Using NICHD Investigative Interview Protocol," PubMed Central, November 19, 2007, https://www.ncbi.nlm.nih.gov/pmc/articles /PMC2180422/.

CHAPTER 9. SOMEONE LIES ABOUT YOU

1. Rob Warden, "Jesse Boorn," National Registry of Exonerations, Pre-1989, https://www.law.umich.edu/special/exoneration/Pages/casedetailpre1989. aspx?caseid=25 (accessed May 4, 2021).

2. "How Snitch Testimony Sent Randy Steidl and Other Innocent Americans to Death Row," A Center on Wrongful Convictions Survey, Winter 2004–2005, https://www.innocenceproject.org/wp-content/uploads/2016/02/SnitchSystem Booklet.pdf.

3. Tony Saavedra, "Prosecutors in Orange County Snitch Scandal Were Intentionally Negligent, DA Probe Concludes," *Orange County Register*, July 20, 2020, https://www.ocregister.com/2020/07/20/ prosecutors-in-orange-county-snitch-scandal-were-intentionally-negligent-da-probe-concludes/.

4. Tony Perry, "4 Convictions in Slaying Called into Question," *Los Angeles Times*, December 23, 1998, https://www.latimes.com/archives/la-xpm-1998-dec-23-mn-56915-story.html.

5. *The Snitch System*, Northwestern University School of Law, Center on Wrongful Convictions, Winter 2004–2005, https://www.innocenceproject.org /wp-content/uploads/2016/02/SnitchSystemBooklet.pdf.

6. Brady v. Maryland, 373 US 83, 87 (1963).

7. *Hanline v. George Galaza, United States District Court, Central District of California*, Western Division. EDCV 00-530-VAJ(AWJ). Report and Recommendation of Magistrate Judge, 46.

8. Ibid., 48.

9. Hanline v. Galaza, 28 U.S.C. §2254, 24, https://www.casemine.com/judgement /us/5914fabdadd7b049349a9cf2.

10. *Michael Hanline Released after 36 Years [of] Wrongful Imprisonment*, https://www.youtube.com/watch?v=BRYUi-8WEi0.

11. Samuel R. Gross et al., "Government Misconduct and Convicting the Innocent: The Role of Prosecutors, Police and Other Law Enforcement," University of

Michigan Law School, 2020, https://repository.law.umich.edu/cgi/viewcontent .cgi?article=1165&context=other.

12. Frazier v. Cupp, 394 U.S. 731, 739 (1969).

13. Maurice Possley, "Martin Tankleff," https://www.law.umich.edu/special /exoneration/Pages/casedetail.aspx?caseid=3675.

14. "Lessons from the Innocent," Innocence Project, Wisconsin Academy Review, Fall 2001, https://media.law.wisc.edu/m/ngm9y/findleywarfall01.pdf.

15. "Rampart Scandal Timeline," *PBS SoCal,* March 18, 1997, https://www .pbs.org/wgbh/pages/frontline/shows/lapd/scandal/cron.html.

16. James Gordon, "Up to 50 Murder Convictions Could Be Quashed as Review Is Launched into Chicago Detective Accused of 'Beating Suspects to Get Confessions and Falsifying Witness Statements,'" *DailyMail.com,* May 16, 2020, https://www.dailymail.co.uk/news/article-8325593/Up-50-murder-convictions-quashed-review-launched-cop-beat-people-up.html.

17. Jennifer Gonnerman, "How One Woman's Fight to Save Her Family Helped Lead to a Mass Exoneration," *New Yorker,* May 21, 2018, https://www .newyorker.com/magazine/2018/05/28/how-one-womans-fight-to-save-her-family-helped-lead-to-a-mass-exoneration.

18. "18 Exonerated in Chicago's Second Mass Exoneration," Innocence Project, September 24, 2018, https://innocenceproject.org/second-mass-exoneration-in-chicago/.

19. "Breaking: 7th Mass Exoneration of Victims of Corrupt CPD Sgt. Ronald Watts," Exoneration Project, https://www.exonerationproject.org/blog/breaking-7th-mass-exoneration-of-victims-of-corrupt-cpd-sgt-ronald-watts/ (accessed May 20, 2021).

20. "'Home Free': How a Wrongfully Convicted Man Taught Himself Law and Won His Freedom," Innocence Project, June 15, 2016, https://innocenceproject .org/how-derrick-hamilton-won-his-freedom/.

21. Sean Piccoli, "A Former Detective Accused of Framing 8 People for Murder Is Confronted in Court," April 1, 2019, https://www.nytimes.com/2019/04/01 /nyregion/nypd-detective-louis-scarcella.html.

22. "500 NYC Convictions to Be Tossed Based on Cop's Alleged Perjury, DA Says," *NBC New York,* January 20, 2022, https://www.nbcnewyork.com/news /local/500-nyc-convictions-to-be-tossed-based-on-cops-alleged-perjury-da-says /3505488/.

23. "Mass Exonerations and Group Exonerations since 1989," National Registry of Exonerations, April 9, 2018, https://www.law.umich.edu/special /exoneration/Documents/NREMassExonConf4418.pdf.

24. "Presunto Culpable: On Its Way to Become the Highest Grossing Doc in Mexican History," Cinema Tropical, February 21, 2011, https://www .cinematropical.com/cinema-tropical/presunto-culpable-on-its-way-to-become-the-highest-grossing-doc-in-mexican-history. See also Jo Tuckman, "Mexican

Film Ban Attempt Elevates Presumed Guilty to Box-office Hit," *The Guardian*, March 7, 2011, https://www.theguardian.com/world/2011/mar/07/mexico-film-ban-presumed-guilty.

25. Elisabeth Malkin, "A Free Man Still Looks Over His Shoulder in Mexico," *New York Times*, March 4, 2011, https://www.nytimes.com/2011/03/05/world/americas/05mexico.html?searchResultPosition=2.

26. "Fernando Carrerra," RedInocente, https://redinocente.org/exoneraciones/fernando-carrera/; http://innocenceprojectargentina.org/fernando-carrera/ (accessed July 27, 2021).

27. "Jailed for a Crime He Didn't Commit," *Independent*, June 8, 2006, https://www.independent.co.uk/news/education/education-news/jailed-for-a-crime-he-didn-t-commit-481421.html (accessed July 27, 2021).

28. Rebecca Camber, "Innocent Man Jailed for 3 Years Over False Rape Claim—Despite Police Knowing 'Victim' Was a Fantasist," *Daily Mail*, June 18, 2010, https://www.dailymail.co.uk/news/article-1287534/Innocent-Warren-Blackwell-served-3-years-false-rape-claim-fantasist.html.

29. Dr. Melanie Heenan and Dr. Suellen Murray, "Study of Reported Rapes in Victoria 2000–2003, Summary Research Report," National Criminal Justice Reference Service, July 2006, https://www.ojp.gov/ncjrs/virtual-library/abstracts/study-reported-rapes-victoria-2000-2003-summary-research-report.

30. Eugene J. Kanin, "False Rape Allegations," *Archives of Sexual Behavior* 23(1) (February 1994): 81(12), https://www.aals.org/wp-content/uploads/2015/06/Bowen-Kanin-False-Rape-Empirical.pdf.

31. "Statistics," National Sexual Violence Resource Center, https://www.nsvrc.org/statistics (accessed July 28, 2021).

32. Cameron Kimble, "Sexual Assault Remains Dramatically Underreported," Brennan Center for Justice, October 4, 2018, https://www.brennancenter.org/our-work/analysis-opinion/sexual-assault-remains-dramatically-underreported.

33. Ibid.

34. Jason Farrell, "Ministers 'Deeply Ashamed' as Review Finds Thousands of Rape Victims 'Are Being Failed,'" *Sky News*, June 18, 2021, https://news.sky.com/story/ministers-deeply-ashamed-as-review-finds-thousands-of-rape-victims-are-being-failed160-12335252.

35. Lisa A. Paul et al., "Does Encouragement by Others Increase Rape Reporting? Findings from a National Sample of Women," PubMed Central, June 2014, https://www.ncbi.nlm.nih.gov/pmc/articles/PMC4243174/.

36. Mark Godsey, *Blind Injustice: A Former Prosecutor Exposes the Psychology and Politics of Wrongful Convictions* (Oakland: University of California Press, 2017), 197–98.

37. Ibid.

38. Daniele Selby, "Only One Prosecutor Has Ever Been Jailed for Misconduct Leading to a Wrongful Conviction," Innocence Project, November 11,

2020,https://innocenceproject.org/ken-anderson-michael-morton-prosecutorial-misconduct-jail/.

CHAPTER 10. YOU ARE POOR AND/OR A PERSON OF COLOR

1. Jeffrey J. Rachlinski and Gregory S. Parks, "Implicit Bias, Election '08, and the Myth of a Post-racial America," *Cornell Law Faculty Publications*, April 1, 2010, https://scholarship.law.cornell.edu/cgi/viewcontent.cgi?article=1177&context=facpub.

2. David Paul Kuhn, "Exit Polls: How Obama Won," *Politico,* November 5, 2008, https://www.politico.com/story/2008/11/exit-polls-how-obama-won-015297.

3. Melissa Alonso and Eliott C. Mclaughlin, "Louisiana Judge Resigns and Apologizes Following Video with Racial Slurs," CNN, January 1, 2022, https://edition.cnn.com/2021/12/31/us/louisiana-lafayette-judge-resignation-racial-slurs/index.html.

4. Stephen Middleton, "Repressive Legislation: Slave Codes, Northern Black Laws, and Southern Black Codes," *Oxford Research Encyclopedia of American History,* February 28, 2020, https://oxfordre.com/americanhistory/view/10.1093/acrefore/9780199329175.001.0001/acrefore-9780199329175-e-634.

5. "Slavery by Another Name: The Origins of Black Codes," *PBS SoCal,* February 12, 2012, https://www.pbs.org/video/slavery-another-name-origins-black-codes/.

6. Ibid.

7. "Examples of Jim Crow Laws—Oct. 1960—Civil Rights," *Jackson Sun,* 2001, https://www.ferris.edu/HTMLS/news/jimcrow/links/misclink/examples.htm.

8. Susan Pearson, "Birth Certificates Have Always Been a Weapon for White Supremacists: Policing the Color Line through Vital Documents," *Washington Post,* September 11, 2018, https://www.washingtonpost.com/outlook/2018/09/11/birth-certificates-have-always-been-weapon-white-supremacists/.

9. "Examples of Jim Crow Laws—Oct. 1960—Civil Rights."

10. Plessy v. Ferguson, 163 U.S. 537, 543.

11. Brown v. Board of Education, 347 US 483,495 (1954).

12. Dan Baum, "Legalize It All: How to Win the War on Drugs," *Harper's Magazine,* April 2016, https://harpers.org/archive/2016/04/legalize-it-all/.

13. Anti-Drug Abuse Act of 1986, NCJRS Library 149074, 1986, https://www.ojp.gov/ncjrs/virtual-library/abstracts/anti-drug-abuse-act-1986.

14. Harmelin v. Michigan, 501 U.S. 957 (1991).

15. Terry v. United States, 593 U.S. ___ (2021).

16. Peter Baker, "Bush Made Willie Horton an Issue in 1988, and the Racial Scars Are Still Fresh," *New York Times*, December 3, 2018, https://www.nytimes.com/2018/12/03/us/politics/bush-willie-horton.html.

17. "Anti-Drug Abuse Act of 1986 Deepened Racial Inequity in Sentencing," *ACLU*, October 26, 2006, https://www.aclu.org/press-releases/aclu-releases-crack-cocaine-report-anti-drug-abuse-act-1986-deepened-racial-inequity.

18. "Clemency Statistics," U.S. Department of Justice, https://www.justice.gov/pardon/clemency-statistics (accessed July 27, 2021).

19. James Cullen, "The United States Is (Very) Slowly Reducing Incarceration," Brennan Center for Justice, January 18, 2017, https://www.brennancenter.org/our-work/analysis-opinion/united-states-very-slowly-reducing-incarceration.

20. Jennifer Bronson and E. Ann Carson, "Prisoners in 2017," Bureau of Justice Statistics, April 2019, https://bjs.ojp.gov/content/pub/pdf/p17.pdf; Zhen Zeng, "Jail Inmates in 2017," Bureau of Justice Statistics, April 2019, https://bjs.ojp.gov/library/publications/jail-inmates-2017.

21. Kaelin Mastronardi, "US Perpetuation of Wealth Inequality," *Grossmont College Journal of Politics* 1(1) (Winter 2021), https://www.grossmont.edu/academics/programs/political-economy/_resources/assets/pdf/2021-winter-journal-of-politics-volume-1-issue-1.pdf#page=22.

22. "Global Comparisons," Prison Policy Initiative, https://www.prisonpolicy.org/prisonindex/us_southafrica.html (accessed July 31, 2021).

23. "Trends in U.S. Corrections," The Sentencing Project, May 17, 2021, https://www.sentencingproject.org/publications/trends-in-u-s-corrections/.

24. "Lifetime Chance of Being Sent to Prison at Current U.S. Incarceration Rates," Prison Policy Initiative, https://www.prisonpolicy.org/graphs/lifetimechance.html (accessed July 31, 2021).

25. Michelle Alexander, *The New Jim Crow: Mass Incarceration in the Age of Colorblindness* (New York: New Press, 2010), 2.

26. MCSO Findings Letter "United States Investigation of the Maricopa County Sheriff's Office," U.S. Department of Justice, December 5, 2011, 2, https://www.justice.gov/sites/default/files/crt/legacy/2011/12/15/mcso_findletter_12-15-11.pdf.

27. MCSO Complaint, May 10, 2012, 2, https://www.justice.gov/sites/default/files/crt/legacy/2012/07/18/mcso_complaint_5-10-12.pdf.

28. Jan Ransom, "Trump Will Not Apologize for Calling for Death Penalty Over Central Park Five," *New York Times*, June 18, 2019, https://www.nytimes.com/2019/06/18/nyregion/central-park-five-trump.html.

29. Amber Phillips, "'They're Rapists.' President Trump's Campaign Launch Speech Two Years Later, Annotated," *Washington Post*, June 16, 2017, https://www.washingtonpost.com/news/the-fix/wp/2017/06/16/theyre-rapists-presidents-

trump-campaign-launch-speech-two-years-later-annotated/; "Trump Pledges to Build a Wall," CNN, January 24, 2017, https://www.youtube.com/watch?v=cBW8mTHDgvk&ab_channel=CNN.

30. Brandon Jett, "Vengeance in a Small Town: The Thorndale Lynching of 1911," *Southwestern Historical Quarterly* (January 2012), https://www.researchgate.net/publication/254965148_Vengeance_in_a_Small_Town_The_Thorndale_Lynching_of_1911_review.

31. Vincent Schilling, "The Traumatic True History and Name List of the Dakota 38," *Indian Country Today*, December 26, 2020, https://indiancountrytoday.com/news/traumatic-true-history-full-list-dakota-38.

32. Sally Kohn, "Nothing Donald Trump Says on Immigration Holds Up," *Time*, June 29, 2016, https://time.com/4386240/donald-trump-immigration-arguments/.

33. David A. Harris, "Racial Profiling: Past, Present, and Future?" American Bar Association, January 21, 2020, https://www.americanbar.org/groups/criminal_justice/publications/criminal-justice-magazine/2020/winter/racial-profiling-past-present-and-future/.

34. Lynne Peeples, "What the Data Say about Police Brutality and Racial Bias—and Which Reforms Might Work," *Nature*, June 19, 2020, https://www.nature.com/articles/d41586-020-01846-z.

35. "Investigation of the Ferguson Police Department," US Department of Justice, March 4, 2015, https://www.justice.gov/sites/default/files/opa/press-releases/attachments/2015/03/04/ferguson_police_department_report.pdf.

36. V. A. Mathur et al., "Neural Basis of Extraordinary Empathy and Altruistic Motivation," *Neuroimage* 51(4) (July 15, 2010):1468–75, https://doi.org/10.1016/j.neuroimage.2010.03.025.

37. Jody Armour, *N*gga Theory: Race, Language, Unequal Justice, and the Law* (Los Angeles: LARB Books, 2020), 97.

38. Samantha Bielen, Wim Marneffe, and Naci H. Mocan., "Racial Bias and In-group Bias in Judicial Decisions Evidence from Virtual Reality Courtrooms," National Bureau of Economic Research, May 2019, https://www.nber.org/system/files/working_papers/w25355/w25355.pdf.

39. Pierre Thomas, John Kelly, and Tonya Simpson, "ABC News Analysis of Police Arrests Nationwide Reveals Stark Racial Disparity," *ABCNews*, June 11, 2020, https://abcnews.go.com/US/abc-news-analysis-police-arrests-nationwide-reveals-stark/story?id=71188546.

40. Douglas Rice, Jesse H. Rhodes, and Tatishe Nteta, "Racial Bias in Legal Language," *Research and Politics*, April–June 2019, https://journals.sagepub.com/doi/pdf/10.1177/2053168019848930.

41. "Demographic Differences in Sentencing," US Sentencing Commission, November 14, 2017, https://www.ussc.gov/research/research-reports/demographic-differences-sentencing.

42. Brian Banks, *What Set Me Free* (New York: Atria, 2019), 94.

43. Dafna Linzer and Jennife LaFleur, "Presidential Pardons Heavily Favor Whites," *ProPublica*, December 3, 2011, https://www.propublica.org/article/shades-of-mercy-presidential-forgiveness-heavily-favors-whites.

44. Jaynie Adams, "The Pioneer Hotel Fire of 1970," Arizona Historical Society, December 18, 2020, https://arizonahistoricalsociety.org/2020/12/18/the-pioneer-hotel-fire-of-1970/.

45. Fernanda Santos, "Advances in Science of Fire Free a Convict after 42 Years," *New York Times*, April 2, 2013, https://www.nytimes.com/2013/04/03/us/advances-in-science-of-fire-set-convict-free-after-42-years.html.

46. Richard Ruelas, "After 42 Years, Freedom," *AZCentral.com*, https://www.azcentral.com/story/news/local/arizona/2017/07/14/after-42-years-freedom/481079001/.

47. Taylor v. County. of Pima, 913 F.3d 930 (9th Cir. 2019).

48. Zach Sommers, "Missing White Woman Syndrome: An Empirical Analysis of Race and Gender Disparities in Online News Coverage of Missing Persons," *Journal of Criminal Law and Criminology* (Spring 2016), https://scholarlycommons.law.northwestern.edu/cgi/viewcontent.cgi?article=7586&context=jclc.

49. Daniel Lathrop and Anna Flagg, "Killings of Black Men by Whites Are Far More Likely to Be Ruled 'Justifiable,'" Marshall Project, August 14, 2017, https://www.themarshallproject.org/2017/08/14/killings-of-black-men-by-whites-are-far-more-likely-to-be-ruled-justifiable.

50. "Executions by Race and Race of Victim," Death Penalty Information Center, https://deathpenaltyinfo.org/executions/executions-overview/executions-by-race-and-race-of-victim (accessed January 26, 2022).

51. "Exonerations by Race/Ethnicity and Crime," National Registry of Exonerations, July 1, 2022, https://www.law.umich.edu/special/exoneration/Pages/ExonerationsRaceByCrime.aspx.

52. Mohammed Imran, Masharrof Hosen, and Mohammad Ashraful Ferdous Chowdhury, "Does Poverty Lead to Crime? Evidence from the United States of America," *International Journal of Social Economics* (August 7, 2018), https://www.emerald.com/insight/content/doi/10.1108/IJSE-04-2017-0167/full/html.

53. Sharon Wolf, Katherine A. Magnuson, and Rachel T. Kimbro, "Family Poverty and Neighborhood Poverty: Links with Children's School Readiness before and after the Great Recession," PubMed Central, June 23, 2017, https://www.ncbi.nlm.nih.gov/pmc/articles/PMC6107082/.

54. Cal. Penal Code §186.22

55. Tara O'Neill Hayes and Margaret Barnhorst, "Incarceration and Poverty in the United States," American Action Forum, June 30, 2020, https://www.americanactionforum.org/research/incarceration-and-poverty-in-the-united-states/.

56. Alysia Santo, "No Bail, Less Hope: The Death of Kalief Browder," Marshall Project, August 9, 2015, https://www.themarshallproject.org/2015/06/09/no-bail-less-hope-the-death-of-kalief-browder.

57. "In Your State," Gideon, http://gideonat50.org/in-your-state#state-funding-level.

58. Daniele Alge, "Pressures to Plead Guilty or Playing the System? An Exploration of the Causes of Cracked Trials," PhD thesis, University of Manchester, 2009, https://repository.uwl.ac.uk/id/eprint/2367/1/Alge_Thesis.pdf.

59. Bernadette Rabuy and Daniel Kapf, "Prisons of Poverty: Uncovering the Pre-incarceration Incomes of the Imprisoned," Prison Policy Initiative, July 9, 2015, https://www.prisonpolicy.org/reports/income.html.

60. Olim v. Wakinekona, 461 U.S. 238 (1983).

61. Alice Speri, "Puerto Rico Wants to Cut the Cost of Incarcerating People by Shipping Them Off the Island," *The Intercept,* March 23, 2018, https://theintercept.com/2018/03/23/puerto-rico-prisons-hurricane-maria/. See also Justin Brooks, "Exile on Main Street . . . Inmate Transfers from Puerto Rico to the Continental United States Violate Due Process," *Interamericana Law Review* 27 (Spring 1993): 1.

62. Li Zhou, "Kamala Harris Wants Public Defenders to Get Paid as Much as Prosecutors," *Vox,* May 17, 2019, https://www.vox.com/policy-and-politics/2019/5/17/18540359/kamala-harris-2020-democrats-public-defenders-prosecutors.

63. Go to www.innocencenetwork.org for a complete list of innocence organizations.

CONCLUSION

1. Steven A. Drizin and Richard A. Leo, "The Problem of False Confessions in the Post-DNA World," *North Carolina Law Review* 82(3) (2004), https://scholarship.law.unc.edu/cgi/viewcontent.cgi?article=4085&context=nclr.

2. Jody Armour, *N*gga Theory: Race, Language, Unequal Justice, and the Law* (Los Angeles: LARB Books, 2020), 20–21.

3. "Innocence and the Death Penalty: The Increasing Nature of Executing the Innocent," Death Penalty Information Center, July 1, 1997, https://deathpenaltyinfo.org/facts-and-research/dpic-reports/in-depth/innocence-and-the-death-penalty-the-increasing-danger-of-executing-the-innocent.

4. Melissa S. Kearney, "The Economic Challenges of Crime and Incarceration in the United States," *Hamilton Project,* December 22, 2014. https://www.hamiltonproject.org/blog/the_economic_challenges_of_crime_incarceration_in_the_united_states.

5. Stephen Raher, "The Company Store: A Deeper Look at Prison Commissaries," Prison Policy Initiative, May 2018, https://www.prisonpolicy.org/reports/commissary.html.

6. Kenny Lo, Betsy Pearl, and Akua Amaning, "Clemency 101: How Sentences Can Be Pardoned or Commuted," Center for American Progress, May 1, 2020, https://www.americanprogress.org/issues/criminal-justice/reports/2020/05/01/484300/clemency-101/.

Index

Note: Page numbers followed by *fig.* indicate photographs.

217